ORGANIZING KNOWLEDGE

ISLAMIC PHILOSOPHY THEOLOGY AND SCIENCE

Texts and Studies

VOLUME LXI

TUTA SUB AEGIDE PALLAS · 1683 ·

ORGANIZING KNOWLEDGE

Encyclopædic Activities in the Pre-Eighteenth Century Islamic World

EDITED BY

GERHARD ENDRESS

PREFACE BY

ABDOU FILALI-ANSARY

BRILL
LEIDEN · BOSTON
2006

Proceedings of a Colloquium held at the Institute for the Study of Muslim Civilisations
The Aga Khan University (International) in the United Kingdom
(London, November14-16, 2003)

This book is printed on acid-free paper

Library of Congress Cataloging-in-Publication Data

Organizing knowledge : encyclopaedic activities in the pre-eighteenth century Islamic world / preface by Abdou Filali-Ansary ; edited by Gerhard Endress.
p. cm. — (Islamic philosophy, theology, and science ; v. 61)
Includes bibliographical references and index.
ISBN-13: 978-90-04-14697-6
ISBN-10: 90-04-14697-0 (hardback : alk. paper)
1. Encyclopedias and dictionaries, Arabic—History and criticism. 2. Islamic learning and scholarship—History. I. Filali-Ansary, Abdou. II. Endress, Gerhard, 1939- III. Series.

AG10.55.O74 2006
039'.927—dc22

2006043937

ISSN 0169-8729
ISBN-13: 978-90-04-14697-6
ISBN-10: 90-04-14697-0

PRINTED IN THE NETHERLANDS

Aga Khan University's **Institute for the Study of Muslim Civilisations (AKU-ISMC)** was established in 2002 in London. The Institute's goal is to strengthen research on, and promote understanding of, the cultures of Muslims, past and present. It works to address important issues of contemporary societies, including social justice, governance, moral and legal thought, and the environment. Its activities and educational programmes apply the methodologies of the humanities and social sciences to the study of Muslim cultures and seek to create opportunities for interaction amongst a wide audience across intellectual disciplines.

Aga Khan University (AKU) is a private, self-governing institution with teaching and research programmes in Egypt, Pakistan, Kenya, Tanzania, Uganda, Afghanistan, Syria and the United Kingdom. The University includes a Medical College, a School of Nursing, two teaching hospitals, an Institute for Educational Development, an Institute for the Study of Muslim Civilisations, and an Examination Board. A Faculty of Arts and Sciences is being built on a new campus near Karachi, and other major developments in Pakistan, East Africa and elsewhere are at the planning stage.

The University is part of the Aga Khan Development Network (AKDN), a group of private international development agencies working to improve living conditions and create opportunities for the disadvantaged in the developing world through social, economic and cultural development.

www.aku.edu/ismc
www.akdn.org

CONTENTS

INTEGRATIVE CONCEPTS

A EUROPEANIST'S PERSPECTIVE

PREFACE

Pre-18th century Muslim cultures may be said to be 'book cultures'. There is little need here to stress the enormous expansion of writing and the accumulation of written compendia in Muslim contexts during the centuries that preceded the 18th century, and the deep influence it had on the making of a social order and the founding of structures of authority. In a novel which has greatly impressed the imagination in recent years, Orhan Pamuk's *My Name is Red* captured the spirit of a time, the ethos of large communities of artists, miniaturists, calligraphers, binders—professionals of bookmaking—who lived for centuries in an area stretching from Central Asia to the Atlantic Ocean. However, what he so strongly conveyed was only one, albeit significant, part of the story.

Miniaturists' workshops spread throughout these areas were probably the tip of an iceberg, encompassing large communities of scholars, copyists, painters, bookmakers, their apprentices, etc. Illuminations and illustrations were designed for relatively small circles of wealthy and powerful clients. However, those who handled and copied texts alone (absent of illuminations or illustrations) enjoyed unchallenged prestige in much wider circles, its men and women (for there were women too) the keepers and transmitters of what the community considered to be its most precious treasure. The vast corpus of knowledge thus transmitted encompassed not only the word of God and the hadith of His Prophet, but also exegesis works, commentaries, compendia of law, books on grammar, etc.; its accumulation over many centuries and across a vast geographic area was impressive not only in its quantity and variety but also its impact on collective consciousness. It defined, as much or more than any other institution, the ethos and worldview of one of the largest, and oldest, communities in the history of mankind. The views and conceptions which were disseminated through written literature were endowed with the authority of what was considered to be *ʿilm* (Science). This literary corpus laid and sustained systems of authority, in terms of conception of the world, history and men, and at the level of norms which were formulated to rule individual and communities' lives.

The aspect that is probably most relevant to us nowadays is the ways in which this immense body of literature entrenched prevailing ideas about the self, the other and the world and shaped the historical consciousness of Muslim communities. Classification, systematisation and dissemination of knowledge played a vital role in the process of transmitting the views of scholars—together with the truths they strongly assumed—to the public. Indeed, systematisation of knowledge was a temptation which came well before the emergence of Muslim cultures. Yet one can safely say that Muslims pushed the endeavour (or endeavours) as far as one can imagine, thereby defining a mindset and attitude which weighed enormously on how individuals and societies felt about their lives and the world around them.

Theirs was a world which seems as remote to us today as the one brought to life by Pamuk. Of course, in some *madrasas* here and there, some impoverished, tattered remnants of this world have survived. But nowadays, forms of knowledge built on pre-eighteenth century accumulations look obsolete even within the most conservative circles, where bits and pieces of this particular heritage are still in use. What prevails and impresses large strata of Muslim societies, are modern reconstructions, which have cast aside the ideal of organising and mastering knowledge as it seemed at the time, in order to preserve as much as possible the sense of a distinct identity, together with a strong drive towards the implementation in real life of what is perceived as the 'Islamic' way.

Thus the influence of the old remains, although not in explicit and easily perceptible ways. There is no strict rupture between past and present. Among those who are permeated by these attitudes, we still do not find the idea of knowledge as a progressive accumulation of facts and continuous adjustment of views about the world, history and ourselves. The attitudes of modesty, openness and acceptance of difference that humans learnt through modern scientific endeavours are conspicuously absent. What we see in fact does not take the form of an easily recognisable, formally traceable link between the massive accumulation of writings in the past and particular views, conceptions or attitudes in what can be observed nowadays. It remains an immense, yet not quite understood presence that acts as an obstacle to the adoption of modern attitudes to knowledge and its role in building representations and attitudes. It is as if the impact of the pre-18th century outlook remains, even though the substance of the then prevailing views has become obsolete, and generally unaccepted. In consequence, the prevailing conceptions that Muslims hold about their religion, their history and their position in the world are, today, at least in good part, built on knowledge that was thus systematised. We are in a situation in which this presence is overwhelming but needs to be clearly acknowledged and its effects clearly assessed.

One can point to the fact that, after the 18th century, the drive to produce encyclopædias survived or returned in force within Muslim contexts. A large number of encyclopædic projects are today in progress in many areas where Muslims constitute a substantive majority. A rapid survey reveals that the number, the scale and the geographic distribution of these projects is impressive. Should we link this fact to some particularity in Islam or Muslim contexts, as many observers do whenever they detect any form of continuity between the past and present in Muslim cultures? Here, one can immediately see that these contemporary projects are designed and implemented with different assumptions in mind, and with different attitudes to knowledge. Contemporary encyclopædic projects are produced within properly modern frameworks, including modern nation-states, institutions (many state-funded), and through distinctively modern scholarship. They seem to be, in a way, attempts to reappropriate knowledge and the control of memory and history, endeavours which remain in line with the nationalist ethos of our times. Many of these projects mobilise new energies, younger generations of active scholars, sometimes under the supervision of older scholars. However, these new accumulations are still in process, and have not yet permeated public consciousness nor even school curricula. They require specific attention, since they are set to bring about an important move in how knowledge about Muslim cultures and societies, both present and past, is apprehended.

At this stage then, and not only for chronological reasons, let us turn to the pre-18th century genre, or complex of genres, which lay behind dominant perceptions. From the wildest dream of collecting all possible 'pieces' of knowledge, which could lead to multi-volume collections such as the monumental *Biḥār al-Anwār* of the 17th century Shiite scholar Muḥammad Majlisī, to summaries and catalogues, sometimes arranged in verse to facilitate assimilation and retention by students, the mass of 'monuments' which defined and shaped the intellectual landscape in many Muslim contexts, lies before us as a substantial part of the heritage which awaits examination.

This is what motivated the organisation of the conference *Organizing Knowledge: Encyclopædic Activities in the Pre-Eighteenth Century Muslim World*. As a first large scholarly gathering organised by the Institute for the Study of Muslim Civilisations, it was intended as a means to initiate a dialogue among scholars and researchers, in the ways in which scholarship, while remaining faithful to its vision, objectives and ethics, can provide clues to understanding the significant ways in which the past can influence the present, and thus the means to approach substantial questions of our time. The follow-up to the reflections endeavoured in this volume should be done in future through a gathering of scholars and a publication which, it is hoped, will bring about new insights into a phenomenon not yet fully acknowledged: the emergence of a large number of new encyclopædic projects in the second half of 20th century Muslim societies.

Abdou Filali-Ansary
Director
Institute for the Study of Muslim Civilisations (AKU-ISMC), London

EDITOR'S NOTE*

Every society seeks ascertainment of its foundations in knowledge, how to attain knowledge, and how to present and promulgate an acknowledged basis of authority in the communities of science and learning. If linked to an institution of learning, the stock-taking, classification, and presentation of its concepts, methods, and matters will take the character of a systematic compilation which we have been accustomed to call an encyclopædia. Depending on the criteria of essential knowledge in the epistemic community, the concept of encyclopædia will vary not only in content, but also in the methodological approaches and in the forms of presentation.

The arrangement of the studies united in the present volume is to take into regard the spheres and milieus of the institutions of learning in mediæval and early modern Muslim societies. The clerical, legal, religious, scientific, and courteous traditions are being presented in view of their approaches to authority and tradition, and the constituents of material knowledge regarded as essential. After a general discussion of the concept of encyclopædia, the first part concerns the basis of authority in the institution of religion and law. The following studies are devoted to the *summæ* of scientific and philosophical learning based on Iranian and Greek sources, which in the first period of classical Islamic civilization developed in separate institutions and traditions of learning, although in constant interaction with the concurrent traditions of the religious community. It was at the courts and in the chancery of the central and provincial administrations—the scope of a third group of studies—, that models of integration and amalgamation were worked out by both secretaries and jurists. The special character of Muslim institutions, their teaching traditions and syllabi is put into perspective by a concluding Europeanist's viewpoint.

Gerhard Endress
University of Bochum (Germany)

* An endeavour has been made to introduce some degree of consistency in style. The transliteration of Arabic names and terms follows the usage of the *Encyclopædia of Islam* (using, however, *j* instead of *dj*, and *q* instead of *ḳ*).

THE CONTRIBUTORS

Mokdad Arfa is Professor of Arabic and Islamic Philosophy at the Faculty of Human and Social Sciences, University of Tunis. He completed his doctorate at Sorbonne in 1976 and Habilitation in 1996 in Tunis. Among his publications are *Kitab ʿilm al-kalam wal-falsafa* (1995) and *al-Kindi, Cinq Epîtres* (1976).

Ann Blair is Professor of History at Harvard University. She specialises in the cultural and intellectual history of early modern Europe (16th–17th centuries), with an emphasis on France. Her publications include *The Theater of Nature: Jean Bodin and Renaissance Science* (Princeton University Press, 1997) and "Reading Strategies for Coping with Information Overload ca. 1550–1700" in *Journal of the History of Ideas* (2003).

Abdesselam Cheddadi is Professor at Institut Universitaire de la Recherche Scientifique, Université Mohammed V, Rabat, Morocco. His research interests include Islamic history and culture, the process of modernity, and the problem of the relationship of non-western societies with it. He obtained his Doctorat d'État en Sciences Humaines et Sociales from the École des Hautes Études en Sciences Sociales, Paris. Among his publications are *Ibn Khaldun, Le Livre des Exemples, I: L'Autobiographie, La Muqaddima, texte traduit, presenté et annoté* (2002) and *Éducation et culture au Maroc, le difficile passage à la modernité* (2002).

Gerhard Endress is Professor of Arabic and Islamic Studies at Ruhr University, Bochum, Germany. He completed his doctorate in 1965 at the University of Frankfurt and his Habilitation from the same institution in 1972. Among his publications are *Islam: an historical introduction*, 2nd ed. (2002) and *A Greek and Arabic Lexicon: materials for a dictionary of the medieval translations from Greek into Arabic* (ed., with D. Gutas, 1992ff.).

Josef van Ess was Professor in Islamic and Semitic Studies at the University of Tübingen from 1968 till his retirement in 1999. He has published innumerable articles and many publications in German.

Among them are *Theologie und Gesellschaft im 2. und 3. Jahrhundert Hidschra: eine Geschichte des religiösen Denkens im frühen Islam*, and *Der Wesir und seine Gelehrten: zu Inhalt und Entstehungsgeschichte der theologischen Schriften des Rašīduddīn Fazlullah (gest. 718/1318).*

ABDOU FILALI-ANSARY is Director of the Institute for the Study of Muslim Civilisations, Aga Khan University, London. He served from 1984 to 2001 as the founding director of the King Abdul-Aziz Foundation for Islamic Studies and Human Sciences in Casablanca, Morocco. His work includes a translation into French of Ali Abderraziq's landmark book, *Islam and the Foundations of Political Power* (1994), and *Reforming Islam? An Introduction to Contemporary Debates* (2003).

DIMITRI GUTAS is Professor of Arabic and Greco-Arabic at Yale University. He obtained his doctorate from Yale in 1974. Among his interests are the processes of the transmission of Greek scientific and philosophical works into the Islamic world. His publications include *Greek Philosophers in the Arabic Tradition* (2000) and *A Greek and Arabic Lexicon: materials for a dictionary of the medieval translations from Greek into Arabic* (ed., with G. Endress, 1992ff.).

SYRINX VON HEES is based at Rheinische Friedrich-Wilhelms-Universität, Bonn. She was previously at the German Academic Exchange Service (DAAD) in Bonn and a visiting scholar at the CMES (Harvard). Her publications include *Enzyklopadie als Spiegel des Weltbildes: Qazwīnīs Wunder der Schöpfung* (2002).

ELAHEH KHEIRANDISH is lecturer at Harvard University's Department of the Classics. She obtained her doctorate from Harvard in 1991 in the History of Science. Her publications include a two-volume work, *The Arabic Version of Euclid's Optics: Kitab Uqlīdis fī Ikhtilāf al-manāẓir* (1999) and *Sources for the History of Mathematical Sciences in the Islamic World* (1991).

WADAD AL-QADI is Professor of Islamic Thought at the Department of Near Eastern Languages and Civilizations at the University of Chicago, and since 1997, The Avalon Foundation Distinguished Service Professor at the same university. Her most recent work is a critical edition of the 10th century prose work *al-Baṣā'ir wa-l-dhakhā'ir*, a nine-volume anthology of various literary topics written by Abū Ḥayyān al-Tawḥīdī.

RIDWAN AL-SAYYID is Professor of Islamic Studies at the Lebanese University. He received his PhD from the University of Tübingen. He is the editor-in-chief of *al-Ijtihād* published in Beirut and author and editor of many books in Arabic and German, including *Die Revolte des Ibn al-Ashʿath und die Koranleser* (1977) and *Azmat al-fikr al-siyāsī al-ʿarabī* (2000).

THE CONCEPT OF ENCYCLOPÆDIA

ENCYCLOPÆDIC ACTIVITIES IN THE ISLAMIC WORLD: A FEW QUESTIONS, AND NO ANSWERS

Josef van Ess
University of Tübingen

"So many summaries, so many new methods, so many indexes, so many dictionaries have slowed the live ardour which made men learned . . . All the sciences today are reduced to dictionaries, and no one seeks other keys to enter them", said Monsieur Huet, bishop of Avranches and member of the Academy, in French, of course, and three centuries ago, when the English did not yet dream of their Encyclopædia Britannica and when the French Encyclopédistes were still innocent (and, as we may hope, godly) youngsters.[1] Our new millennium is less prone to such misanthropic scepticism. The book market is flooded with handbooks and "encyclopædias" of all sorts, for scholars as well as for lay people like politicians, journalists, or managers. Theologians, academics rather than bishops, still produce encyclopædias of their different denominations, the Protestants as well as the Catholics or the Copts, in spite of their constant talk about their ecumenicity and their preaching one and the same truth. Blurbs written by the publishers praise encyclopædias as the last word of scholarship while a new edition is already on the way, and what is said there in one article is totally unconnected with what is said in the next one. Therefore Monsieur Huet's problem is still with us: Are encyclopædias in reality a latter day phenomenon, or do they open the horizon for further glorious development?

Neither seems to be the case, and the question is probably not an important one. Encyclopædias are not restricted to one particular period; they are ubiquitous and insofar perhaps fairly negligible. But the role played by encyclopædias in a non-Western civilization is a rewarding topic. Looking at people different from ourselves,

[1] Pierre Daniel Huet (1630–1721); cf. *Huetiana ou pensées diverses de M. Huet* (Paris 1722), p. 171 § 74, quoted after Ann Blair, 'Reading Strategies for Coping with Information Overload ca. 1550–1700', in: *Journal of the History of Ideas* 64 (2003): 22.

geographically or chronologically, tells us something about our own situation. Do we live in an encyclopædic age or are we simply uncultivated, having replaced encyclopædias by quiz shows? Were other ages or other civilizations more cultivated than we are, and how did those people look at encyclopædias? Did they ever use them, and who had them at his disposition? Did the scholars of the Mamluk period, of a period then which has frequently been called the classical age for encyclopædias in Islam (ʿUmarī, Nuwayrī and others), have the feeling that they were latecomers and that the achievements of earlier, more original and more creative centuries were about to get lost? Did they consider it their duty to save what could be saved, especially after Baghdād had been destroyed by the Mongols, just as the Abbasid caliph, who had been killed by the pagan intruders, had been replaced in Egypt (and only there, not in other countries) by a political phantom in order to make up for the loss of the spiritual centre? Or did they merely lack any new ideas, profiting instead from relative political stability and their personal affluence in order to keep themselves busy by collecting masses of old and worn out stuff? Did they perhaps understand themselves as the registrars and salesmen of a collective memory? Yet the material they brought together was mostly Arabic in kind whereas they themselves frequently happened to be of Turkish descent, members of a special social class, i.e. *awlād al-nās*, the "children of the Mamlūk gentry".[2] Did they therefore want to show that they had been completely assimilated or that they knew more about the past of the country their fathers had been governing than the aborigines who were Arabs? Should we regard then, in certain cases, an encyclopædia as a symbol of identity?

The possibility exists, but it rather applies to modern examples. After the Islamic revolution, one of the first things the new Iranian government thought about was an encyclopædia. This is how we got the (useful and quite learned) *Dāʾirat ul-maʿārif-i buzurg-i islāmī*[3] and,

[2] The historians Ibn al-Dawādārī (died 713/1313), Khalīl b. Aybak al-Ṣafadī (died 764/1363) and Ibn Taghrībirdī (= Tanrı-verdi, died 874/1470) are interesting specimens, in a way also Ibn Aydamir who will be mentioned later (below, n. 26). Cf. U. Haarmann, 'Väter und Söhne im Herrschaftssystem der Mamluken', in: *Berliner Wissenschaftliche Gesellschaft*, Jahrbuch 1995, p. 211ff.

[3] Tehran 1367/1988ff; there is also an Arabic version of it.

in addition to that, another more specifically Shīʿī encyclopædia.[4] These works replaced the enterprise started under the Shāh's regime, Ehsan Yarshater's *Encyclopædia Iranica* (first: *Encyclopædia Persica*) which still had a Latin, "Western" name, obviously in imitation of the *Encyclopædia Britannica.* Somewhat less ambitious were the Turks who, in 1939, started their *İslam Ansiklopedisi*, at a moment when Atatürk had been dead for less than one year. But they, too, wanted to show their particular physiognomy by defining their attitude towards Islam. They simply translated the European *Encyclopædia of Islam* (presumably in its French version) with its articles written by Western orientalists—with exception of those on Turkey and its civilization which were now written by Turks. Something similar happened in Pakistan where the *Encyclopædia of Islam* was translated into Urdu after the creation of the state in 1947; in our days, half a century later, nobody would conceive any more such an idea. Yet even if these "nationalist" incentives may be gone by now they always served—or pretended to serve—an older and more respectable purpose. The *İslam Ansiklopedisi* has a long programmatic preface which is introduced by a quotation from the *Kutadgu Bilig*: "bilig kıymetini biliglig bilig", "Only wisdom knows the value of wisdom".[5] This slogan had the advantage of coming from Central Asia from where the Anatolian Turks claimed to be descended, but it also pointed to acquiring and preserving knowledge as a value in itself. This is a motive to which, as it seems, we all can subscribe, less transitory and time-bound than those mentioned before. We should, however, not forget that in Western countries which like to identify themselves as having proceeded beyond nationalism, an encyclopædia is at present first and foremost a commercial enterprise.

Modern Oriental encyclopædias have been, until now, mainly governmental projects. This is why the search for identity has become so prominent a feature. For the same reason we should be cautious in projecting this incentive back into the medieval past. The term "encyclopædia" itself is, in a way, modern and certainly Western. The Arabs translated it into *Dāʾirat al-maʿārif* (*dāʾira* corresponding to

[4] The *Dāʾirat ul-maʿārif-i tashayyuʿ*.
[5] Volume I, printed Istanbul 1950, p. i.

Greek κύκλος, the "cycle" in "encyclopædia") or into *mawsūʿa*, a neologism which rather emphasizes the comprehensiveness.[6]

Mawsūʿa is also the term used for the corresponding entry in the *Encyclopædia of Islam*. Charles Pellat wrote the article, with all his enthusiasm for *adab*, and he starts with the "encyclopædism" of authors like Jāḥiẓ or Ibn Qutayba. But this propels us right away into the centre of the problem. Could it be that such a start is responsible for the inflationary manner in which the term is used in our discipline? Are Jāḥiẓ and Ibn Qutayba, as *udabāʾ*, also "encyclopædic"? Is Ṣafadī's *Wāfī bil-wafayāt* an encyclopædia or merely an extremely "comprehensive" biographical dictionary? Is ʿAbd al-Jabbār's *Mughnī* a Muʿtazilī encyclopædia or simply a *summa theologica*? Is Qudāma b. Jaʿfar's *K. al-Kharāj wa-ṣināʿāt al-kātib* rightly called an encyclopædia by Paul Heck in his Ph.D. thesis,[7] or is it simply a manual? And what about Qazwīnī's *ʿAjāʾib al-makhlūqāt*? Is this book really an "encyclopædia of natural science" as Syrinx von Hees labels it in her dissertation,[8] or is it merely a cosmography as it has always been called? In this last case, we are even confronted with a twofold semantic charade: can we talk about "natural science" with regard to this author? Qazwīnī deals with the angels in one of his chapters, the angels which belonged to the cosmos as it was understood in the Middle Ages (thence "cosmography") but never made it into natural science the way this word is understood when it falls upon a modern person's ear.[9] I do not want to say that speaking of "encyclopædias" in these cases is totally wrong. Nobody can prevent us from using the word in a looser and less determined way. But what we need is a definition. Otherwise what is going to happen might

[6] Mention should be made here of the *Mawṣūʿa Filasṭīniyya* (1–3, Beirut 1978; ²Damascus 1984) which, as a symbol of identity, is unique insofar as the identity is not kept awake by an independent nation but by refugees and victims of an occupation.

[7] *The Construction of Knowledge in Islamic Civilization* (Leiden 2002), p. 1: "Qudāma's work must then be understood as an encyclopædia".

[8] *Enzyklopädie als Spiegel des Weltbildes. Qazwīnī's Wunder der Schöpfung, eine Naturkunde des 13. Jahrhunderts* (Wiesbaden 2002).

[9] Von Hees defends her usage of the term, p. 109ff. For the sake of justice, we have to admit that, in German, "Naturkunde" is not the same as "Naturwissenschaft". The word avoids the anachronism which is always implied when "natural science" is used with respect to the Middle Ages; it means something like "physiography", a description of nature. But this is not my point here; the question is rather whether the angels belong to nature.

be what happened to the term "humanism" as used by George Makdisi, Joel Kraemer, Marc Bergé or Mohammed Arkoun: it sounds good but it is extremely difficult to pin down, and everybody understands it according to his own gusto.[10] We would be left with vague associations.

Such a definition (*taʿrīf*) can, of course, only be a descriptive one, a *rasm*, not a *ḥadd*. Is dimension, bulkiness, the only criterion? Or is it comprehensiveness, in the sense that a certain "encyclopædic spirit" has to go with it? What does an encyclopædia have to contain, not only for us but according to the perspective of the age in which it was produced? The word was coined by the European humanists, at about 1490, the time when Columbus discovered America. Its origin went back to the ἐγκύκλιος παιδεία of the Greeks. But this ἐγκύκλιος παιδεία did not primarily materialize in books; it was rather a "Bildungsideal", the cultural code of a period, a normative standard of intellectual formation which developed into a *studium generale*, the "general education" of the kind I still witnessed at the American University of Beirut (a former missionary institution) when teaching there in the 1960s. When books were written for this purpose in ancient Greece they reflected something present in the author's and the reader's mind. In other words: an encyclopædia was always the work of one author, and it was in harmony with the wisdom expected from every contemporary, or rather: from every member of a certain class, namely the aristocrats. Is this also true for early Islam, and should we therefore call a book an "encyclopædia" when it reflects the *adab* of its time? This was Pellat's assumption. However, according to our usage of the term, an "encyclopædic" mind stores and masters the gist of several and different disciplines whereas under the early Abbasids the wisdom of the early days had just started differentiating into the "sciences" of the later period. When did the *ʿilm* of the Qurʾān and the *Ṣaḥāba* thus change into the *ʿulūm* of the future generations so that one person could be "encyclopædic" whereas others were not? Should we rather call a man like Ibn al-Jawzī an "encyclopædist" who lived a few centuries later and who, though being a Ḥanbali preacher and jurist in the first place, was able to express himself in *kalām* terms or compose poetry? He was certainly

[10] Cf. Marco Schöller, "Zum Begriff des «islamischen Humanismus»", in: *ZDMG* 151 (2001): 275ff.

aware of the fact that he was well-versed in a plurality of things. Nevertheless we find him narrow-minded rather than encyclopædic.

This dilemma may have been the reason why Gerhard Endress, in his chapter on encyclopædias written for the *Grundriß der Arabischen Philologie*, does not mention any endeavour of this sort before al-Fārābī. For him it was the philosophers who developed the concept, inspired by the cycle of commentaries written on the Aristotelian corpus which formed the basis of their curriculum.[11] Aristotle had been universal in his teaching and in his writings, they thought; following him meant presenting all available knowledge in a new, non-theological discourse. All available *theoretical* knowledge, to be precise. Professional practice was something else; this belonged to the realm of special training, in medicine for instance or in astronomy. Nevertheless collections of specialized knowledge were possible, too, and, if combined with practical advice, even desirable. Ibn Sīnā used for his medical compilation the word *Qānūn*, a Greek term which seems to have got into Arabic by way of the Islamic tax system.[12] Conversely, he gave his most "encyclopædic" work a medical title taken from Arabic: *K. al-Shifāʾ* (The Book of Healing), a medication for the soul, not for the body. We may doubt, however, whether the *Shifāʾ* tallies with our understanding of an encyclopædia; the book was rather a huge commentary on the Aristotelian corpus. Ibn Sīnā's *Dānishnāma-yi ʿAlāʾī* comes closer to what we mean by our expression; this book, of much smaller size than the *Shifāʾ*, contains, in a nutshell, the essential issues of the philosophical curriculum put together for a person who was not a specialist, and presented in a language intelligible to him, namely Persian. *Dānishnāma* (Book of [the necessary] Knowledge) is a title which elegantly meets this intention and therefore may be seen as a kind of fore-runner to our term "encyclopædia." As for the *al-Qānūn fī l-ṭibb*, it is rather what we would call an encyclopædia "of" something: of medicine, in this case, as we have them nowadays for cookery, for tax regulations or for Islamic studies. But since this work was written for the practitioner and specialist we would prefer calling it a handbook or a manual.

[11] *GAP*, vol. III 57ff. We should, of course, keep in mind that Endress was responsible, in this multi-authored work, only for the chapter on philosophy; *adab* was written by somebody else (vol. II: 208ff, by H. Horst). Cf. now also H. H. Biesterfeldt, "Medieval Arabic Encyclopedias of Science and Philosophy", in: St. Harvey (ed.), *The Medieval Hebrew Encyclopedias of Science and Philosophy* (Dordrecht 2000): 77ff.

[12] Cf. *EI*[2] IV 556 (Y. Linant de Bellefonds).

Or is systematisation the main criterion for encyclopædias: putting things in the right order, arranging the sciences according to a hierarchical concept? Fārābī's *Iḥṣāʾ al-ʿulūm* would be a good example. But what about Khwārazmī's *Mafātīḥ al-ʿulūm* then which lists a great number of sciences but in print only counts some 150 pages? Or Ibn Farīghūn's *Jawāmiʿ al-ʿulūm* where the author does not *say* so much about the disciplines he enumerates but rather presents them in Porphyrian trees, the *tashjīr* system as it was called in Arabic? And what about Ghazzālī's *Iḥyāʾ ʿulūm al-dīn*? Can we read this impressive work as an encyclopædia of practical religious behaviour, a kind of counter-project ("Gegenentwurf") against Ibn Sīnā's plainly theoretical *Shifāʾ*, counter-project also insofar as its author tended to reduce philosophy to mere propædeutics, in his *Maqāṣid al-falāsifa*? Was the "project" as conceived by the philosophers thus early on hijacked by the theologians who took over what they could use from philosophy and left everything else aside? Endress rightly points to the importance of Najm al-dīn al-Kātibī's *Ḥikmat ʿayn al-qawāʿid* in this respect. But what about Majlisī's *Biḥār al-anwār*? Is this an encyclopædia?

Islamic philosophy also provides us with the first example of an encyclopædia being organized and elaborated not by one author only, but by several people who worked together: the *Rasāʾil Ikhwān al-Ṣafāʾ*. The Ikhwān were dilettanti, people who loved philosophy (and perhaps used it for a religious purpose) but never made their living out of it, in some respect comparable to Abū Ḥayyān al-Tawḥīdī (who knew them but did not think very highly of them).[13] Living in Baṣra, far from the court at Baghdād, they tried to fix the state of the art in all the disciplines an educated layman should be conversant in, like a team working on a "project", continuing in their own way the tradition of the bourgeois "salon" which had been so typical for this town during the time of al-Jāḥiẓ. In classical Islam such cooperation was a singular event, never to be repeated until the rediscovery of their corpus by Western scholars.[14] We feel reminded

[13] Cf. his *K. al-Imtāʿ wal-muʾānasa*, ed. Aḥmad Amīn and Aḥmad al-Zayn (²Cairo 1373/1953), vol. II, p. 4ff; Abū Ḥayyān's own interest in philosophy comes out best in his *K. al-Muqābasāt*.

[14] Friedrich Dieterici, *Die Abhandlungen der Ichwān aṣ-ṣafāʾ in Auswahl zum ersten Mal aus arabischen Handschriften herausgegeben* (Leipzig 1886), with German translations of the most important parts being published from 1858 onward.

of the French Encyclopédistes who, following the initiative of d'Alembert and Diderot, cooperated as a "société de gens de lettres". They, too, were amateurs in philosophy; today we would call them intellectuals. When they posed as "philosophers" they resembled early Islamic theologians and literati like al-Naẓẓām who, at Baghdād and during the highest efflorescence of the Muʿtazila, was called a philosopher by his Christian contemporary Job of Edessa.[15] They were philosophers insofar as they understood their enterprise as a step forward towards emancipation; knowledge meant enlightenment. In a way, this was similar to what Aristotle had had in mind (and, in his wake, the Islamic philosophers) when they said that knowledge enhances a person's εὐδαιμονία or *saʿāda*—knowledge as a contribution to man's happiness. But the Europeans pursued this ideal with a certain missionary spirit, a "mission civilisatrice". This new and ultimately, somewhat militant tendency reached the Islamic world only with the Turkish *İslam Ansiklopedisi*. In Europe the *Encyclopædia Britannica*, with its pretentious name, added an element of national glory to it, at least for our ears; Diderot and his people had never thought of naming their project an "Encyclopédie Française". The French published their last volume in 1765, the British started only three years later, in 1768. I do not want to say that they had an empire in mind; there had been an attempt in England before, by Ephraim Chambers who had called his work a "Cyclopedia or a Universal Dictionary of Arts and Sciences" (1728), and the French had originally thought of simply translating this book. But in any case knowledge meant power here, and encyclopædic knowledge had to encompass the entire world (which, to the Europeans, ended at the borders of their continent at that time). The French included numerous and long articles on technology; in classical Islam this has almost never been done.

The history of the *Encyclopædia Britannica* is a success story; the last edition came out in 2002. It is dedicated "(by permission) to George W. Bush, president of the United States and to Her Majesty Queen Elizabeth II". The editors follow an ancient habit; in 1974 the 15th edition mentioned the same Queen together with president R. W. Reagan. Our question is therefore not whether the two addressees of the year 2002 will ever waste much time studying this awe-inspiring

[15] Cf. my *Theologie und Gesellschaft im 2. und 3. Jahrhundert Hidschra* (Berlin 1991–1997), vol. III: 299 and 334; also vol. IV: 733.

book of 29 volumes (and far more than 30,000 pages, if we include the introductory volume and the indexes), but whether Islamic encyclopædias could also be dedicated to somebody and why this was done. Half of the question has already been answered; we mentioned the *Dānishnāma-yi ʿAlāʾī* where the epithet *ʿAlāʾī* hints at the Kākūyid ruler ʿAlāʾ al-dawla Muḥammad ibn Rustam Dushmanziyār who reigned from before 398/1008 until 433/1044 and whom Avicenna served as vizier. No Islamic book started without an invocation of God (and usually also the Prophet), but this habit never hindered anybody from uttering profuse praise of a prince or a sponsor if this turned out to be timely or necessary.

In Avicenna's case it was necessary, for he had written his compendium at the order (*be-fermān*) of his master as he says in his preface. The title itself was added later, by a pupil of his.[16] Another—and even better—example is Fakhr al-dīn al-Rāzī (died 606/1210) who, in 574/1179, wrote his *Kitāb-i sittīnī*, a kind of encyclopædia for beginners which enumerated 60 different disciplines and was called *Jāmiʿ al-ʿulūm*, again in Persian, and dedicated to the Khwārazmshāh Abū l-Muẓaffar Tekish (reigned 567/1172–596/1200). He says in his introduction that he "has gathered together there all the sciences of his age in order to establish a repertoire for scholars at the court to use".[17] We may assume that these "scholars" were not very fluent in Arabic,[18] but as far as Persian was concerned they may at least have used their reading ability. For they were offered, among other things, a chapter on military science which dealt with the production of kettle-drums (*ṭubūl*) and (permitted) means of mass-destruction like inflammable sulphur compounds.[19] The noise made by these formidable instruments helped Tekish to defeat the last representative of the Great Seljuks in Persia; consequently, in 595/1199, one year before his death, he was invested by the caliph al-Nāṣir with the Sultanate of Iraq. We must admit, though, that this experience with technology did not bring his successors much luck; the caliph was in the end not deposed and killed by the Khwārazmshāhs but by the Mongols.

[16] *Encyclopaedia Iranica*, 6 (1993): 651 f. s. v. *Dāneš-nāma* (H. Dabashi).

[17] Ž. Vesel in *EI*² VI 908 s. v. *Mawsūʿa*; cf. also id. in *Encyclopaedia Iranica*, 8 (1998): 436 s. v. *Encyclopædias, Persian.*

[18] The book exists, however, also in an Arabic version (cf. GAL² 1/669, S 1/924).

[19] *Jāmiʿ al-ʿulūm* (lith. Bombay 1906, reprint Tehran 1346 H. sh./1967), pp. 157–160.

When, more than a century later, the Mongols had equally transgressed the peak of their power in Iran Shams al-dīn-i Āmulī composed an even bigger encyclopædia, the *Nafā'is al-funūn fī 'arā'is al-'uyūn* which covered 120 sciences altogether;[20] he dedicated it to Abū Isḥāq Īnjū, the prince of Shiraz whose liberal rule was, as is well-known, nostalgically remembered by Ḥāfiẓ. Iran was a productive area in this respect; Āmulī had doubled the number of disciplines in comparison to Rāzī's catalogue. In Iran, Ibn Sīnā's impetus remained effective during the centuries, and there was always an audience who wanted to be educated. Mamlūk society provided such an audience, too, but Egypt had a different past. There was no Avicenna available; the Egyptians were not particularly philosophically-minded, and the hey-day of their cultural achievement had been under the Fāṭimids. This was a precarious heritage for a Sunni community; it is true that Maqrīzī revived it, but other authors preferred a different canon to shape the collective memory. The Islamic West had been in a similar situation. Pre-Islamic Spain had nothing to offer with regard to Greek philosophy, and there was only one Latin author whose work was taken up in an Arabic translation: the historian Orosius.[21] In their collective memory, the people of al-Andalus remembered their Syrian origins as long as they were under Umayyad rule; this is why we feel tempted to interpret Ibn 'Abdrabbih's *'Iqd al-farīd* as a kind of encyclopædia for the "New World", *sit venia verbo.* But we would certainly be using the term in a metaphorical way then. The only work of Maghribī origin which deserves the compliment of being "encyclopædic" is Ibn Khaldūn's *Muqaddima*; the author profits from the (rather short-lived) rise of philosophy in Spain when he, besides talking about history, describes and evaluates, in the sixth part of his introduction to the *K. al-'Ibar*, a number of other

[20] Lithograph Tehran 1309; edited by Abū l-Ḥusayn-i Sha'rānī 1–3, Tehran 1377/1957–1379/1959. The chapter on *futuwwa* was published by Morteza Sarraf in: *Rasā'il-i Javānmardān/Traités des Compagnons-Chevaliers* (Bibl. Iranienne 20, Tehran/Paris 1973), p. 58ff; cf. the Persian introduction by the editor, p. 19ff and the French introduction by H. Corbin, ib. 27ff. In contrast to Fakhr al-dīn al-Rāzī, Āmulī includes sufism among the "sciences".

[21] Ed. 'Abd al-Raḥmān Badawī, *Orosius: Ta'rīkh al-'ālam. Al-Tarjama al-'arabiyya al-qadīma* (Beirut 1982); cf. G. Levi Della Vida, 'La traduzione araba delle storie di Orosio', in: *al-Andalus* 19 (1954): 257ff. Another Latin work which has certainly been used was the agronomical treatise *De re rustica* by Columella, but it always remained anonymous, and the contents were not philosophical either.

sciences in a systematic order.[22] However, his reputation is founded on his ideas about the growth and decay of civilizations. As for the rest, he rather displayed a respectable knowledge of Eastern material; he summarized without saying much new.

Encyclopædias were, of course, always only as good as the expertise of their authors. They could serve as an instrument of education, but then it all depended on what the audience wanted to learn. Every area had its own cultural background. In Fakhr al-dīn al-Rāzī's *Jāmiʿ al-ʿulūm* Arab *adab* boiled down to dry terminology and occasional advice of poetical or rhetorical craftsmanship; the only artistic pastime which was found worth being mentioned in greater detail was, except warfare, playing chess.[23] In Egypt, on the contrary, Ibn Faḍl Allāh al-ʿUmarī (700/1301–749/1349), not a theologian and philosopher like al-Rāzī, but a rather unsuccessful government official, concentrated, in his *Masālik al-abṣār*, mainly on history and geography. He fulfilled his promise to describe "the earth and its inhabitants", i.e. to follow the paths (*masālik*) visible to everybody's eye (*baṣar*), but he had nothing to say about war technique. What he offered instead were remarks about administration, a topic exhaustively handled later on by his fellow-countryman al-Qalqashandī.[24] And Ibn Khaldūn was mainly a solitary and homeless thinker who, after some unhappy experiences as a diplomat, wrote his work in seclusion at Qalʿat Ibn Salāma and ended up as a jurist. The examples are good altogether for showing one thing: what we should never expect from any encyclopaedia, whether medieval or modern, is originality.

Moreover, there were fields of cultural interest which, as separate and independent subjects, were never incorporated into an encyclopædia. Poetry was one of them, in spite of its relevance even for the common man. Poems had been collected all the time, in *dīwāns* first and later in anthologies; the most comprehensive works of this sort have become available only recently: Ibn Maymūn's *Muntahā l-ṭalab*[25]

[22] Cf. the old English translation by F. Rosenthal, vol. II, p. 409ff and the new French one by Abdesselam Cheddadi (Paris 2001), vol. I, p. 832ff. Ibn Khaldūn quotes Orosius, by the way, though not in his *Muqaddima* but in the later parts of his *K. al-ʿIbar* (cf. Badawī, previous note, p. 35ff and 469ff).

[23] *Jāmiʿ* p. 220ff, with numerous diagrams.

[24] The topoi of Islamic world-history are treated by B. Radtke, *Weltgeschichte und Weltbeschreibung im mittelalterlichen Islam*; Beirut 1992 (Beiruter Texte und Studien, 51).

[25] This work was completed in Baghdād in the year 589/1193 (*GAL* S 1/494); ed. Muḥ. Nabīl Ṭarīfī, 1–9, Beirut 1999.

and Ibn Aydamir's *Durr al-farīd*.[26] But this remained a world by itself, being not so much a matter of education but of aesthetic pleasure. Something similar may be said of lexicography. From the beginning, the Arabs had been obsessed by the analysis of their language (their own one only); they were much better at that than Isidore of Seville. But this predilection, for understandable reasons, merely resulted in dictionaries, though sometimes of encyclopædic size, like an "ocean" (Fīrūzābādī's *Qāmūs* which, however, still needed Murtaḍā al-Zabīdī's "bridal garland", *Tāj al-ʿarūs*, in order to be really crowned with ultimate success).[27] And finally biographical literature, "famous men", the celebrities modern encyclopædias and contemporary newspapers are so fond of this genre also largely remained something apart. Ṣafadī was, as Hellmut Ritter fully recognized for the first time, the greatest protagonist in this field, especially since he wrote, in addition to his *Wāfī*, another dictionary in which he enumerated his contemporaries, the *Aʿyān al-ʿaṣr*; there he could no longer build on earlier sources.

We have to bear in mind, though, that European encyclopædias varied in their approaches, too. In the Western world the cultural background and the reading public mattered as much as everywhere else. When the Germans published their first encyclopædias their country did not yet exist as a nation; nobody therefore thought of a name corresponding to that of the *Encyclopædia Britannica*. They were latecomers in this like in other respects, and their encyclopædias did, at that moment, not commemorate a people but the individuals who financed and published them: Brockhaus (in 1796) and Meyer (in 1840). Both persons were not scholars but entrepreneurs like Ephraim Chambers in early 18th-century England. Interestingly, they both did not call their project an encyclopædia; they called it a "Konversationslexikon", something useful for conversation, culti-

[26] The autograph dates from 680/1281. The author had witnessed the fall of Baghdād; his father had been killed when the Mongols entered the town (*GAL* S 1/444; cf. G. J. H. van Gelder in *EI*² Suppl, 635 s.n. *Muḥammad b. Sayf al-Dīn* with further literature). The most famous anthology is, of course, Abū Tammām's *Ḥamāsa*. The book was edited as early as 1828 by G. Freytag (Bonn, with Latin translation, 1857–61). The Būlāq edition of 1284/1867 depends completely on this German one. And for Spain we should not forget Ibn Bassām's *Dhakhīra* (ed. Iḥsān ʿAbbās, 1–8, Beirut 1399/1979).

[27] The metaphorical connection between the "ocean" and the "bridal garland" is made in the title of the commentary: *Tāj al-ʿarūs min jawāhir al-Qāmūs*; the pearls which are found in the ocean are put into the crown of the bride.

vated conversation, of course, "Meyers Conversations-Lexikon für die gebildeten Stände" as the second one of them formulated it, "a book of reference for the cultivated people"—or rather "Stände", the upper classes, not just "people", since "Bildung" (culture) was conceivable only with a certain elevated status. This brings us back to the early Arabs: the encyclopædia as a tool for practicing *adab* in conversation.[28] Everybody who wants to talk with other people has to show interest, and in order to show interest he has to know something about everything; otherwise he would be boring, as boring as a modern specialist. Specialists are possibly competent, but they are also isolated. They are not "gesellschaftsfähig" as educated people used to say in the earlier days. The word is difficult to translate ("sociable" is not enough. You can be sociable and an ignoramus at the same time). Baldesar Castiglione has described this elitist attitude which fits so badly into our modern democratic societies, in his famous *Libro del Cortegiano* at the beginning of the 16th-century: you have to keep your conversation going with witty anecdotes and pertinent comparisons. To take only one example: you should know something about music and demonstrate an exquisite taste with regard to it, but you should avoid sounding the trumpet during a party because you would have to blow up your cheeks for that and you would look funny. Did Ibn Qutayba think this way? *Adab* as a normative ideal then, and Ibn Qutayba's *Adab al-kātib* or his *K. al-Maʿārif* as "encyclopædias" for somebody who had to know something about everything? Not too much in any case—and the right things, of course, things which are socially correct; Castiglione talks about love, Ibn Qutayba does not.

Castiglione wrote his book not only about the *cortegiano* but also for the *cortegiano*, the courtier, the cultivated aristocrat of the Italian renaissance who excelled not only by his *finesse d'esprit* but also by his *virtú*, his morality. Similarly, the ἐγκύκλιος παιδεία was originally destined for the free man, at least in the circles of the Sophists. Was *adab* then originally something for Arabs only, not for the clients, the *mawālī* who were merely specialists, like the slaves? This is, of course, the question: to what extent and from which moment onward was Islamic society an egalitarian society, as far as non-Arabs were concerned. However, analogies are dangerous, and we should avoid

[28] Cf. H. Kilpatrick, "A Genre in Classical Arabic Literature: the *adab* Encyclopedia", in: Proceedings 10th Congress UEAI, Edinburgh (1982): 34ff.

indulging in vague omnicomparatism. We only want to ask questions. Was *adab* really encyclopædic? With Ibn Qutayba or Qudāma ibn Jaʿfar it seems rather to have been practical, like the "Konversationslexikon". With respect to their *adab* people wanted to have, as for anything else, something where they could look up everything they needed or where they found all they had to learn. In German we call this a "Nachschlagewerk", a reference-work. This is much more modest than "encyclopædia"—and in a number of cases perhaps more appropriate. There are other words we can think of, "Sammelwerk" for instance or, in lexicography, "thesaurus".[29]

Should we leave then the grandiloquent term "encyclopædia" for a few ambitious specimens the criteria of which we would still have to define? Talking about encyclopædias in terms of reference works brings us down to the level of practical usage; conceived in this way encyclopædic activities have always been necessary, in the Middle Ages as well as in our days, in the East as well as in the West. The conditions of working, however, have changed. Do we have to assume, as we normally do, that all the medieval authors we mentioned, whatever the size of their literary production, represented the type of the lonely scholar, a type revered in the West (in Europe rather) for centuries but dying out at present, just before our eyes? As far as Ṣafadī is concerned, to take only one example, this seems to be true; we still possess the brouillon (*muswadda*) of his *Wāfī bil-wafayāt*, and we can see how he inserted leaflets with material he had found somewhere, perhaps on his many journeys in Syria or Egypt. But we know from our own experience that complex societies also need the other type, the impresario, the scholar who finances or tries to find money for pretentious projects. What about ʿUmarī then who died at the relatively young age of 48 years and who left, besides his *Masālik al-abṣār*, still another, possibly more original work, the *Taʿrīf bi-muṣṭalaḥ al-sharīf*? Was he, as *ibn al-nās*, rich enough to afford some research assistants (whom he never mentions, of course), as did Leone Caetani, the *principe di Teano, poi duca di Sermoneta*, for his *Annali dell' Islam*.[30] Or was he simply quick and active, though not so much

[29] A dictionary would be a "thesaurus", however, only when it has some historical dimension. In order to find a "treasure" one has to dig deeply; insofar the metaphor differs from "ocean" which emphasizes the breadth rather than the depth.

[30] Cf. G. Levi Della Vida, *Fantasmi ritrovati* (Venice 1966), p. 19ff: "La soffitta delle Botteghe Oscure."

in "writing" (in the sense of composing) but in compiling? And what about Rashīd ul-dīn, the vizier of the Īlkhānid rulers Ghāzān Khān and Öljeitü? We cannot suppress the feeling that, as far as his *Jāmiʿ ul-tavārīkh* is concerned, a world-history of encyclopædic format including China and even unimportant Europe, he did not write it all by himself. He did not have the time for that; he seems to have had ghost-writers. The book was copied at his expense and illustrated with precious (and costly) miniatures. For his theological treatises, which, compared to his historical "encyclopædia", were of minor value but important for his prestige, he left money in his famous *waqf* at Tabrīz;[31] the scholars of his time were invited to write blurbs *(taqārīẓ)*—and did not blush to do so.[32]

There were certainly more such examples. We still have to find out how, under similar circumstances, but in an earlier period, Jayhānī, the supposed author of a geographical "encyclopædia", got his work done; he was the minister of the Sāmānid ruler Naṣr II. b. Aḥmad (reigned 301/914–331/943) and probably had an entire staff at his disposition. A book on geography which also dealt with the non-Islamic, the unknown world (for practical purposes, of course; it is difficult to trade or make war in an area which is unknown) had to be readjusted and enlarged all the time; this is why other members of Jayhānī's family who equally functioned in the Samānid administration apparently added further material to it. For a member of the secretarial class an encyclopædic approach to the world he had to administer was a professional necessity. Muṭahhar b. Ṭāhir al-Maqdisī's *K. al-Badʾ wal-taʾrīkh* is worth some further investigation in this respect.[33] He worked for a Sāmānid governor in the province of Sīstān, at Bust, and his book, of moderate dimensions, though published in six volumes, comprises history as well as geography, a lot of (Muʿtazila-inspired) theology together with Greek philosophy and cosmology, unknown information about non-Islamic religions and civilizations in addition to a (somewhat conventional) survey of

[31] Cf. my *Der Wesir und seine Gelehrten*, Wiesbaden 1981 (Abhandlungen für die Kunde des Morgenlandes XLV 4); now also Birgitt Hoffmann, *Waqf im mongolischen Iran: Rashīduddīns Sorge um Nachruhm und Seelenheil* (Stuttgart 2000).

[32] Compare F. Rosenthal, "«Blurbs» (taqārīẓ) from fourteenth-century Egypt", in: *Oriens* 27–28 (1981): 177ff.

[33] Cf. *EI*[2] VII 762, where the work is called a "historical encyclopædia".

the most important Islamic denominations or "heresies", a "Konfessionskunde" as Rudolf Strothmann used to call it.[34] The conservative title hides an astonishing amalgamation of indigenous and foreign knowledge; "whoever has a look into this book", says al-Maqdisī, "gets as-it-were a bird's-eye view of the world."[35] As a historian, Maqdisī is more cosmopolitan but less detailed than Ṭabarī. In any case, he was a keen observer and a very independent thinker—an Arab (a man from Jerusalem?) in the service of the Iranians, as Ṭabarī was a Persian working for an Arab audience in Iraq.

Finally, there is one fact which we should not forget: all the authors we mentioned lived in a world which did not yet know the art of printing. Knowledge had a high reputation; acquiring it was encouraged by the religious ethos: *uṭlub al-ʿilm wa-law fī l-Ṣīn*, "Look out for knowledge, be it in China".[36] But manuscripts were not always available, and books could disappear completely; knowledge was vulnerable and perishable. Collecting the wisdom of the age, even without any originality, was a cultural exploit, in a way even a necessity. The identity of the society was at stake, its "civilization" in the original sense of the word; there were not many other ways to have it survive. However, the task became increasingly more difficult. Assiduity was an important virtue then, but also curiosity, though curiosity with regard to the past rather than to the future. The reception depended on the linguistic medium; in Iran (and later on in India) encyclopædias, like poetry, had to be presented in Persian. The immediate motive for getting to work could change: from practical reasons in the case of Ibn Qutayba to programmatic considerations like those of the philosophers or, perhaps, nostalgia and personal identity problems in the Mamlūk period.

This variety of incentives and realizations suggests that too rigid a definition would not be of much help. What we rather need is a variety of terms and an attempt at periodization. For encyclopædism

[34] The term "heresiography" which we tend to use nowadays is much less appropriate. The *Mafātīḥ al-ʿulūm* of al-Khwārazmī, a contemporary of Maqdisī's, and again a Sāmānid *kātib*, also contains a list of the Islamic denominations.

[35] *Fa-l-nāẓir fī hādhā l-kitāb kal-mushrif al-muṭṭaliʿ ʿalā l-ʿālam*; cf. *Badʾ*, ed. Huart, vol. I, p. 17, l. 10. For Greek thought Maqdisī uses, by the way, a source which was otherwise only rarely available in the Islamic world: Pseudo-Plutarch's *Placita philosophorum* (cf. H. Daiber, *Aëtius Arabus. Die Vorsokratiker in arabischer Überlieferung*, Wiesbaden 1980).

[36] Cf. F. Rosenthal, *Knowledge Triumphant* (Leiden 1970).

is in itself a historical phenomenon, and history is a world of change. The only common denominator underlying this time-bound but, in a way, also timeless process is perhaps the undying illusion that knowledge is able to achieve something. "Illusion" insofar as knowledge has to be spread for that. The old way of achieving this goal was reading, a cultural device of venerable reputation which reached its culmination in the Gutenberg galaxy. Will the Internet be encyclopædic? For the moment encyclopædias seem mainly to be functioning as reference works for scholars who are searching, in an alphabetical jungle, for a synthesis which they themselves are no longer able to achieve. We are not "encyclopædic" ourselves. But have we ever been? The problem is rather that the specialist is still expected to give, as an "expert", encyclopædic answers; this is something he, by definition, cannot live up to. Monsieur Huet would probably have nodded in sarcastic agreement. But who cares?

THE ARABIC ISLAMIC TRADITIONS

BIOGRAPHICAL DICTIONARIES AS THE SCHOLARS' ALTERNATIVE HISTORY OF THE MUSLIM COMMUNITY

Wadad al-Qadi
The University of Chicago

> History is divided into two kinds: a kind in which the main interest is in kings, chiefs, wars, campaigns, conquests of lands, and public events like prices, rains, thunderbolts, misfortunes, calamities, earthquakes, dynastic change, religious and sectarian turns, affairs of notables . . . and so forth; and a kind in which the purpose is the elucidation of the conditions of the scholars, judges, pious leaders and rulers, and Ṣūfīs of praiseworthy conduct: the dates of their births and deaths, some of their doctrines and narrations, and their teachers and transmitters; this kind is the concern of the scholars of *ḥadīth*. Al-Rāfiʿī, *Tāʾrīkh Qazwīn*, I, 2.

In the past three decades, the body of scholarship on Arabic Islamic biographical dictionaries has grown substantially.[1] The scholars studied

---

[1] See, in chronological order, Hartmut Fähndrich, "The *Wafayāt al-Aʿyān* of Ibn Khallikān: A New Approach," *Journal of the American Oriental Society* 93 (1973), 432–445; Tarif Khalidi, "Islamic Biographical Dictionaries: A Preliminary Assessment," *Muslim World* 63 (1973), 53–65; I. Hafsi, "Recherches sur le genre "*ṭabaqāt*" dans la littérature arabe," *Arabica* 23 (1976), 227–65 and 24 (1977), 1–41, 150–86; Fedwa Malti-Douglas, "Controversy and its Effects in the Biographical Tradition of al-Khaṭīb al-Baghdādī," *Studia Islamica* 46 (1977), 115–131; Hartmut Fähndrich, "Compromising the Caliph," *Journal of Arabic Literature* 8 (1977), 36–47; Malak Abiad, "Origine et développement des dictionnaires biographiques arabes," *Bulletin d'Etudes Orientales* 31 (1979 [1980]), 7–15; Fedwa Malti-Douglas, "Dreams, the Blind, and the Semiotics of the Biographical Notice," *Studia Islamica* 51 (1980), 137–162; idem, "Biography, Islamic," *Dictionary of the Middle Ages* (New York, 1982), II, 237–239; M. J. L. Young, "Arabic Biographical Writing," in *Cambridge History of Arabic Literature: Religion, Learning and Science in the 'Abbasid Period* (Cambridge: Cambridge University Press, 1983), 168–187; Paul Auchterlonie, *Arabic Biographical Dictionaries: A Summary Guide and Bibliography* (Durham: Middle East Libraries Committee, 1987); D. Marcia, K. Hermansen, "Survey Article: Interdisciplinary Approaches to Islamic Biographical Materials," *Religion* 18 (1988), 163–182; Ruth Roded, *Women in Islamic Biographical Collections* (Boulder & London: Lynne Reinner Publishers, 1994); Wadād al-Qāḍī, "Biographical Dictionaries: Inner Structure and Cultural Significance," in *The Book in the Islamic World*, ed. George N. Atiyeh (The Library of Congress: State University of New York Press, 1995), 93–122; R. Stephen Humphreys, *Islamic History: A Framework for Inquiry* (Revised edition, Princeton: Princeton University Press, 1991), esp. 188–193;

the origins and development of biographical dictionaries, the areas they cover, their arrangement, selection criteria, methods, contents, styles, the motivations for compiling them, their cultural significance, and their usefulness and shortcomings, sometimes surveying them with various degrees of detail and with varying interests in mind. This does not mean, however, that we are at a point in research where the field has been exhausted, nor that the observations posited by the various scholars are all certain or have received general acceptance. Far from it. Indeed, some of the basic issues connected with biographical dictionaries, like origin, purpose, and style, are still controversial,[2] despite the fact that some of the ideas about them have been in circulation for many than decades. More basically, biographical dictionaries, as a kind of writing, do not have what we might call a "standard" appellation in the scholarly literature. Most scholars do not give this kind any name at all; some give it general appellations like "literature," "composition," or "writing;" some call it a "genre," others a "form" or "literary form," and still others use for it "form" and "genre" interchangeably. More specifically, the term "prosopography" was applied to biographical dictionaries in 1983 by Young and was recently adopted by Robinson;[3] but while Robinson distinguished between biography (*sīra*) and "biographical notices" in "prosopographies," Cooperson applied the term "biography" to both *sīra*

Tarif Khalidi, *Arabic Historical Thought* (Cambridge: Cambridge University Press, 1996), esp. 204–210; F. Eickelman, "Tardjama," in *Encyclopaedia of Islam* 2, X [1998], 224–225; R. S. Humphreys, "Ta'rīkh: Historical Writing," *Encyclopaedia of Islam* 2, X, [1998], 271–280; Michael Cooperson, *Classical Arabic Biography* (Cambridge: Cambridge University Press, 2000), esp. 1–23; Chase Robinson, *Islamic Historiography* (Cambridge: Cambridge University Press, 2003), esp. 66–74. Earlier works, most of which remain influential, are, in alphabetical order, W. Heffening, "Ṭabaḳāt," in *Encyclopaedia of Islam* (first edition), Supplement [1927], 214–15; Sir Hamilton Gibb, "Islamic Biographical Literature," in *Historians of the Middle East*, ed. B. Lewis and P. M. Holt (London and New York: Oxford University Press, 1962), 54–58; idem, "Ta'rīkh," in *Encyclopaedia of Islam* (first edition), Supplement [1927], 233–45; G. Levi Della Vida, "Sīra," in *Encyclopaedia of Islam* (first edition), IV, 439–43; Ilse Lichtenstadter, "Arabic and Islamic Historiography," *The Moslem World* 35 (1945), 126–132; Otto Loth, "Ursprung und Bedeutung der Ṭabaḳât vornehmlich der des Ibn Saʿd," *Zeitschrift der Deutschen Morgenländischen Gesellschaft* 23 (1869), 593–614; Franz Rosenthal, *A History of Muslim Historiography* (Leiden: Brill, second edition, 1968); idem, "Literature," in *The Legacy of Islam*, ed. J. Schacht and C. E. Bosworth (Oxford: Oxford University Press, 1974), 321–349.

[2] On the controversies, see Roded, 4–5; Malti-Douglas, "Dreams," 138–139; Cooperson, 1ff.

[3] See Robinson, xxv, n. 3.

and entry in a biographical dictionary. Even in the two generally accepted observations—that biographical dictionaries are a branch of historical writing, and that they are an indigenous creation of the Muslim community—there is room for reflection and elaboration.

What I would like to do here is to start from these last two observations in order to understand the manner in which biographical dictionaries expressed the attitude towards knowledge and its organization in pre-modern Islamic civilization. I plan to begin by comparing the two forms of historical writing in Islam, the chronicle and the biographical dictionary, as a prelude to suggesting that the scholars, who first created the biographical dictionaries, wanted those dictionaries to be the communal historical alternative to the largely political chronicle. This creation, I further suggest, entailed assumptions by the scholars about knowledge that posed historicization problems for them. The complex ways in which they overcame these problems through biographical dictionaries betrayed their understanding of the place of knowledge in society. These ways are all expressed in biographical dictionaries: their alignment, which is related to the scholars' vision of the organization of knowledge; their scope, which is related to the scholars' vision of the pervasiveness of knowledge; their structure, which is related to the scholars' vision of the configuration of knowledge; and their style, which is related to the scholars' vision of the channelling of knowledge. Furthermore, the scholars' recognition of the importance of permitting society to have access to knowledge made them, with the passage of time, make structural changes to their biographical dictionaries. The study shall conclude with some remarks on the positive and negative consequences of organizing knowledge through biographical dictionaries in Islamic civilization.

I

That biographical dictionaries are a branch of historical writing is a matter that has been pointed out by many medieval Muslims who authored these dictionaries, and some of these, like al-Sakhāwī (d. 902/1496), were themselves historians.[4] This point has been

[4] For a survey based on the introductions of some authors of biographical dictionaries, see Khalidi, "Biographical Dictionaries," 55–58.

repeatedly mentioned in the scholarly literature,[5] and, more often than not, one section or more are devoted to biographical dictionaries in surveys of Islamic history and historiography.[6] While most scholars took this observation to be self-evident, one scholar, Stephen Humphreys, went beyond that, offering a perceptive, though brief, comparison between biographical dictionaries and the other most obvious form of historical writing, namely the chronicle.[7] According to him, "... chronicles and biographical dictionaries ... are very distinct genres as to sources, methods, and subject matter, and they convey very different kinds of information."[8] If we were to develop this idea, we can say that biographical dictionaries are, by their very nature, free from almost all of the outside strictures with which the chronicle is shackled. The element of chronology or time, for example, is crucial for chronicles while it is irrelevant to biographical dictionaries in principle, for their defining feature is people—men—not chronology;[9] and whereas the ground which the chronicle covers is

[5] Rosenthal, *Muslim Historiography*, 93–95, 100–106; Gibb, "Ta'rīkh," 235, 238–239, 241; idem, "Biographical Literature," 54; Khalidi, "Biographical Dictionaries," 53, 55–57; idem, *Historical Thought*, 184, 207; al-Qāḍī, 94; Humphreys, "Ta'rīkh," 271, 273, 278–279; idem, *Islamic History*, 188ff; Cooperson, 1–23; Robinson, 66–74.

[6] Gibb, "Ta'rīkh," 233–245; Rosenthal, *Muslim Historiography*," 93–95, 100–106; Humphreys, "Ta'rīkh," 271–280; idem, *Islamic History*, 188–193; Khalidi, *Historical Thought*, 204–210; Robinson, 66–74.

[7] In Cooperson, 22–23, there is a somewhat useful comparison between what he calls "the functions of biographical discourse as opposed to historical dicourse" (p. 22). But Cooperson uses biography in a very broad sense, no matter where it occurs, and that includes the *sīra*, which is normally an independent work on the life of one person. Robinson, xxiv–xxv, 59, on the other hand, divides historiography into three categories: chronography, biography, and prosopography. Prosopography includes the works that this paper deals with, namely biographical dictionaries. Robinson, however, divides this category into two sub-categories: biographical dictionaries ("name lists, annotated ... and arranged in accordance with the compilers' design and purpose;" 68) and *ṭabaqāt* works (whose biographies are arranged in "successive cohorts", 72). Since the difference between the two sub-categories is fundamentally structural, I shall point to it in this paper only if need arises. As for Robinson's third category, biography (i.e., the *sīra*; 61), it shall not be dealt with here since it is a stand-alone work, and thus does not constitute a part of a larger work, the biographical dictionary in this case. More importantly, its origin and purpose are quite different from the origin and purpose of biographical dictionaries.

[8] Humphreys, *Islamic History*, 189.

[9] This is less true of the *ṭabaqāt* (classes/generation) structure (see below) than of the alphabetical. Robinson, 66, mentions that biographical dictionaries ("prosopographies"), particularly the *ṭabaqāt* works, point in the direction of chronography. But, as he notes also, the length of a class/generation is far from uniform. The defining feature of biographical dictionaries remains people, rather than time.

confined to a relatively small number of individuals or groups whose actions affect the lives of the broad societies they govern or lead, the ground which the biographical dictionaries cover is wide open, almost limitless in principle, for their authors can choose any group of individuals to compose works on and make their works as long as they wish.[10] In a similar manner, whereas the chroniclers are profoundly influenced by political change, the authors of biographical dictionaries, in principle, are not;[11] when they are, that would be by accident, not of necessity.[12] Again, once a chronicler has decided what ground he is going to cover, he has little room for manoeuvre—an annalist cannot add a year or subtract one, and a dynastic chronicler cannot change the sequence of rulers in a dynasty; but the writer of a biographical dictionary has almost boundless room for additions and deletions, and the only thing he has to be concerned about is where to make these emendations before he puts his book into circulation.[13] And even within one biography, the author of a biographical dictionary has much greater freedom to choose his material than the chronicler. It is true that biographical dictionaries, by the mere fact that they are dictionaries, are constrained by the stricture of some structure that permits readers to access them. But this stricture is, on the one hand, one of choice, and, on the other, one that carries numerous options.

What all this tells us is that biographical dictionaries are a very flexible form of historical writing, much more than the chronicle. For this reason they can attract, by their very nature, many historically minded authors and hence be widespread. But, in Islamic civilization, biographical dictionaries are not only extensive and very widespread; they are practically a *creation* of that civilization, especially in the *ṭabaqāt* form, as the scholarly literature has agreed. For, although one can find a biographical component in the Greek and Roman historical literatures, as Rosenthal has mentioned,[14] and in the Chinese dynastic histories and Syriac martyrologies, as Gibb has

[10] Cf. Cooperson, 14, on the "open-endedness" of biographical works.

[11] According to Gibb ("Ta'rīkh," 243), "[i]n contrast to the historical tradition, the biographical tradition [is] less dependent upon political changes . . ."

[12] See Gibb, "Biographical Literature," 54.

[13] Cf. Cooperson, 14, where he talks about the possibility of keeping a book "up to date" through additions by later transmitters.

[14] In his *Islamic Historiography*, 101–102. See also Young, 169; Robinson, xxv.

pointed out,[15] the biography "achieved a dominating position" in Muslim historiography, according to the former scholar,[16] and, according to the latter, ". . . the true genius of the Arabic historiography shows itself rather in biography than in chronicle;"[17] Khalidi even called the biographical dictionary "a unique product of the Arab Muslim culture."[18] The reasons for this phenomenon are, obviously, difficult to pin down, but they must be rooted in the very nature of Islamic civilization; without that it would be difficult to explain why biographical dictionaries became so pervasive there and there alone.[19] And this is indeed what Rosenthal proposed, at least to some extent, rooting it in several phenomena. The first is the politico-religious experience of the early Muslim community (the interest in the Prophet Muḥammad's biography, the importance of knowing the lives of the transmitters of the Prophetic tradition). The second is the dogmatic struggle in Islam, which was waged in the name of individuals. The third is the practical aspect of the chroniclers' lives and livelihoods (the desire of the historians to be useful and employable). The fourth is the readers' demand—from the rulers to the educated people—to learn about the exemplary men of the past. And the fifth is the mentality of the Muslims (their "firm conviction that all politics was the work of individuals and understandable in the light of their personal qualities and experiences"). Rosenthal then added rather abruptly and curtly another, sixth, reason without elaborating on it: "Under the influence of theology, even the history of the various branches of learning was conceived as a collection of biographies of the outstanding scholars."[20] It is this last vague reason that brings us to our subject here.

Perhaps the first question that we should ask is: who were the authors of biographical dictionaries in pre-modern Islamic civiliza-

---

[15] In his "Biographical Literature," 54. See also Robinson, xxv.
[16] Rosenthal, *Islamic Historiography*, 101–102.
[17] Gibb, "Ta'rīkh," 241.
[18] Khalidi, "Biographical Dictionaries," 53.
[19] Note Gibb's opening statement in his "Biographical Literature," 54: "It is probably a truism that every kind of literary production which is regularly cultivated in a society expresses some enduring element in both the conscious motivations and unconscious orientations of the society as a whole or of its public exponents." Al-Qāḍī, in her "Biographical Dictionaries," 94, argues that biographical dictionaries reflect "some important aspects of the intellectual and cultural development in the Islamic community, at least in the first nine centuries of Islamic civilization."
[20] Rosenthal, *Islamic Historiography*, 101. See also Gibb, "Biographical Literature," 54.

tion? The answer is clear: they are the scholars, *ʿulamāʾ*, of the Muslim community.[21] The next question is: how many of these scholars were "professional" historians—called *akhbārīs* first then *aṣḥāb al-taʾrīkh* or *aṣḥāb al-tawārīkh*—i.e., writers of chronicles? The answer is unequivocally: very few, for most of the scholars were religious scholars of a wide variety of specializations,[22] and that from the earliest times biographical dictionaries came to exist.[23] What were the chroniclers

[21] Humphreys, in his *Islamic History*, 187, dicusses biographical dictionaries in the chapter entitled "A Cultural Elite: the Role and Status of the ʿUlamāʾ in Islamic Society." On the role of the scholars in creating biographical dictionaries, see Gibb, "Taʾrīkh," 258.

[22] It is important to emphasize the variety of specializations of the scholars who initially authored biographical dictionaries, and not to restrict those scholars to the specialists in *ḥadīth* and *ḥadīth* criticism, as has often been stated (see Loth, 593–614; Gibb, "Taʾrīkh," 235, 238; Rosenthal, "Literature": 327–328; Hafsi, 227; Khalidi, "Biographical Dictionaries," 53, 55, 58, 64; Young, 169). There is no doubt that *ḥadīth* scholars in particular played a major role in launching the biographical dictionaries in the formative period of Islam, due to their having become a self-conscious group quite early, certainly by the beginning of the third/ninth century (see below). But it was not they alone who launched this project. After all, one of the authors of the two earliest dictionaries that we have, *al-ṭabaqāt al-kubrā* and *ṭabaqāt fuḥūl al-shuʿarāʾ*, namely Ibn Sallām (d. 232/846), was a scholar of poetry, not of *ḥadīth*, and his book is a dictionary of poets, not of *ḥadīth* scholars; and an even earlier book which has not survived, namely al Wāqidī's (d. 207/822) *Taʾrīkh al-fuqahāʾ* (cited in Ibn al-Nadīm's *al-Fihrist* [ed. Riḍā Tajaddud, Tehran, 1971], 111) is a biographical dictionary of jurists, not of *ḥadīth* scholars. See also the next note. For a cautious approach to the role of *ḥadīth* scholars, see Gibb, "Biographical Literature," 55; Robinson, 67: ". . . although *ḥadīth* criticism cannot explain the appearance of prosopography, it certainly gave an impetus to its elaboration." Rosenthal (in "Literature," 327–328) also talked about biography being the "handmaiden" of the "religious sciences" in general, not of *ḥadīth* in particular.

[23] Cooperson, 1–13, argues, following Willi Heffening, that the rise of the biographical dictionary occurred in the milieu of the *akhbārīs*, i.e., the early chroniclers, and is thus related to the pre-Islamic interest in narrating genealogy and producing lists of feats of famous men. Again following Heffening, he attracts attention to the existence of collections of biographies before Ibn Saʿd (all now lost) which deal with "poets, singers, Qurʾān readers, and jurisprudents [as well as] *ḥadīth* scholars" (p. 1). He takes this idea further, however, and tries to make the authors of the first extant biographical dictionaries—al-Wāqidī's/Ibn Saʿd's *al-ṭabaqāt al-kubrā* and Ibn Sallām al-Jumaḥī's *ṭabaqāt fuḥūl al-shuʿarāʾ*—write their dictionaries as *akhbārīs*, chroniclers, rather than *ḥadīth* transmitters (p. 4: "it seems more accurate to suggest that al-Wāqidī and Ibn Saʿd were *akhbārīs*"). His discussion runs into problems which he often finds himself admitting and trying hard to circumvent, with only partial success. This interpretation is flawed on two main accounts. First, because it bases the assertion of the origin of biographical dictionaries on texts that have not survived, and in the case of those which have survived partially (as in al-Jāḥiẓ's *ṭabaqāt al-mughannīn*), there is no indication at all as to how the texts could have looked like. I am also quite skeptical that al-Jāḥiẓ or Ibn Sallām, or even al-Wāqidī and Ibn Saʿd, would have considered themselves *in writing their respective biographical*

interested in? Mainly in the state: with the political rulers managing the affairs of the Muslim community, and the policies, personnel, and events connected with those events.[24] But was this what the scholars were interested in? Only marginally. The scholars, in fact, mostly had a problematic relationship with the state and its folks in the formative period of Islam: working with the government was frowned upon in general; and the rift between the scholars and the rulers after the infamous *miḥna* ("inquisition") in the third/ninth century resulted in the practical independence of the scholars from the state for such a long time that it took centuries for the scholars to make their peace with the state and join its ranks. Most importantly, one of the consequences of this *miḥna* was that the scholars became conscious of their collective identity as leaders and spokesmen of the masses of the community,[25] whose welfare they believed they could

dictionaries as *akhbārīs*. We might even further note that, among al-Wāqidī's now lost works, is a certain *Tārīkh al-fuqahā'*, a biographical dictionary of the jurists, as was mentioned above (n. 22). Second, Cooperson assumes that there could be only two groups at the root of the creation of the biographical dictionary: the chroniclers (the *akhbārīs*) and the *ḥadīth* folk. But this need not have been the case. The chroniclers' nemesis could very well be not merely the *ḥadīth* folk but *all* other scholars who were not primarily chroniclers. It is in this sense that I am using the term "scholars" here. It is also what explains that the pre-Wāqidī/Ibn Sa'd biographical collections dealt with "poets, singers, Qur'ān readers, and jurisprudents [as well as] *ḥadīth* scholars." For, all the groups mentioned in this sentence, with one exception, are actually "scholars" in the sense of non-chroniclers, including the poets, who, as Cooperson himself notes (p. 9), wrote their works in their capacity as "scholars" and "experts." The one exception is the singers, about whom al-Jāḥiẓ wrote a treatise in 215/830, of which only the introduction has survived, but not the text (see *Rasā'il al-Jāḥiẓ*, ed. 'Abd al-Salām Muḥammad Hārūn, Cairo: Maktabat al-Khānjī, 1979, 3: 131–136; Cooperson, 8–9). But it would be very surprising if this work turns out to be a biographical dictionary; if it does, it would indeed be quite different from all of al-Jāḥiẓ's numerous other work. Heffening's article referred to in this note is his "Ṭabaḳāt," in the supplement to the first edition of the *Encyclopaedia of Islam* (see n. 1 above), which appeared in 1927. About two decades later, in 1945, an article by Ilse Lichtenstadter (see n. 1 above) intimated independently a relationship between the rise of the biographical dictionary and the pre-Islamic Arabian interest in genealogy and the battles (*ayyām*) of the pre-Islamic Arabs. On this idea see also Abiad, 7–15.

[24] The vast majority the book titles which Ibn al-Nadīm mentions in the section on the early *akhbārīs*, like al-Madā'inī, Ibn al-Kalbī, and al-Haytham b. 'Adī, in his *Fihrist*, 101–128, are related in one way or another to people in government, including their tribes, genealogies, virtues (*manāqib*), vices (*mathālib*), battles, administrators, and so forth.

[25] On the affinity between the scholars and the people, it is worthwhile to cite Humphreys' perceptive statement: ". . . the vast majority of the *'ulamā'* did not stand out so clearly from the crowd, and indeed had no desire to do so. In their ideal self-image, they embodied the values of the Community . . ." (*Islamic History*, 195).

safeguard against the incursions of the state. Furthermore, they regarded themselves better than the rulers, since they—at least the religious scholars among them—were the guardians of the faith, and the heirs to the Prophet[26]—an idea which, they affirmed, had its roots in the Qur'ān. Viewed from this perspective, the Islamic chronicles must have looked skewed for the scholars, for not only is their presence in them almost non-existent; the presence of most of the community—the entity that matters—is practically non-existent too. They had no problem with history as such; on the contrary, it was from their very own ranks that historical writing began in the community with the Prophet's biography, *sīra*, and campaigns, *maghāzī*; and the community's history must be recorded. The problem lies with the shift which history, in the form of the chronicle, made when its focus became the state rather than the community. The scholars, thus, had to find an alternative to the chronicle, one in which they, the scholars, and other sectors of the community, had a presence. And since the scholars were the *de facto* leaders of the community since the beginning of the *miḥna*, it fell to them to select this alternative.

But what options did the scholars have in choosing a form of writing that would serve as an alternative to the chronicle? These options had to be viable in the early, formative period of Islamic civilization, when the scholars had become conscious of their identity as a group and when the need for an alternative first became pressing. The scholarly treatises or books which they authored in their various fields could not serve as the desired alternative, since such works do not have a historical dimension. *Siyar*, or works devoted each to the biography of one individual, was not a viable option since, by focusing on a single individual, the *sīra* effectively denied all scholars other than the biographee the opportunity to be recognized; and, besides, the *sīra* remained identified with the Prophet for a long time before it was applied to Muslims other than him. Works on the branches of knowledge, or the *aqsām al-ʿulūm*, take the option a step forward, but they also lack the historical contextualization required in the desired enterprise and neglect the necessary human element in it. A much more viable alternative, theoretically, could be works

---

[26] Cooperson, *passim*. See also Gibb, "Ta'rīkh," 258: "For the lives of the *ʿulamā'*, "the heirs of the Prophet," represented in the eyes of the learned the real history of the *ummat Allāh* on earth much more truly than the ephemeral (and sometimes ungodly) political organizations."

on the various institutions in which the scholars served, like mosques, courts, libraries, schools, or colleges. But this was not a realistic option in the formative period, because of the amorphous nature of mosques, the informal nature of courts, the limited spread of libraries, and the delay in the emergence of schools and even further delay in the emergence of colleges. And certainly the history of other institutional avenues, such as the *ḥisba, qaḍāʾ*, or the *dīwān*, in which some of the scholars were active, were not an option, due to the firm connection between these avenues and the state. And a form of writing along the lines of the historians' political chronicle was surely not possible due to the diffuse activities of the scholars, their spread all over the empire, and their lack of recognizable symbols of power and institutional infrastructure. It is thus that the scholars fell upon the idea of the biographical dictionary.[27]

This form of historical writing was the only truly viable alternative, both theoretically and practically, since it is a kind of writing in which the history of the Muslim community is written through the achievement of its authentic non-political leaders, the scholars—in the same way as the chronicle had proposed to write the history of the same community through the feats of its political leaders. In this regard, Gibb's eloquent words ring loud: ". . . the conception that underlies the old biographical dictionaries is that the history of the Islamic community is essentially the contribution of the individual men and women to the building up and transmission of its specific culture; that it is these persons (rather than the political governors) who represent or reflect the active forces in Muslim society in their respective spheres; and that their individual contributions are worthy of being recorded for future generations."[28] By so doing, the scholars made of themselves, consciously or unconsciously, the effective historians of the Muslim community, relegating the chroniclers largely to the position of the historians of the Islamic state, for, as Gibb remarked, "[a]lthough the scholar and the traditionist had yielded

[27] This interpretation for the rise of biographical dictionaries in Islamic civilization agrees in its skeletal form with Gibb's interpretation. Khalidi, in "Biographical Dictionaries," 54–58, took a different approach in his study of the "motive" for compiling biographical dictionaries in Islam. He studied the introductions written by selected authors of such dictionaries and derived from them the authors' "motives." Not unexpectedly, the results with which he came out were so mixed and differentiated that it would be difficult to form a homogenous picture from them.

[28] Gibb, "Biographical Literature," 54.

place to the official in political historiography, there still remained in their hands the even more extensive field of biography."[29] And the biographical dictionary was indeed the perfect vehicle for the scholars' purposes, both formally and historically. For one thing, the biographical dictionary had the potential of being taken in all directions and filled with all kinds of information, due to the flexibility of its form and its freedom of methodological and other constraints. For another, the biographical dictionary could be picked up at any time, because its primary unit is the biography of an individual, and thus all that was needed for its launching was the emergence of sufficient consciousness of an identifiable body of individuals, without reference to such matters as development or institutionalization. And indeed, historically, group consciousness did take place early in Islamic society, when the *ḥadīth* transmitters in the first decades of the third/ninth century found themselves unmistakably on the opposite side of the fence with the state in the affair of the *miḥna*, which began in 218/833. That consciousness required that they introduce their own alternative history for the state's history, the chronicle, quickly, without delay; and at that early stage in the development of Islamic society and civilization, there was nothing available to them other than the biographical dictionary. It is thus not by coincidence that the first biographical dictionary we have, the *al-ṭabaqat al-kubrā*, is devoted to *ḥadīth* transmitters, and that it was compiled by a scholar, Ibn Saʿd, who died, significantly, in the last years of the *miḥna*, in 230/844.[30]

When the early third/ninth century scholars decided to write the alternative history of the Muslim community specifically through biographical dictionaries, they were implicitly making two assumptions about knowledge. The first is that knowledge represents the true achievement of the Muslim community, and that, as a result, the history of that community is the history of its scholarly achievement,

[29] Gibb, "Ta'rīkh," 258.

[30] There is an earlier work on the *ḥadīth* transmitters, but it has not survived: the *ṭabaqāt al-muḥaddithīn* by al-Muʿāfā b. ʿImrān b. Nawfal al-Mawṣilī, who died in 184/800 (Hafsi, 241), Fuat Sezgin, *Geschichte des arabischen Schrifttums*, 1 (Leiden: Brill, 1967), 348. But cf. Chase Robinson, "Al-Muʿāfā b. ʿImrān and the Beginnings of *Ṭabaqāt* Literature," *Journal of the American Oriental Society*, 116 (1996), 114–120. Robinson rejects the attribution of this book to al-Muʿāfā. Also, as was mentioned above (nn. 22, 23), al-Wāqidī (died in 207/822) compiled a book entitled *ṭabaqāt al-fuqahā'* on another group of religious scholars, namely the jurists (Ibn al-Nadīm, 111). It, too, however, has not survived.

as opposed to its political achievement portrayed in the chronicles. The second assumption is that knowledge resides in people not in institutions. It is they, as individuals, who produce knowledge, carry it, organize it, transmit it, and ultimately control it. These two assumptions put challenges before the scholars, and the way they reacted to those challenges left their mark on biographical dictionaries, betraying, in the process, the scholars' attitude towards knowledge.

The first assumption meant that those sectors of the community that do not participate in the production of knowledge have no place in the making of the community's history. The scholars, the authors of the dictionaries, thus, faced a dilemma similar to that of the chroniclers, perhaps even greater. For, when the chroniclers decided to devote their works mainly to the ruling classes and their appendages, they in effect divided the community into two groups: the rulers and the ruled, with their interest lying, unapologetically, in the former group. Could the scholars, with their initially all-inclusive, communal vision, avoid the discriminatory attitude of the chroniclers in their own histories, their biographical dictionaries? They could not, for no sets of biographical works, no matter how numerous and copious, could account for all the activities of all the people of a community, any community, at any time or any place. And the scholars were, not unlike the chroniclers, an interest group. They therefore, too, had to divide the community into two groups: the carriers of knowledge and the non-carriers of knowledge, i.e., the scholars and the non-scholars; and their biographical dictionaries could not but be confined to their own kind to the exclusion of others. Because of that, their biographical dictionaries did not account for the activities of very large sectors of the community: "the productive classes in society—the farmers, merchants, and artisans," in the words of Humphreys,[31] but also the labourers, skilled and unskilled, most of the military, middle- and low-level government employees, and generally the amorphous "masses" and the riff-raff, among others. The only exceptions to that arise when a member of these groups engages in some scholarly activity—and examples of this crossover abound; but then this member would be mentioned in the biographical dic-

[31] Humphreys, *Islamic History*, 189. See also Gibb, "Biographical Literature," 58: "[a]griculture and the industrial arts are as thinly represented as in a *Who's Who* . . .;" Cooperson, 15: "no one to my knowledge ever composed biographies of prayer-callers, midwives, or garbage collectors . . ."

tionaries only because of that knowledge-related activity, in the same manner that the masses, for example, get mentioned in the chronicles when their path crosses that of the rulers. Of course, the scholars could argue that they could live with this discrimination since they were the veritable leaders of the Muslim community, and leaders define the ethos of society. But there is no question that the scholars had to find ways to face up to this challenge of exclusiveness in their biographical dictionaries.

The second assumption made the scholars face another, much bigger dilemma. For, in writing a *history* of any entity, some kind of continuity must be present in that entity. But how can individuals, no matter how endowed with knowledge, ensure the element of continuity in scholarly achievement, when individual achievements cannot but be confined to the individuals' limited capabilities and life spans? And how can the history of scholarship be written when scholars are such an amorphous, fluid group, whose members are scattered all over a vast empire and work in innumerable ways and areas?[32] This is a problem the chroniclers did not face, because political leadership is, in one way or another, clearly definable, and its continuity is ensured by the attractiveness of political office. Besides, there is an institutional aspect to political leadership, and it has a bureaucratic infrastructure that remains in place even though changes may occur at the top at times of transfer of power. And this is certainly not the case with the scholars. Again here the scholars had to face up to this challenge of continuity in their biographical dictionaries.

II

The ways in which the scholars responded to the two challenges of exclusiveness and continuity were quite complex and they were expressed in biographical dictionaries in a manner that betrays the

[32] See Humphreys' apt statement on the scholars is his *Islamic History*, 187: "[The ʿulamāʾ] are neither a socio-economic class, nor a clearly defined status group, nor a hereditary caste, nor a legal estate, nor a profession . . . In short, they cut across almost every possible classification of groups within Islamic society, playing a multiplicity of political, social and cultural roles. But in spite of this ambiguity, they are plainly a crucial element in Islamic society . . ."

scholars' vision of knowledge. Four such ways are identifiable. They deal with the dictionaries' alignment, which reflects the scholars' vision of the organization of knowledge; scope, which reflects the scholars' vision of the pervasiveness of knowledge; structure, which reflects the scholars' vision of the configuration of knowledge; and style, which reflects the scholars' vision of the channelling of knowledge.

II 1

Let us begin with the most conspicuous way, *alignment.* The scholars' biographical dictionaries intimate that, although knowledge resides in individuals not institutions, *groups* of individuals who engage in similar activities which can be called scholarly share features that make them constitute an institution-like body. Taken together, they ensure the element of continuity, and make possible the writing of the history of Islamic scholarship in the Muslim community through biographical dictionaries. In other words, once knowledge is organized in categories, each of which has a common denominator, it is possible to historicize it just like any other institution. For, the Prophet's biography aside, it is noteworthy that the scholars did not write stand-alone biographies of individual scholars for a relatively long time after they had launched their biographical dictionaries project; and when they did, they did so very sparingly indeed, writing only about very few luminaries of the faith and/or of scholarship; they also, significantly, did not give those biographies titles that start with "*tārīkh* (history of) so-and-so,"[33] as they did in so many of their

[33] Among the earliest of the scholars' stand-alone biographies, we have, in chronological order, *Ādāb al-shāfiʿī wa-manāqibuhū* by Ibn Abī Ḥātim al-Rāzī, who died in 327/938 (Beirut: Dār al-Kutub al-ʿIlmiyya, n.d.); *Akhbār abī ḥafṣ ʿumar ibn ʿabd al-ʿazīz* by Abū Bakr al-Ājurrī, who died in 360/970 (Beirut, 1979); *Akhbār abī ḥanīfa wa-aṣḥābihī* by Abū ʿAbd Allāh al-Ṣaymarī, who died in 436/1044 (Beirut: Dār al-Kitāb al-ʿArabī, 1976); *Sīrat wa-manāqib ʿumar ibn ʿabd al-ʿazīz* by Ibn al-Jawzī, who died in 597/1200 (Beirut: Dār al-Kutub al-ʿIlmiyya, 1984); *Manāqib amīr al-muʾminīn ʿumar ibn al-khaṭṭāb* by the same author (Beirut: Dār al-Kutub al-ʿIlmiyya, 1987); *ʿUmar ibn ʿabd al-ʿazīz* by Ibn Kathīr (Cairo: al-Dār al-Qawmiyya, n.d.). I am not certain where to place *Sīrat ʿumar ibn ʿabd al-ʿazīz* by Abū Muḥammad ʿAbd Allāh b. ʿAbd al-Ḥakam, who died in 214/829 (Beirut: Dār al-ʿIlm li-l-Malāyīn, 1954), whether with the historians or the scholars. The version that we have of it is the work of his son ʿAbd al-Raḥmān b. ʿAbd Allāh b. ʿAbd al-Ḥakam, the famous historian of Egypt, who died in 257/871. Whether the published *Sīrat al-imām aḥmad ibn ḥanbal* (Riyadh: Dār al-Salaf, 1995) is indeed the work of Ibn Ḥanbal's son, Ṣāliḥ (d. 265/878), is questionable. It is a collection of narrations on Aḥmad that

biographical dictionaries. Rather, right from the beginning of this—their own—dictionaries enterprise, they perceived their work as the collective work of *groups* of scholars, not of individuals.[34] This attitude on the part of the scholars did not arise from their ignorance of the single-person biography form. Their nemeses, the *akhbārīs*, had written scores of works—almost a hundred of them according to Ibn al-Nadīm's lists—on individual public figures in the second–third/eight–ninth centuries, before and at the time the project of biographical dictionaries was launched, and had given these works titles that do *not* start with the word *tārīkh*, history, starting rather with generic words: "book," ("*Kitāb* so-and-so") "reports," ("*Akhbār* so-and-so") "slaying," ("*Maqtal* so-and-so") "virtues," ("*Faḍā'il* so-and-so") "biography," ("*Kitāb sīrat* so-and-so"), and "story," ("*ḥadīth* so-and-so") in descending order of frequency.[35] In the very rare cases that the word "tārīkh" is used in their titles, the meaning of the word there is almost certainly dating (i.e., "ta'rīkh"), not history.[36] Had the scholars, thus, wanted to write stand-alone biographies in the formative period, they most certainly could have. But they did not. They, instead, chose to write about groups of scholars in books of multiple biographies—biographical dictionaries. This indicates that they viewed their work as a collective, institution-like activity in which

go back to Ṣāliḥ and that must have been put together much later, possibly as late as 432/1040 (see p. 29).

[34] See Humphreys' perceptive statement: "In their ideal self-image, they embodied the values of the Community and saw their work as a collective enterprise" (*Islamic History*, 195). See also Robinson, 66.

[35] In Ibn al-Nadīm's *Fihrist*, 101–128, I have counted **40** titles of works by Abū Mikhnaf (d. 151/768), al-Madā'inī (d. 225/839), Ismā'īl b. Mujammi' (d. 227/841), Ibn 'Abda (death date unknown), and 'Umar b. Shabba (d. 262/875) that have the standard title *kitāb* so-and-so (pp. 105, 110, 114, 115, 116, 118, 124); **23** titles of works by Ibn al-Kalbī (d. 206/821), al-Haytham b. 'Adī (d. 207/822), al-Wāqidī (d. 207/822), al-Madā'inī, al-Zubayr b. Bakkār (d. 256/869), 'Umar b. Shabba, and Aḥmad b. al-Ḥārith al-Kharrāz (d. 258/871) that have the standard title *Kitāb akhbār* so-and-so (pp. 108, 109, 112, 112, 115, 116, 117); **14** titles of works by Abū Mikhnaf, Naṣr b. Muzāḥim (d. 212/827), al-Wāqidī, al-Ghallābī (death date unknown), and 'Umar b. Shabba that have the standard title *Kitāb maqtal* so-and-so (pp. 105, 106, 111, 113, 115, 121, 125); **3** titles of works by al-Madā'inī that have the standard title *kitāb faḍā'il* so-and-so (p. 114); **2** titles of works by 'Awāna b. al-Ḥakam (d. 147/764) and al-Wāqidī that have the standard title *Kitāb sīrat* so-and-so (pp. 103, 111); **1** title of a work by Abū Mikhnaf that begins with "*ḥadīth*" (*ḥadīth al-azāriqa*; p. 105).

[36] Ibn al-Nadīm mentions three books that have the word "tā'rīkh" in their titles: two by 'Awāna b. al-Ḥakam and Ibn al-Kalbī both entitled *Kitāb al-tā'rīkh* (pp. 103, 109), and one by Ibn al-Kalbī entitled *Kitāb tā'rīkh akhbār al-khulafā'* (p. 109).

groups of scholars participate, and although knowledge according to them resides in the individual, it is produced collectively by those groups. And when scholarly activity is broken down into separate areas, each of which consists of scholars who partake of one particular aspect in their work, then knowledge comes to play an organizing role in delineating these areas, and the quasi-institutional aspect of scholarly activity becomes even more conspicuous, permitting it easily to overcome the challenge of historicization.

An examination of the extant biographical dictionaries indicates that the scholars identified three major areas in which scholarly activities are similar enough to be grouped together and hence to have the semblance of an institution which can be historicized. These areas are, in rough chronological order of appearance in Islamic civilization: field, place, and time.

a. In the first area, *field*, the scholars grouped together in single biographical dictionaries the biographies of those scholars who worked in the same scholarly discipline. Given that most biographical dictionaries are dedicated to scholars who share one field of inquiry, it is clear that the scholars were deeply convinced that knowledge is primarily organized according to subjects of specialization. Thus, when the achievements of scholars who work in one subject are recorded in a biographical dictionary, a brick in the edifice of knowledge is uncovered; and when the achievement of all the scholars who work in all subjects in the community are recorded, then the entire edifice of knowledge in that community is uncovered, making its history, in effect, open for recording.

Biographical dictionaries of scholars working in the same specialized field were the earliest to appear in Islamic civilization.[37] The earliest extant works are Ibn Saʿd's (d. 230/844)[38] *al-ṭabaqāt al-kubrā*, in which he put together the biographies of people who worked in the field of *ḥadīth* transmission, and Ibn Sallām al-Jumaḥī's (d. 232/846)

[37] See al-Qāḍī, 101ff.: "one of the most striking things about biographical dictionaries is that they were, right from the start of the genre, and for at least the following four centuries, solely of the "restricted" rather than the "general" kind: most of them dealt with specific fields mostly, although some of them were restricted by criteria other than field" (p. 102).

[38] The contribution of al-Wāqidī, Ibn Saʿd's master, to the latter's book is enormous, though difficult to pin down precisely. This has made some scholars refer to the author as "al-Wāqidī-Ibn Saʿd." I shall use the name of Ibn Saʿd alone, since this is how the book was transmitted and eventually circulated.

*ṭabaqāt fuḥūl al-shuʿarā*ʾ, which recorded the biographies of people involved with the field of poetry. Both of these dictionaries were followed by many other dictionaries on these same two groups; but biographical dictionaries devoted to the former group, the *ḥadīth* transmitters, by far outnumbered those of the latter, the poets. This observation made several modern scholars make the connection between biographical dictionaries and *ḥadīth* transmission a vital one, so vital that one scholar claimed that biographical dictionaries are inseparable from *ḥadīth*.[39] But this is surely an exaggeration. The preponderance of biographical dictionaries devoted to *ḥadīth* transmitters has to do with the nature of the religious foundation of Islamic civilization, with the disproportionately large number of scholars working in this field, with the methodologically sensitive issues and problems connected with it, and with the grave consequences resulting from knowing or not knowing these problems. In reality, the scholars wrote specialized dictionaries for almost all the fields in which Muslim and non-Muslim scholars were productive in Islamic civilization. Thus we have biographical dictionaries for people working in Qurʾān recitation, Qurʾān exegesis, *ḥadīth* transmission, law, theology, sectarianism, Ṣūfism, language, grammar, poetry, prose, philosophy, science, astronomy, medicine, among others.

We also have dictionaries for people in professions related to a specific scholarly field, like the judges (whose practice falls in the field of law) or a general scholarly field, like the oneirocritics (dream interpreters) who are endowed with special powers derived from religion.[40] As time passed, even more specialized dictionaries began to appear, indicating the scholars' awareness of developments within fields, and hence of the emergence of sub-groups within the original groups. In the field of poetry, for example, a dictionary was devoted specifically to "modern" poets (Ibn al-Muʿtazz's [d. 296/908] *ṭabaqāt al-shuʿarā*ʾ); and, as we shall see below, in the field of law, dictionaries were compiled for the members of the various schools of law, and, in *ḥadīth* transmission, dictionaries specifically devoted to sub-groups of varying degrees of reliability were also compiled. Conversely, as time passed, the scholars started to write general dictionaries that are not confined to particular disciplines, as we shall

[39] Hafsi, 227. See also above, n. 22.

[40] On the oneirocritics in particular, see Young, 174; Malti-Douglas, "*Dreams*."

see; but there, the specification of the field of specialization of all the subjects entered in them remained central.

b. In the second area, *place*, the scholars grouped together in single biographical dictionaries the biographies of those scholars who worked in the same locality. By choosing this criterion for some of their biographical dictionaries, the scholars were conveying their conviction that locality does contribute to the production of knowledge and that it can play a unifying role in the otherwise disparate forms of scholarly activity. Locality, thus, becomes a criterion for the organization of knowledge. And when the contributions of the scholars of a particular locality are recorded in biographical dictionaries, the sum total of those contributions constitute a veritable history of that locality. In so doing, the scholars were, again, posing as alternate historians to the chroniclers, some of whom had written political histories of some localities quite early in Islamic civilization, like Ibn Ṭayfūr's (280/893), *Kitāb Baghdād.*

Biographical dictionaries of scholars working in the same place emerged not long after the emergence of the biographical dictionaries based on field of specialization, and the first to have survived of them is Baḥshal's (d. 292/905) *Tārīkh Wāsiṭ*. This book is somewhat disappointing in the sense that the entries included in it consist only of the persons' names and the *ḥadīth* each one of them transmitted. Thus, in a way, it falls under the category of books bound together by subject. But, this is not really so, since, in addition to its title, specifically anchoring it in a particular locality, it has an introductory exposé of the city of Wāsiṭ: its foundation, topography, history, and scholarly pedigree. These two features—title and introduction—of the book are what became typical of the later biographical dictionaries based on localities. And these were compiled in abundance by the scholars from various cities and regions of the Islamic world, each one of them writing normally about his own town or province. We have, thus, biographical dictionaries of Baghdad, Damascus/Syria, Cairo/Egypt, Cordoba, Granada, Sabta, Fez, Bijāya, Ifrīqiya (Tunisia), Yemen, Mecca, Medina, Jerusalem, Dārayyā (near Damascus), Aleppo, Raqqa, Wāsiṭ, Qazwīn, Iṣfahān, Nishapur, Jurjān, Harāt, and Samarqand, among others.[41] In the case of some cities, we have more than

[41] For a comprehensive list of such books, as listed by al-Sakhāwī in his *al-Iʿlān bi-l-tawbīkh*, see Rosenthal, *Historiography*, 381–408.

one biographical dictionary devoted to its scholars, as in the case of the city of Iṣfahān. Such works, almost always entitled *Tā'rīkh*..., "history of...," and mostly composed of several volumes, could no doubt give the impression of unity and continuity needed for the writing of history.

c. In the third area, *time*, the scholars grouped together in single biographical dictionaries the biographies of those scholars who worked in the same period. The selection of this criterion by the scholars for some of their dictionaries indicates that the scholars believed that time periods do influence the production of knowledge and, as in the case of localities, confer a unifying aspect on the scholars' varied activities in them. Time period, thus, becomes a criterion for the organization of knowledge. And, as in the case of field and place, the scholars could claim that their time period-based dictionaries in fact record the history of the periods they cover.

Biographical dictionaries based on time did not emerge until very late in Islamic civilization, although the way was prepared for them by other works. Some early third/ninth century political annals, particularly those of Khalīfa b. Khayyāṭ (d. 242/856) and Ṭabarī (d. 311/923), often included at the ends of many of the years they covered "obituary notices" of the scholars who died in those years, though practically always without elaboration. Almost three centuries later, the historian scholar Ibn al-Jawzī (d. 597/1200), in his *al-Muntaẓam fī l-tā'rīkh*, developed this feature greatly, making the historical narrative of each year followed by the biographies/obituaries of those people who died that year, often allowing much more room for biographies than for historical narrative. The same method was followed by later historian scholars, like Ibn Kathīr (d. 774/1372) in his *al-Bidāya wa-l-nihāya*. But in the meantime another method had been developed by al-Dhahabī (d. 748/1348) in his *Tā'rīkh al-islām*. There, al-Dhahabī broke down the history of Islam mainly into decades, rather than years, and, in the manner of his predecessors, made the narrative historical part of each decade followed by a much longer biographical one. But, despite their heavy biographical content, all these books cannot be called biographical dictionaries because their governing structural principle is not the individual biography. It took the scholars almost a century to pick up a specific time period as a unifying element of their biographical dictionaries. And when they did, the time period was not a short period like the single year, or a more extended one, like the decade, but rather a very long one: the century. The length of time is indeed striking and must be related to the scholars' desire to anchor their form of historical writing, biographical dictionaries, in sufficiently long temporal stretches to warrant historicization and to make that historicization meaningful. This form of writing, the centennial biographical dictionary, proved to be quite popular ever since the famous scholar Ibn Ḥajar al-ʿAsqalānī (d. 852/1448) wrote his *al-Durar al-kāmina*, devoted to the biographies of the scholars of the eighth/fourteenth century, although two centennial biographical dictionaries from the previous century are also known.[42] Ibn Ḥajar's work opened the way for centennial dictionaries of the ninth/fifteenth century (al-Sakhāwī's *al-Ḍawʾ al-lāmiʿ*), the tenth/sixteenth century (al-Ghazzī's [d. 1061/1651] *al-Kawākib al-sāʾira*), the eleventh/seventeenth century (al-Muḥibbī's [d. 1082/1699], *Khulāṣat al-athar*), the twelfth/eighteenth century (al-Murādī's [d. 1206/1791] *Silk al-durar*), and the thirteenth/nineteenth century (al-Ālūsī's [d. 1342/1924] *al-Misk al-adhfar*). All signals one hears from scholars and publishers indicate that one or more centennial dictionaries are being prepared for the past fourteenth/twentieth century.

II 2

Let us turn now to the second way in which the scholars responded to the challenges of exclusiveness and continuity in writing their alternative history of the Muslim community, namely *scope*. This way consists of making their biographical dictionaries encompass a broad sector of that community, thus suggesting that scholarship—the production of knowledge—is not an isolated, elitist phenomenon but is pervasive and diffused in society much more than is first assumed. It is also a continuous phenomenon there and does not stop at the demise of scholar after scholar, no matter how important any given individual scholar or group of scholars is. As such, the scholars could speak loudly to the challenge of continuity, and hence historicizability, and at the same time indicate that the pervasive nature of scholarship in the community allows the biographical dictionaries to be more representative of that community than what appears on the surface. The scholars expressed this position in three ways: broad-

[42] See Rosenthal, *Historiography*, 85.

ening the sphere of inclusiveness in their biographical dictionaries, aiming at comprehensiveness in more ways than one, and creating forms that allow for continuity.[43]

a. One of the readily observable features of biographical dictionaries in general is their casting the net very wide indeed to include in their ranks wide-ranging and diverse groups of scholars, religious and secular, Arab and non-Arab, Muslim and non-Muslim, orthodox and sectarian, free and slave, rich and poor, pious and impious, old and young, men and women, people of sound health and people with physical defects, and much more. As we have seen in the previous paragraphs, the scholars wrote biographical dictionaries for people from a wide range of disciplines, localities, and time periods. But further scrutiny of the people mentioned in those dictionaries suggests that much more was involved in the process. In the area of field, we find biographical dictionaries not only for people who work in the main disciplines of law, poetry, *ḥadīth* transmission, and so forth; we also find many more biographical dictionaries for scholars who work in sub-disciplines. Thus, while we have only one major biographical dictionary devoted to the jurists, namely Abū Isḥāq al-Shīrāzī's (d. 476/1083) *Ṭabaqāt al-fuqahā'*, we have over a dozen biographical dictionaries that have survived of jurists of particular legal schools, and that only among the Sunnīs: at least two for the Ḥanbalīs (by Ibn Abī Ya'lā al-Farrā' [d. 526/1131], Ibn Rajab [d. 795/1392]), four for the Mālikīs (by al-Qāḍī 'Iyāḍ [d. 544/1490], Ibn Farḥūn [d. 769/1368], Aḥmad Bābā al-Tunbuktī [d. 1036/1627]), five for the Shāfi'īs (by al-'Abbādī [d. 458/1066], al-Subkī [d. 771/1369], al-Asnawī [d. 772/1370], Ibn Qāḍī Shuhba [d. 874/1469], and Ibn Hidāyat Allāh [d. 1014/1605]), and two for the Ḥanafīs (by Ibn Abī l-Wafā [d. 775/1373], Ibn Quṭlubghā [d. 879/1474]). And while we do have biographical dictionaries on

[43] Cf. Khalidi, "Biographical Dictionaries," 64: "To justify this exclusivity, they made an explicit or implicit appeal to a doctrine of the élite, by whose labors and in whose lives religion subsists and is transmitted from one generation to the next." In the same article, 62, Khalidi concludes that "we find that the over-all trend is from exclusivity to inclusiveness and then back to exclusivity . . ." (see also his *Historical Thought*, 209). But Khalidi was concentrating on a selected number of "general" biographical dictionaries, rather than on the whole corpus of such dictionaries; he also depended greatly on the authors' introductions to their works. The elitist tendency is also mentioned by Robinson, 66. On the other hand, Auchterlonie, 2, attributed the "widening scope of the biographical dictionary" to "the growing confidence of the *Ummah* or Islamic community."

poets in general (by Ibn Qutayba [d. 276/889], al-Marzubānī [d. 384/994]), many of the other biographical dictionaries devoted to poets enter only poets of special artistic traits, such as the bullish, traditional ones (Ibn Sallām's) and the "modern" ones (Ibn al-Mu'tazz's), mentioned above; even those poets whose first name happens to be "Muḥammad" have a dictionary devoted to them (al-Qifṭī's [d. 646/1248] *al-Muḥammadūn*). Similarly, in *ḥadīth* transmission, while most of the biographical dictionaries are general in nature (Bukhārī's [d. 256/869] *al-Tāʾrīkh al-kabīr*, Ibn Abī Ḥātim's [d. 327/938] *al-Jarḥ wa-l-taʿdīl*, and Dhahabī's *Mīzān al-iʿtidāl*), many more are devoted to specific categories of *ḥadīth* transmitters: only those who are outstanding (*ḥuffāʾ*) in knowledge of *ḥadīth* (Dhahabī's *Tadhkirat al-ḥuffāẓ*), or only those who are mentioned in the six canonical books (Ibn ʿAsākir's [d. 571/1175] *al-Muʿjam*, al-Ḥāfiẓ ʿAbd al-Ghanī's [d. 600/1206] *al-Kamāl*, al-Mizzī's [d. 742/1341] *Tahdhīb al-kamāl*, and Ibn Ḥajar's *Thadhīb*), or those who are known to be sound and reliable in their transmission (al-ʿIjlī's [d. 261/874], *Kitāb al-thiqāt*), or, conversely, those who are known to be weak or unreliable in their transmission (Ibn Ḥibbān's [d. 245/858] *Kitāb al-majrūḥīn*, Ibn ʿAdī's [d. 365/975] *Kitāb al-ḍuʿafāʾ al-kabīr*, and Ibn Ḥajar's *Lisān al-mīzān*). In fact, when we come to the theologians, almost all of the biographical works we have on them are about specific groups of them, like those for the Khārijites (Abū Zakariyyāʾ's [d. between 450 and 500/1059 and 1107] *Siyar al-aʾimma*, and al-Darjīnī's [d. ca. 670/1271] *Ṭabaqāt al-mashāyikh*), the Muʿtazilīs (Abū l-Qāsim al-Balkhī's [d. 319/931], al-Qāḍī ʿAbd al-Jabbār's [d. 415/1024], and al-Ḥākim al-Jushamī's [d. 494/1100] works in *Faḍl al-iʿtizāl*, and Ibn al-Murtaḍā's [d. 840/1436] *Ṭabaqāt*), and the Imāmī Shīʿīs (al-Kashshī's [4th/10th century] *Rijāl*, al-Ṭūsī's [d. 460/1067] *Rijāl*, al-Najāshī's [d. 450/1058] *Kitāb al-rijāl*, and Ibn Shahr-Āshūb's [d. 588/1192] *Maʿālim al-ʿulamāʾ*). Remaining in the area of field of specialization, other observations can be made. There are some dictionaries that are devoted to people who are not, strictly speaking, in fields of scholarship but are professionals whose work derives from one or more fields, as we have seen above in the case of oneirocritics (al-Khallāl's [d. 532/1137] *Ṭabaqāt al-muʿabbirīn*) and judges (Wakīʿ's [d. 306/918] *Akhbār al-quḍāt*). And here again, further branching is observable, for we have a dictionary devoted specifically to the judges of Cordoba, namely al-Khushanī's (d. 366/976) *Quḍāt qurṭuba*.

In the area of locality and time period, the biographical dictionaries cast their net even wider, in part due to the fact that they are, by their very nature, not restricted to specific fields of knowledge. The dictionaries devote most of their entries to scholars of all fields, but they also make room for individuals who are not scholars. Thus, al-Khaṭīb al-Baghdādī's (d. 463/1070) biographical dictionary on the city of Baghdad includes, in addition to the religious and non-religious scholars, biographies of caliphs, viziers, bureaucrats, merchants, military leaders, rebels, ascetics, among others. Ibn ʿAsākir's (d. 571/1175) biographical dictionary on Damascus and Syria has all such features and more; we find there even biographies for prophets (e.g., Adam [7:373], Abraham [6:164], Lot [50:306], Jeremiah [8:27], among others). As for the centennial dictionaries, they are by their very nature comprehensive, and thus we find in them biographies of kings, merchants, entrepreneurs, notables, among others, in addition to scholars of all kinds.

Outside the areas of field, place, and time, we have another widening-of-the-net phenomenon in biographical dictionaries, namely the compilation of dictionaries specifically for people who share some defects or marvels that mark them as different from the rest of people in society. Thus we have dictionaries for people who lived conspicuously long lives (Abū Ḥātim al-Sijistānī's [d. 248/862] *al-Muʿammarūn wa-l-waṣāyā*), for those who are blind (al-Ṣafadī's *Nakt al-himyān fī nukat al-ʿumyān*), and for the leprous, lame, cross-eyed, and blind scholars, to whom al-Jāḥiẓ (d. 255/869) devoted his *al-Burṣān wa-l-ʿurjān wa-l-ḥulān wa-l-ʿumyān* (al-Jāḥiẓ, in fact, takes up more defects than is indicated by the title of the book.) Now, most of those included in such dictionaries are Muslim scholars or litterateurs, but some of them are not: some are pre-Islamic tribal leaders or heroes, some are Muslim political leaders, others are singers, beggars, and so forth; and even some prophets come, here again, to have entries in these books.

But there is no doubt that the area which had the greatest effect on widening the range of people entered in biographical dictionaries is the emergence of the "general" biographical dictionary, as opposed to the specialized one we have been discussing so far. This kind of dictionary emerged much later than the specialized one, as I have mentioned in an earlier work:[44] it makes its appearance for the first time in the second half of the seventh/thirteenth century with the famous work of Ibn Khallikān (d. 681/1282), *Wafayāt*

[44] See al-Qāḍī, 103.

al-aʿyān. In the introduction to this book, the author states clearly that his book is a book of history, and that it includes entries for a wide range of people (with specific exceptions) from all walks of life: "I did not limit this concise work to a specific group, like the scholars or the rulers or the viziers or the poets; rather, I mentioned all those who possess some fame among people and about whom questions may be asked," adding that he aimed at entertainment in addition to edification.[45] Thus, while one finds in Ibn Khallikān's book biographies of scholars of all fields, places, and times, one finds also entries for singers (e.g., Ṭuways; no. 519), entertainers (e.g., Ibrāhīm al-Mawṣilī; no. 87), people known for a certain demerit (e.g., Ashʿab the greedy man; 294); eloquent speakers (e.g., Ibn al-Qirriyya; no. 106); storytellers/preachers (e.g., Ibn al-Sammāk; no. 469), script designers (e.g., Ibn Muqla; no. 698); missionaries (e.g., Abū ʿAbdallāh al-Shīʿī; 199); *zindīq*s/Manichaeans (e.g., Ibn al-Rāwandī; no. 35); rebels claiming divinity and other non-Islamic dogma (al-Muqannaʿ; no. 420), among other groups, not only of men but of women, too. Ibn Khallikān's book gave rise to other general, or encyclopaedic biographical dictionaries, as will be discussed later.

b. The second way in which the scholars expressed their emphasis on the pervasiveness of knowledge can be gleaned from their tendency to make their biographical dictionaries comprehensive. Due to some laxity in using this term in modern literature, let me hasten to say that what I mean by comprehensive is simply the attempt to be all-inclusive. This tendency is obvious in the late general, "encyclopaedic" dictionaries; but it is also present in earlier specialized dictionaries as well, and is attested to by the sheer large number of the biographies included in each.[46] Al-Khaṭīb al-Baghdādī's (d. 463/1070) *Tāʾrīkh Baghdād* contains almost 8,000 biographies for the scholars and other notables of Baghdād from the foundation of that city until his time, and Ibn ʿAsākir's (d. 571/1175) larger *Tāʾrīkh madīnat Dimašq* contains more than 10,000 Syrian scholars and other figures. Indeed, the very first biographical dictionary which has survived, the above-mentioned *al-Ṭabaqāt al-kubrā* by Ibn Saʿd, was

[45] Ibn Khallikān, *Wafayāt al-aʿyān*, ed. Iḥsān ʿAbbās (Beirut: Dār Ṣādir, 1978), 1:20.

[46] Robinson, 71, talks about the "massiveness" of biographical dictionaries, and on p. 68 calls their sizes "gargantuan," giving examples further down on the same page.

clearly intended to be comprehensive,[47] with over 4,700 biographies of *ḥadīth* transmitters to its credit over a period of only two centuries—and that figure does not take into account the recently discovered missing parts of that book which could contain over 1,000 additional biographies.[48]

But comprehensiveness should not be always measured by number of entries and how large this number is. Rather, it should be seen as the attempt by the authors of biographical dictionaries to be as exhaustive as they can in making entries for people who fit the criteria they had set for their respective dictionaries. After all, these authors came normally from the cities they write about, and they want to emphasize their own cities' contribution to scholarship. Thus, when we find that the biographical dictionary devoted to the town of Dārayyā—ʿAbd al-Jabbār al-Khawlānī's (d. after 365/975) *Tāʾrīkh dārayyā*—includes less than 40 biographies of Dārānī *ḥadīth* transmitters, we should not conclude that the author had been lax in seeking comprehensiveness. Rather, we should conclude that, in all probability, the town was not a magnet for visiting *ḥadīth* transmitters from outside it, and that only some locals engaged in this scholarly activity. What further confirms this conclusion is that the town was very small: it was the second largest village in the suburb of al-Ghūṭa, near Damascus. And when Ibn ʿAsākir, writing two centuries after *Tāʾrīkh Dārayyā*'s author, came to add other biographies of Dārānīs to that book, he could produce an additional thirteen names but no more than 8 biographies.[49] The relative size of the town and its relation to the biographical dictionary compiled about it can be seen also in Baḥshal's *Tāʾrīkh Wāsiṭ*, which was mentioned above. The book is not large and the sum of its biographies is in the

[47] Humphreys, *Islamic History*, 189: "The earlier dictionaries attempted to provide comprehensive coverage for those broad classes (hadith specialists or poets, usually) which they included in their purview."

[48] The parts of the book missing from the Sachau edition include the following: (1) *al-Ṭabaqa al-rābiʿa min al-Ṣaḥāba mimman aslama ʿinda fatḥ makka wa-baʿda dhālika: al-baṣriyyīn wa-l-baghdādiyyīn wa-l-shāmiyyīn wa-l-miṣriyyīn wa-ākharīn* (Beirut: Dār Iḥyāʾ al-Turāth al-ʿArabī, n.d.); (2) *al-Ṭabaqa al-khāmisa min al-Ṣaḥāba* (in two parts), ed. Muḥammad Ṣāmil al-Sulamī (Ṭāʾif: Maktabat al-Ṣiddīq, 1993); (3) *Tatimmat al-ṭabaqa al-thālitha ilā muntaṣaf al-sādisa wa-man baʿdahum*, ed. Ziyād Manṣūr (Medina: al-Jāmiʿa al-Islāmiyya, 1983).

[49] See the section entitled "al-ziyāda ʿalā tāʾrīkh Dārayyā," pp. 115–118 of ʿAbd al-Jabbār al-Khawlānī's *Tāʾrīkh Dārayyā*, ed. Saʿīd al-Afghānī (Damascus: Dār al-Fikr, second edition, 1984).

hundreds not the thousands. But this is quite expected. As an active, middle-sized town that was the governor's seat for some time in the first/seventh-early eighth century under the Umayyads, the town did indeed attract outside scholars, especially in *ḥadīth* transmission, and that made it a reasonably vibrant scholarly milieu for a while before its slow deterioration after the fall of the Umayyads. All in all, although the author of its biographical dictionary lived more than 70 years before the author of the biographical dictionary on Dārayyā, it should not be surprising that the former book is at least ten times the size of the latter in terms of the number of biographical entries.

c. The third way in which the authors of biographical dictionaries widened the extent of their inclusiveness, and faced up to the continuity issue, consists of their creating new forms of biographical dictionaries that aimed at "updating" earlier dictionaries. By creating such forms, the scholars were implicitly stating that knowledge is cumulative and continuous, and hence can be both pervasive and permitting of being historicized through biographical dictionaries. Now, it is not uncommon for prospective authors of biographical dictionaries to begin their works by lamenting the deficiencies in the works of their predecessors. Such statements could sometimes have a grain of truth to them; but they aimed mainly at self-justification rather than anything else, and they appear in practically all branches of composition in pre-modern Islamic civilization, not only biographical dictionaries. In the latter sphere, in particular, they gave way to the scholars' creation of two forms of writing: the "supplement," the *dhayl*, *ṣila*, *takmila*, or *tālī*; and the "encyclopaedia," "definitive/exhaustive work," the *wāfī* or the *dhayl wa-takmila*.

The "supplement" phenomenon (which is also known in the other form of historical writing, the chronicle, like, for example, the two supplements of Tabarī's history, the *Ṣila* by ʿArīb b. Saʿd al-Qurṭubī [d. after 331/942] and the *Takmila* by Muḥammad b. ʿAbd al-Malik al-Hamadhānī [d. after 367/977]) consists of an author taking a biographical dictionary authored by someone before him and bringing it up to date, so that it covers scholars who lived after the predecessor's death, often adding in the process people whom the predecessor failed to mention for one reason or another; and this phenomenon my happen in more than two successive works. A well-known and early example of this phenomenon comes from Andalusia, where Ibn Bashkuwāl (d. 578/1183) wrote his *Kitāb al-ṣila* in order to supplement Ibn al-Faraḍī's (404/1013) *Ṭabaqāt al-fuqahāʾ wa-l-ruwāt li-l-ʿilm bi-l-Andalus*, on the Andalusian religious scholars. A century or so later, Ibn Bashkuwāl's book itself was supplemented by Ibn al-Abbār's (d. 658/1259) *Kitāb al-takmila li-kitāb al-ṣila*. This phenomenon is even more prevalent in the East, and particularly conspicuous in influential and large books. Perhaps the most famous example comes with regard to the above-mentioned 14-volume *Tāʾrīkh Baghdād* by al-Khaṭīb al-Baghdādī. This book was supplemented by numerous scholars, only some of whose works have survived. Al-Samʿānī (d. 562/1166), we are told, wrote the first supplement (his *Dhayl*) on this book, which fell in 15 volumes. ʿImād al-Dīn al-Kātib (d. 597/1200) then wrote a 3-volume book entitled *al-Sayl ʿalā l-Dhayl*, in which he supplemented al-Samʿānī's supplement. Ibn al-Dubaythī (d. 637/1239) then compiled his own *Dhayl*, in which he complemented both al-Khaṭīb's and al-Samʿānī's books. Then came Ibn al-Qaṭīʿī (d. 739/1338) who wrote a supplement, his *Ṣila*, on the supplement of Ibn al-Dubaythī. And this is only some of the supplemental activity that revolved around al-Khaṭīb's book.[50] Another very influential book that generated supplements is Ibn Khallikān's (d. 681/1282) *Wafayāt al-aʿyān*, mentioned above. Three supplements and a supplement to a supplement are mentioned in *Kashf al-ẓunūn*,[51] not including Ibn al-Suqāʿī's (d. 726/1326) *Tālī kitāb Wafayāt al-aʿyān*, and *Fawāt al-wafayāt* (literally, "what was missed in the *Wafayāt al-aʿyān*") by Ibn Shākir al-Kutubī (d. 763/1361).

The other form which the scholars created in order to ensure continuity and to display inclusiveness was what we may call the "encyclopaedia" form. By that I mean that an author would, in addition to updating a previous work, incorporate the entries of that work (or at least many of them), and come out with a book (normally a multi-volume one) which is avowedly exhaustive, and its title normally reflects this precious value of almost absolute comprehensiveness. Furthermore, the entries in these encyclopaedic dictionaries are normally concise, filled frequently with quotations from earlier sources, and are original only when dealing with their authors' contemporaries; because of that they can be veritably considered reference works. The series of three Andalusian books mentioned in the previous

[50] See Ḥājjī Khalīfa, *Kashf al-ẓunūn ʿan asāmī l-kutub wa-l-funūn* (offset copy of the Istanbul edition, Baghdad: Maktabat al-Muthannā, n.d.) 1:288 (under the rubric "Tāʾrīkh baghdād"). See also the next paragraph, under Ibn al-Najjār.

[51] See Ḥājjī Khalīfa, 2:2017–2018. See also the next section, under al-Ṣafadī.

paragraph, for example, were followed by an all-encompassing book in which are recorded the biographies of all the Andalusian and Maghribī scholars known to the author until his time, including many of those that had been mentioned in the previous three books. This is Ibn ʿAbd al-Malik al-Marrākushī's (d. 703/1303) *al-Dhayl wa-l-takmila wa-l-mawṣūl baʿd al-ṣila* (literally, "the supplement and complement and the attachment subsequent to the *Kitāb al-ṣila*"). Again, al-Khaṭīb al-Baghdādī's *Tāʾrīkh Baghdād*, mentioned in the same paragraph above, generated an encyclopaedic complement, namely Ibn al-Najjār's (d. 643/1245) reportedly 30-volume *Dhayl Tāʾrīkh Baghdād*, parts of which have survived. Although its title indicates that it is a mere supplement, it is in fact much more than that, since it does include, in addition to new biographies for later Baghdādīs, some of the biographies mentioned by al-Khaṭīb in his original book.[52] But the most famous of this sort of encyclopaedic books is al-Ṣafadī's (d. 763/1361) *al-Wāfī bi-l-wafayāt*, a 30-volume all-inclusive "encyclopaedic supplement" to Ibn Khallikān's *Wafayāt al-aʿyān*, one which incorporates most of the biographies in the latter book and has fortunately survived.

Interestingly enough, some scholars who lived after some of the authors of encyclopaedic biographical dictionaries noted that those dictionaries could be all-encompassing only up to a point, i.e., up to the various authors' death dates, and, therefore, "the last word" or "the definitive biographical dictionary" is by definition an impossibility. What they tried to do, then, was to accomplish what is possible, namely to keep on updating these dictionaries in the ubiquitous form of the "supplement." Two examples here should suffice. The first is Ibn Taghri-Birdī's (d. 874/1469) *al-Manhal al-ṣāfī wa-l-mustawfā baʿd al-wāfī*, which is an "exhaustive" supplement to al-Ṣafadī's encyclopaedic *al-Wāfī bi-l-wafayāt*. And the second is Ibn Rāfiʿ's (d. 774/1372) *al-Dhayl ʿalā dhayl Ibn al-Najjār*, which, as its title indicates, a supplement to Ibn al-Najjār's encyclopaedic supplement to al-Khaṭīb's *Tārīkh Baghdād*.[53] Ḥājjī Khalīfa informs us that even that supplement generated two other "supplements."[54]

[52] See Ḥājjī Khalīfa, 1:288.
[53] See Ḥājjī Khalīfa, 1:288.
[54] See Ḥājjī Khalīfa, 1:288.

II 3

The third way in which the scholars met the challenge of exclusiveness and continuity in making of their biographical dictionaries the alternative history of the Muslim community is the structure they chose for a large number of their dictionaries, beginning from the earliest of such dictionaries. This has to do with the scholars' perception of the transmission of knowledge.

When one tries to think of the technical term the Arab Muslim scholars used for biographical dictionaries, regardless of their structure, in pre-modern times, the term that readily comes to one's mind is the rather peculiar *kutub al-ṭabaqāt*, literally, "books of classes." The expression *kutub al-tarājim*, literally, "books of biographies," which is certainly clearer in designating biographical dictionaries, did indeed exist then, but that came much later than *kutub al-ṭabaqāt*. This fact is fundamental for understanding how the scholars viewed the transmission of knowledge, and how that view served them in transforming the individualistic aspect of scholarship into a veritable institution that can be historicized through biographical dictionaries.

The use of the term *ṭabaqāt* to designate a biographical dictionary appears very early in Islamic civilization, in the second half of the second/eighth century, for the sources mention a book on the "classes" of *ḥadīth* transmitters entitled *Ṭabaqāt al-muḥaddithīn* and written by a certain al-Muʿāfā b. ʿImrān b. Nawfal al-Mawṣilī, who died in 184/800, as was mentioned above. This book, however, has been lost and its attribution to al-Muʿāfā is uncertain. Thus, in order to understand what the scholars meant by "classes," we have to go to the first surviving biographical dictionary which used this term in its title, namely Ibn Saʿd's *al-Ṭabaqāt al-kabīr*; it was written in the first half of the third/ninth century, and is also a dictionary of *ḥadīth* transmitters. The conclusion with which one comes out, even after a cursory browse, is that the term *ṭabaqāt* refers to the *structure* of the dictionary. For, despite the fact that the author uses several criteria for organizing his biographies (*sābiqa* [merit; seniority in Islam], place, tribe),[55] his overriding criterion is that of "classes:" after the initial biography of the Prophet, the biographies are placed within "classes" inside all of the work's units (except the last unit on women)

[55] See al-Qāḍī, 97–99.

and most of its sub-units. This is something that the author himself mentions in the two short "introductions" he wrote to these units:

> We have written down in the *Maghāzī* all the names of God's Messenger's companions that have reached us: those Arabs who visited God's Messenger and those who narrated *ḥadīth* from him . . . After God's Messenger's companions came the successors, children of the Muhājirūn and the Anṣār as well as others, among whom were jurists and scholars knowledgeable in the transmission of *ḥadīth* and reports (*āthār*), and in legal knowledge (*fiqh*) and rulings (*fatwā*). Then these passed away. They were succeeded by another CLASS (*ṭabaqa ukhrā*), then by other CLASSES (*ṭabaqāt*), until this our present time [emphasis mine].[56]
>
> Naming those whom we have counted from the companions of God's Messenger, from the Muhājirūn and the Anṣār, and those who lived after them from their children and their successors, of the people of knowledge (*fiqh*), learning (*ʿilm*), and transmission of *ḥadīth*, and what has come down to us about their names, genealogies, agnomens (*kunā*), and conditions (*ṣifātihim*), CLASS BY CLASS (*ṭabaqatan ṭabaqa*; [emphasis mine]).[57]

After the second "introduction," the author starts using headings that contain the term *ṭabaqa*. Thus, he introduces the first unit, which consists of the biographies of the earliest companions from the Muhājirūn and the Anṣār, with a heading that reads: "The first class (*ṭabaqa*) based on seniority in Islam (*sābiqa*) from among those who witnessed [the battle of] Badr from the Muhājirūn and the Anṣār" (3/1:2). After finishing the biographies of the Muhājirūn, he puts another heading for the sub-unit on the biographies of the Anṣār, again using the term *ṭabaqa*: "The first class (*ṭabaqa*) of the Anṣār" (3/2:1). In the next unit, which includes the biographies of the Muhājirūn and the Anṣār who did not participate in the battle of Badr but participated in the later battles of the Prophet, he brings another heading, again using the term *ṭabaqa*: "The second class (*ṭabaqa*) of the Muhājirūn and the Anṣār who did not witness [the battle of] Badr but converted early to Islam (*wa-lahum Islām qadīm*); most of them (*ʿāmmatuhum*) emigrated to the land of Abyssinia and witnessed [the battle of] Uḥud and the following battles (*al-mashāhid*)" (4/1: 1). These units conclude the section of the book on the Prophet's companions. The use of *ṭabaqa* here clearly refers to a structural

[56] Ibn Saʿd, *al-Ṭabaqāt al-kabīr*, ed. E. Sachau (Leiden: Brill, 1905–40), 2/2:128.
[57] Ibid., 3:1.

principle, according to which, first, people who partake in the same level of activity (in this case, seniority in Islam) are grouped together in one class, and, second, people who succeed each other in the same activity are placed one after the other, thereby indicating difference in rank or standing (within the criterion of seniority in Islam).

The following units of Ibn Saʿd's biographical dictionary shed more light on the principle of "class" and its significance, for there we get not only far more headings but also the headings clearly show how one class is related to other classes. These units (again excluding the final unit on women) include biographies of some of the Prophet's companions who took up residence mainly outside of Arabia after the conquests and of the *ḥadīth* transmitters who succeeded those companions there, i.e., the "successors" (*tābiʿūn*) and their successors (*tābiʿū l-tābiʿīn*). These units are divided essentially according to place. Thus we get the biographies of these transmitters in the following order: Medina, Mecca, Ṭāʾif, Yemen, Yamāma, Baḥrayn, Kūfa, Baṣra, Wāsiṭ, Madāʾin, Baghdād, Khurāsān, Syria, the Jazīra, Egypt, then Ayla. Now, within each of these units, the biographies are arranged in classes, *ṭabaqāt*. Each of these classes is introduced by a heading that usually carries an ordinal number: the first *ṭabaqa*, the second *ṭabaqa*, the third *ṭabaqa*, and so forth. Thus, *ṭabaqa* here, first, signifies a generation, and, secondly, there is a clear temporal element in the succession of those generations.[58] Now it is clear what Ibn Saʿd had in mind when he placed the biographies of *ḥadīth* transmitters in classes: the field of *ḥadīth* transmission was first covered by a group of the Prophets' companions. Those passed their knowledge of the field to another generation of *ḥadīth* transmitters in the various centres of learning in the Islamic world. The "first class" of *ḥadīth* transmitters then passed their knowledge of the field to the next generation of *ḥadīth* transmitters, the "second class," in each centre of learning. Those in turn passed their knowledge to a "third class," and those in turn to a "fourth class," and so on,

[58] Several scholars who wrote about biographical dictionaries (see n. 1 above) had something to say about Ibn Saʿd's *ṭabaqāt*. Still, I think it is important to mention here what could have been mentioned earlier for the sake of clarifying my point in the overall context of biographical dictionaries in this paper. Furthermore, I would like to give some details which are important for my argument but which were not important for most of the previous writers on Ibn Saʿd.

until the time of the author. Viewed this way, the *ḥadīth* transmitters constitute a chain of specialized scholars that functioned without interruption for two centuries. Because of this, it is possible to write a history of *ḥadīth* transmission through recording the biographies of its men: their carrying their knowledge over successive generations had transformed them collectively into a veritable institution, an institution that can be historicized.

But there is more in Ibn Saʿd's *ṭabaqāt*. Ibn Saʿd suggests that, in the major centres of learning, it is even possible to historicize particular "trends," or "schools of thought," among *ḥadīth* transmitters. This suggestion can be seen clearly in his grouping together biographies of transmitters who belong to sub-groups within one class, where each set of biographies is preceded with a sub-heading identifying the sub-group by the particular teacher(s)-transmitter(s) each of them had or did not have. Thus, within the "first class" of the transmitters of Kūfa, for example, we find ten sub-headings that begin with "Among those of this class who narrated *ḥadīth* from . . . (*wa-min hādhihi l-ṭabaqa mimman rawā ʿan*)," followed by the name(s) of the subsequent sub-group's teacher(s)-transmitter(s). Thus in this class we get the biographies of those who narrated *ḥadīth* from

> Abū Bakr, ʿUmar, ʿUthmān, ʿAlī, Ibn Masʿūd, and others;
> then those who narrated from ʿUmar, ʿAlī, Ibn Masʿūd, and others;
> then those who narrated from ʿUmar and Ibn Masʿūd but not from ʿAlī;
> then those who narrated from ʿUmar and ʿAlī;
> then those who narrated from ʿUmar and but not from ʿAlī and Ibn Masʿūd;
> then those who narrated from ʿUmar only;
> then those who narrated from ʿAlī and Ibn Masʿūd;
> then those who narrated from Ibn Masʿūd;
> then those who narrated from ʿUthmān, Ubayy, Muʿādh, Ṭalḥa, al-Zubayr, Ḥudhayfa, Usāma b. Zayd, Khālid b. al-Walīd, Abū Masʿūd al-Anṣārī, ʿAmr b. al-ʿĀṣ, Ibn ʿUmar, and others, but not from ʿUmar, ʿAlī, and Ibn Masʿūd;
> then those who narrated from ʿAlī only.

The number of biographies under each sub-heading varies: 10, 16, 12, 14, 2, 55, 35, 71, 25, 109, respectively. Despite that, the message Ibn Saʿd is communicating is clear: there is sufficient continuity even in *trends* of *ḥadīth* transmission to allow for their recording, in the form of biographies, as historicizable institutions.

Ibn Sa'd's unmistakable message about historicizing *ḥadīth* transmission through its people has led some scholars to suggest a genetic relationship between the discipline of *ḥadīth* and the form of biographical dictionaries; this is a matter that was alluded to above.[59] Some scholars supported this position by noting that the *ṭabaqāt* structure was pervasive in the biographical dictionaries of *ḥadīth* transmitters in particular. While this is not untrue, it is important to note that this structure does exist in almost all kinds of biographical dictionaries. Thus we have dictionaries structured by classes/generations for legal scholars (Abū Isḥāq al-Shīrāzī's *Ṭabaqāt al-fuqahā'*), for legal scholars of specific legal schools (al-Subkī's *Ṭabaqāt al-Shāfi'iyya al-kubrā*), for Qur'ān reciters (al-Dhahabī's *Ṭabaqāt al-qurrā'*), for theologians (Ibn al-Murtaḍā's *Ṭabaqāt al-mu'tazila*), for Ṣūfīs (al-Sulamī's [d. 412/1021] *Ṭabaqāt al-Ṣūfiyya*), and even for scholars of non-religious disciplines, like those for linguists and grammarians (Abū Bakr al-Zubaydī's [d. 379/989] *Ṭabaqāt al-naḥwiyyīn wa-l-lughawiyyīn*), and for physicians (Ibn Abī Uṣaybi'a's [d. 668/1270] *'Uyūn al-anbā' fī ṭabaqāt al-aṭibbā'*). We also find it in some dictionaries of scholars of a particular locality (Abū l-Shaykh al-Anṣārī's [d. 369/979] *Ṭabaqāt al-muḥaddithīn bi-Iṣbahān*). And this structure can be found in many dictionaries that do not have the word *ṭabaqāt* in their titles (like Abū Sa'īd al-Sīrāfī's [d. 368/978] *Akhbār al-naḥwiyyīn al-baṣriyyīn* and al-Dhahabī's *Siyar a'lām al-nubalā'*), or have words there that might suggest that the dictionaries are not structured in classes (al-Dhahabī's *Tadhkirat al-ḥuffāẓ*), or in which the "classes" structure is implicit rather than explicit (Abū Nu'aym al-Iṣfahānī's [d. 430/1038] *Ḥilyat al-awliyā'*). And while most authors of those dictionaries, especially after the establishment of the meaning of "classes," did not bother to state the rationale for the "classes" structure of their works outside their introductions, some continued to highlight its significance in transitions from one class to another, as we find it clearly in Abū Isḥāq al-Shīrāzī's *Ṭabaqāt al-fuqahā'*, for after each class he would say: "then legal knowledge passed to another class (*thumma intaqala/ḥaṣala l-fiqh ilā ṭabaqa ukhrā/thāniya/thālitha*)."[60] In some Twelver Shī'ī

[59] See n. 22 above.

[60] Abū Isḥāq al-Shīrāzī's *Ṭabaqāt al-fuqahā*, ed. Iḥsān 'Abbās (Beirut: Dār al-Rā'id al-'Arabī, 1970), 63, 66, 70, 71, 81, 82, 89, 109, 114, 119, 137, 140, 141, 142, 143, 153, 157, 159, 165, 166, 167, 168, 172, 177, 178. See also 48 (*thumma ḥaṣala*

biographical dictionaries, particularly al-Ṭūsī's *Rijāl*, the principle of graded classes of scholars manifested itself in the form of structuring according to "discipleship" to the imāms, beginning with the earliest (first) imām, ʿAlī, and ending with the latest (twelfth) imām, al-Ḥasan al-ʿAskarī. But this structure did not have the clarity of the "classes" structure since many of the "disciples" (*aṣḥāb*) of one imām were "disciples" of other imāms as well. Still, the significance of using this structure—to point out to continuity in an area of scholarship that makes historicizing it possible—is sufficiently clear, just like the structure by classes.

Despite its clear message and its usefulness, the classes (and imām) structures gave way rather early in Islamic civilization to the simpler alphabetical order, as we shall see below. But, even with the pervasiveness of this latter structure, structuring biographical dictionaries according to classes continued to thrive until quite late in that civilization, as is observable in Dhahabī's *Siyar aʿlām al-nubalāʾ*.

II 4

The fourth way in which the scholars responded to the challenge of continuity that allows for historicization deals with the way they channelled the expression of knowledge. By that I mean their choice of a particular *style* in presenting biographies in their biographical dictionaries, a style in which focus becomes a fundamental characteristic.

Modern scholars have often lamented the repetitive, formulaic, dry, narrow, and impersonal style of the biographies in biographical dictionaries, about their inability to impart holistic, personalized depictions of individual scholars' personal lives, inner selves, and character development[61] and consequently about their usefulness being

ʿilm hāʾulāʾ fī ṭabaqa ukhrā); 74 (*thumma intaqala ilā* . . .); 76 (*thumma intaqala al-fatwā bi-l-shām ilā* . . .); 78 (*thumma intahā ʿilm hāʾulāʾ ilā* . . .); 84 (*thumma ḥaṣala l-fiqh wa-l-futyā fī* . . .); 91 (*thumma baʿda hāʾulāʾ*); 97 (*fa-ammā l-shāfiʿī fa-qad intaqala fiqhuhu ilā aṣḥābihi*); 104 (*thumma qāma bi-fiqhihi baʿda hāʾulāʾ jamāʿa*); 134 (*wa ammā Abū Ḥanīfa* . . . *fa-innahu intaqala fiqhuhu ilā jamāʿa min aṣḥābihi*); 146 (*wa ammā mālik* . . . *fa-qad intaqala fiqhuhu ilā aṣḥābihi* . . .); 169 (*wa ammā aḥmad ibn ḥanbal* . . . *fa-qad naqala ʿanhu l-fiqh jamāʿa*); 171 (*thummā ḥaṣalat al-riwāya ʿan aḥmad fī ṭabaqa ukhrā*); 175 (*wa ammā Dāwūd* . . . *fa-qad intaqala fiqhuhu ilā jamāʿa min aṣḥābihi* . . .).

[61] Gibb, "Biographical Literature," 56–57. Rosenthal, in "Literature," 327–328, says that biography "was expected to provide only a limited number of dry data." Young, 172, says: "the emphasis [is] on the outer events, rather than the mental development, of a person's life," adding on p. 180: "This concentration on names,

confined to quantitative and prosopographical analysis.[62] Some scholars went even father than that, claiming that biographical dictionaries treated individuals as "ideal types"[63] or "models of behaviour,"[64] who share "somewhat stereotypical generalities."[65] In the words of Marcia Hermansen, ". . . biographical notices serve to . . . display a person's type or example through presenting his or her discrete actions or sayings,"[66] and "[t]he concept of a biographical process of exemplification/embodiment is particularly germane to Islamic biographical materials which are shaped by an explicit set of genres and types."[67] Such attitudes troubled some scholars: it led them to

dates, education, writings and assessments of orthodoxy and reliability as a witness tended to narrow the biographer's view of his subject, and to lessen the possibilities for describing the development of personality." Hermansen, 165, says: "Recent Western concepts of what a life is tend to be diachronic, linear, stretching from birth to death, and told so as to reveal character development. In contrast, . . . Islamic biographical material does not present a series of events or cumulative reflections as contributing to character development." Humphreys, in *Islamic History*, 192, speaks about the "repetitive, formulaic character of their data," and "the impersonality of the biographical dictionary, and of its cousin the chronicle obituary," adding: "as for writing about one's personal life and inner experience—the very stuff of biography as we know it—that was crude and indiscrete; it was simply not done by people who cared about their dignity." Roded, 9, says that biographies "have a relatively uniform format." Robinson, 71, says: ". . . works of prosopography are by convention both formulaic . . . and massive . . ."

[62] Humphreys, in *Islamic History*, 190–192, presents the biography of a certain al-Ghāfiqī from Ibn al-Abbār's *Takmila*, then comments (p. 190): ". . . what are we to do with this biographical data? If it is a question of al-Ghāfiqī as an individual, the answer is plainly very little. But if we are willing to see him as just one member in a collectivity, then we might take a more hopeful view . . . [The] kind of data given in the typical biographical dictionary can almost never support a detailed biographical study of an individual; for a serious investigation of a man's career and personality, a great many other materials must be available. On the other hand, it is precisely the repetitive, formulaic character of their data that permits quantitative and prosopographic approaches to the *'ulamā'* . . ." Robinson, 71, also speaks about the biographical dictionaries lending themselves "particularly well to quantitative approaches."

[63] The expression was used by Fedwa Malti-Douglas in her "Biography," 238, in the context of discussing Ibn Khallikān's presentation of his subjects. Hermansen, 171–172, after quoting M. Hodgson and M. Waldman, says: "In the context of Islamic materials, the correspondence of life and role-depiction to an ideal type or set of criteria is a feature of Qur'ānic narrative . . ."

[64] Roded, 6, says: "the role of the biographies as presenting models of behavior for Muslims has been emphasized by some scholars." This is an opinion she disagrees with, and refers generally to Khalidi's article "Biographical Dictionaries," which indeed displays a thrust in that direction.

[65] Gibb, "Biographical Literature," 56–57.

[66] Hermansen, 165.

[67] Ibid. 171.

discuss variations in style of some authors of biographical dictionaries, and to emphasize the role of anecdotes in the biographies of the biographical dictionaries.[68]

While such responses help us understand the Arabic biographical dictionaries better, they do not tackle the methodologically serious consequence for the adherents to the "ideal/model theory." For, does it not follow that, if what is said about a person in a biography is merely ideal, the information contained in the biographies of biographical dictionaries is possibly exaggerated, false, unreliable, and hence unusable in research? What I would like to propose here is that both the stereotype and the variant are true features of the biographies of the biographical dictionaries, and that they co-exist harmoniously, despite their difference, because of the nature of the scholars' understanding of how knowledge ought to be channelled in order to permit those dictionaries to be the alternative history of the Muslim community.

Let us begin with the idea of the stereotype. As was noted above, the scholars needed to establish institution-like continuity in the areas of their activities so that they could write the history of these activities, and when they chose biographical dictionaries as the form in which this history is written, they needed to show that this continuity existed despite the limited nature of the contribution each individual scholar can offer to those activities. Now, one way in which such continuity could be projected is by showing that scholars, though individually different, share features that, when taken together, highlight this continuity. This is why, I think, the scholars chose to emphasize, in the presentation style of their biographies, the features that convey *similarity* between scholars, ones that make them members "in a collectivity," as Humphreys put it.[69] In order to achieve that air of similarity, the scholars had to be selective in the information they included about their subjects, to channel that informa-

---

[68] See in particular the work of Hartmut Fändrich and Fedwa Malti-Douglas, both theoretical and applied, in the former's "The *Wafayāt al-Aʿyān* of Ibn Khallikān" and "Compromising the Caliph," and the latter's "Controversy and Its Effects," and "Dreams." On the role of anecdotes in enlivening biographies, see Gibb, "Biographical Literature," 57; Khalidi, "Biographical Dictionaries," 64; Young, 180.

[69] Humphreys, *Islamic History*, 190. Young, 170: ". . . prosopography seeks to record a group of individuals having certain features in common, and these individuals are viewed in relationship to the prevaling characteristics of the group." See also Gibb, "Biographical Literature," 55; Robinson, 66.

tion in the direction of homogeneity, and to make it constantly focused on what ensures this homogeneity and avoids diffusion and heterogeneity. Furthermore, it was important for the scholars to establish clear connections between their subjects and the scholarly activities they were engaged in, for it is precisely these activities that allowed the subjects to have a place in the "history" the scholars were writing, and to belong to institution-like entities. The result of all that is that the biographical entries in the biographical dictionaries appeared to be formulaic or stereotypical—formulas and stereotypes emphasize commonality—and also impersonal—personal elements emphasize difference, not similarity; they came to have similar rough structures, similar concerns, and similar areas of investigation. And this is precisely what the scholars wanted, for the sake of establishing continuity. This, however, does *not* mean the biographical dictionaries made of their subject unreal ideals or types, nor that the specific *contents* of biographies were fundamentally the same, for they most certainly were not; if this were the case, the whole project of the scholars would be a sham. It would also be self-destructive for the scholars, ridding them of the pride they took in their contributions, individual scholar after individual scholar, and generation after generation, in various times and places, and in a multiplicity of fields or disciplines.

This brings us to the other aspect of the scholars' style of presentation in the biographies they recorded in their biographical dictionaries, namely their difference. Here one must start by stating what has already been alluded to indirectly above, namely the awareness of the scholars that the similarities between scholars are most prominent among those of them who work in the same field, and, to some extent, those who come from the same city or time period. This means that the similarities between scholars who work in different fields are less pronounced. It also means, by implication, that the field dictates to a large extent what may or may not be included in single biographies. The result of this conception is that the biographies of scholars belonging to the same field included specific items related to the field concerned. Thus, whereas all biographies provide, of course, vital information about an individual scholar (name, genealogy, field, profession, travels, books), biographies of physicians or litterateurs do not normally record whom the particular physician or litterateur studied with, unlike the biographies of the *ḥadīth* transmitters, for whom such information is vital. Similarly, it would be not meaningful for a grammarian's biography to include a record of his miraculous acts or his existential reflections on the nature of human existence, contrary to a Ṣūfī's biography, or to include in it his opinions on free will versus predestination, contrary to a theologian's biography. And, actually, the authors of biographical dictionaries did keep to the discipline-related information to a great extent—though not fully. This is due to several reasons: the excessive amount of copying scholars tended to do from each other's works;[70] the interference of the particular interests of the dictionaries' authors themselves; and the fact that many subjects were active in more than one field or discipline.[71] This is a rather complex phenomenon in biographical dictionaries, and the best way to clarify it is to take the biography of one subject and see how it was presented in different biographical dictionaries which deal with different disciplines and whose authors have different interests.

The subject I have chosen is Abū Ḥayyān al-Tawḥīdī (d. 414/1023), who was an author of many works, a prose writer, a poet, a *ḥadīth* transmitter, a Shāfiʿī legal scholar, a Ṣūfī, and a philosopher of sorts. By profession he was a copyist. He was active mainly in Baghdād, but was buried in Shīrāz. He was a staunch Sunnī who forged an anti-ʿAlī "historical" treatise about the incident of the Saqīfa. He was also prickly by temperament, a vocal misanthropist who antagonized people, a recurring failure at seeking patronage, an occasional sceptic in matters of faith, and one who in old age burned his books and wrote a letter justifying his action. Let us see how he was presented in various biographies.

We have 13 biographies of Tawḥīdī. Three of those (Ibn Khallikān, Ṣafadī, Ṭāshköprüzāda)[72] occur in general dictionaries—dictionaries

---

[70] Humphreys, *Islamic History*, 189, discusses the phenomenon of copying, saying: "Even more than in other genres, biographical compilers copy from their predecessors and even contemporaries. As a result, several of the lives devoted to a particular individual are likely to be paraphrases or abridgements of a single origical text. There are relatively few examples where we have truly independent lines of testimony about a given person . . . This feature of the biographical literature can be very frustrating, obviously, but it also means that a great many texts that are otherwise lost—some of them of great antiquity—can be reconstructed quite reliably."

[71] Contradicting herself, Hermansen, 172, says: "it is important to note that the same individual will be portrayed variously in various role contexts: for example, the same person functioning as a poet and a scholar . . ."

[72] Ibn Khallikān, 5:112–13; Ṣafadī, *al-Wāfī bi-l-wafayāt*, 22, ed. Ramzī Baʿalbakī (Beirut/Wiesbaden: Franz Steiner Verlag, 1983), 39–41; Ṭāshköprüzāda, *Miftāḥ al-saʿāda* (Cairo: Dār al-Kutub al-Ḥadītha, 1968), 1:234–235.

not confined to scholars who belong to a specific field, city, or time period; they shall not be considered here since they do not shed light on the matter under investigation. The remaining ten biographies occur in biographical dictionaries as follows:

Three in biographical dictionaries of Shāfiʿī legal scholars (al-Subkī, al-Asnawī, Ibn Hidāyat Allāh);
Two in biographical dictionaries of *ḥadīth* transmitters (al-Dhahabī, Ibn Ḥajar);
One in a biographical dictionary of authors and litterateurs (Yāqūt);
One in a biographical dictionary of linguists and grammarians (Suyūṭī);
One in a biographical dictionary of Ṣūfī master scholars (Khwānsārī);
One in a biographical dictionary of scholars of the city of Baghdād (Ibn al-Najjār).
One in a biographical dictionary of people associated with the mausoleum of the city of Shīrāz (Junayd-i Shīrāzī);

Of these ten dictionaries, only one presents Tawḥīdī's biography in a manner that does not reflect the specific interest/area of the dictionary in which it occurs, namely Suyūṭī's *Bughyat al-wuʿāt fī ṭabaqāt al-lughawiyyīn wa-l-nuḥāt.*[73] Being devoted to the biographies of linguists and grammarians, one would expect its author to highlight Tawḥīdī's genuine contributions to Arabic language, grammar, and lexicography. Suyūṭī, however, does nothing of the sort, and presents, instead, a bland, short biography of Tawḥīdī's, filled with familiar information that is culled from earlier sources, in Suyūṭī's usual manner in many of his books. The reason for that is clear: Suyūṭī did not know Tawḥīdī's works firsthand, for it is there that Tawḥīdī's contributions to the study of language and grammar appear.[74] He knew Tawḥīdī only from his biographies in earlier biographical dictionaries, and none of these had been interested in highlighting Tawḥīdī's linguistic accomplishments.

Tawḥīdī's biography in Ibn al-Najjār's *Dhayl Tāʾrīkh Baghdād*, a biographical dictionary on the scholars of Baghdād, is the earliest biography we have of Tawḥīdī, and it does highlight the Baghdādī aspect of his scholarly activities by stating that he is a Baghdādī, despite the fact that he originally came from Nishapur and lived in

[73] Suyūṭī, *Bughyat al-wuʿāt fī ṭabaqāt al-lughawiyyīn wa-l-nuḥāt* (Cairo: Aḥmad Nājī l-Jamālī and Muḥammad Amīn al-Khānjī, 1326), 548–349.
[74] See Wadād al-Qāḍī, "Dirāsa fī kitāb al-baṣāʾir wa-l-dhakhāʾir," in Tawḥīdī, *al-Baṣāʾir wa-l-dhakhāʾir*, ed. Wadād al-Qāḍī (Beirut: Dār Ṣādir, 1988), 9:252–256.

Shīrāz, and by enumerating the scholars he studied with in Baghdād. Since, however, the version we have of this biography is available only in an abridgement of Ibn al-Najjār's book, namely Dimyāṭī's *al-Mustafād min dhayl Tā'rīkh Baghdād*, the biography is conspicuously short.[75]

Al-Khwānsārī's biography of Tawḥīdī, in his *Rawḍāt al-jannāt fī aḥwāl al-ʿulamā' wa-l-sādāt*,[76] is a mishmash sort of biography, although it does dwell on the Ṣūfī aspect of Tawḥīdī's life, the aspect which the author was fundamentally interested in documenting in his book. This author starts by citing what earlier authorities had said about Tawḥīdī, pointing out the difference of opinion among them about his creed. He then proceeds to state his own evaluation of Tawḥīdī in this regard. There he concentrates, as expected, on the titles of some of Tawḥīdī's works on Ṣūfī subjects, and attracts attention to the similarity between Tawḥīdī's take on Ṣūfism and al-Ḥallāj's, concluding that that take was the cause of al-Ḥallāj's being put to death. The biography closes with more citations from earlier sources about conflicting reports on Tawḥīdī's death. Clearly what we have here is a mixed bag, the message being: Tawḥīdī has made several laudable contributions but he was possibly a misguided Ṣūfī.

When we come to the three biographical dictionaries on Shāfiʿī legal scholars,[77] we find a reasonable amount of correspondence between their interests and the biographies they present of Tawḥīdī: the older two (eighth/fourteenth century) of them, al-Asnawī's and al-Subkī's, mention Tawḥīdī's contribution to legal matters while the more recent (eleventh/seventeenth century) one, Ibn Hidāyat Allāh's, does not, allocating to his biography only a few lines that give skeletal information about him.

Tawḥīdī's biographies in al-Subkī's *Ṭabaqāt al-Shāfiʿīyya l-kubrā* and al-Asnawī's in *Ṭabaqāt al-Shāfiʿiyya* are clearly independent of each

[75] Shihāb al-Dīn Aḥmad b. Aybak al-Dimyāṭī, *al-Mustafād min dhayl tā'rīkh baghdād li-l-ḥāfiẓ muḥibb al-dīn ibn al-najjār*, ed. Muḥammad Mawlūd Khalaf (Beirut: Mu'assasat al-Risāla, 1986), 346–347.

[76] Al-Khwānsārī, *Rawḍāt al-jannāt fī aḥwāl al-ʿulamā' wa-l-sādāt*, ed. Asad Allāh Ismāʿīlian (Qom, 1970–1972), 8:92–93.

[77] Al-Asnawī, *Ṭabaqāt al-shāfiʿiyya*, ed. ʿAbd Allāh al-Jubūrī (Riyadh: Dār al-ʿUlūm, 1981), 1:301–303; al-Subkī, *Ṭabaqāt al-shāfiʿiyya al-kubrā*, ed. Maḥmūd al-Ṭanāḥī and ʿAbd al-Fattāḥ al-Ḥulw (Cairo: ʿIsā al-Bābī l-Ḥalabī, 1967), 5:286–289; Ibn Hidāyat Allāh, *Ṭabaqāt al-shāfiʿiyya*, ed. ʿĀdil Nuwayhiḍ (Beirut: Dār al-Āfāq al-Jadīda, second edition, 1979), 114–116.

other. The latter author gives a short biography, most of which is general and derived from earlier sources. At its end, however, he mentions Tawḥīdī's contribution to law, and Shāfiʿī's for that matter: Tawḥīdī reported that his Shāfiʿī jurist-teacher, Abū Ḥāmid al-Marwarrūdhī (d. 362/972) ruled that usury does not apply in the case of saffron. Al-Asnawī comments that the accepted (*al-maʿrūf*) Shāfiʿī position on this subject is contrary (*khilāf*) to what Tawḥīdī reported.

Tawḥīdī's biography in al-Subkī's biographical dictionary is longer and more elaborate. He starts it by giving basic information about him, adding to that, for the first time, the names of five scholars from the city of Shīrāz and one from the city of Iṣfahān who narrated *ḥadīth* from him, thus making him a veritable *ḥadīth* scholar. He then cites Ibn al-Najjār's brief positive assessment of his creed[78] then moves to al-Dhahabī's detailed, rationalized negative assessment of that creed: Tawḥīdī is basically an anti-Muslim heretic who advocates the suspension of the *sharīʿa* and attributes disgraceful things to the Prophet's companions. Another brief negative assessment of Tawḥīdī's creed by Ibn al-Jawzī—his *zandaqa*, heresy—follows. Al-Subkī then launches a defence of Tawḥīdī, attributing al-Dhahabī's motive for maligning him to al-Dhahabī's hatred of the Ṣūfīs. He then adds a sentence which indicates that he knew Tawḥīdī's works, or at least some of them, firsthand: he, Subkī, had read much of Tawḥīdī's words (*wa waqaftu ʿalā kathīr min kalāmihi*), and these indicated that he was a morally courageous person (*qawiyy al-nafs*) who defied (*muzdariyan*) his contemporaries. This need not bring him such slander (*nayl*), though. In support of his position, al-Subkī ends this section of Tawḥīdī's biography by citing his own father's agreement with his evaluation. Al-Subkī then comes to the contribution of Tawḥīdī to Shāfiʿī legal thought. He mentions his reporting on the above mentioned issue of usury in saffron, and adds another ruling he said he read in Tawḥīdī's book, *al-Imtāʿ wa-l-muʾānasa*. This concerns the issue of rabies, which originally strikes dogs but can also strike camels. The legal ruling about camels who are rabid is that they should be slaughtered, and their flesh should not be eaten. Al-Subkī ends this section by evaluating Tawḥīdī's legal contribution.

[78] This assessment ("*wa-kāna ṣaḥīḥ al-ʿaqīda*") does not occur in Tawḥīdī's biography in Dimyāṭī's abridgement of Ibn al-Najjār's book (see n. 75 above).

He, Subkī, is not aware of any original contribution by Tawḥīdī to the field of law (*wa-lā aʿrifu lahū min qibal nafsihi kalāman fī l-fiqh*); Tawḥīdī has several useful legal statements, but they are only reports from his teacher Abū Ḥāmid al-Marwarrūdhī. As for the matter of not eating the flesh of rabid camels, this is quite well known, but only if physicians say that eating it is harmful. It is not so certain that rabid camels should be slaughtered if their flesh is not meant to be eaten (*ammā l-naḥru li-gayri maʾkalatin fa-fīhi waqfa*). What should be legally done is that rabid camels, just like other harmful animals, should be killed, and not slaughtered. Thus, al-Subkī's biographical dictionary presents the legal contribution of Tawḥīdī, no matter how limited, and that tallies well with the nature of his dictionary dedicated to Shāfiʿī legal scholars.

When we come to the two biographical dictionaries on *ḥadīth* transmitters which included biographies of Tawḥīdī,[79] we find even greater correspondence between the dictionaries' areas of interest and the biographies themselves. Al-Dhahabī's *Mīzān al-iʿtidāl* is devoted to *ḥadīth* transmitters in general but has a special interest in entering biographies of weak transmitters. Tawḥīdī's biography there is short, but al-Dhahabī makes sure that it proves why Tawḥīdī should be considered a weak transmitter. After giving the basic information about Tawḥīdī, he cites the saying of an authority, a certain al-Mālīnī, to the effect that he heard Tawḥīdī admitting that he had authored the epistle on the incident of the Saqīfa as a response to the Shīʿites' exaggerated claims about ʿAlī. Al-Dhahabī comments that this clearly indicates that Tawḥīdī was a forger, and indeed a certain vizier, al-Muhallabī (d. 352/963), expelled him because his creed was bad; he also delved in philosophy (*wa-kāna yatafalsaf*). Al-Dhahabī then gives further support for his negative assessment of Tawḥīdī's creed: as earlier authorities have said, he was an impious liar, a vocal adherent of suspending the *sharīʿa* [meaning that he was an extreme Ṣūfī], and a heretic (*zindīq*). Al-Dhahabī, thus, by maligning Tawḥīdī's character and creed, declares him unfit to be trusted in *ḥadīth* transmission.

Ibn Ḥajar's dictionary, *Lisān al-mīzān*, is especially dedicated to the biographies of unreliable *ḥadīth* scholars. He includes in Tawḥīdī's

---

[79] Dhahabī, *Mīzān al-iʿtidāl*, ed. ʿAlī Muḥammad al-Bajāwī (offset copy of the Cairo edition, Beirut: Dār al-Maʿrifa, n.d.), 4:518–519; Ibn Ḥajar al-ʿAsqalānī, *Lisān al-mīzān* (Ḥaydarabād, 1331), 7:38–41.

long biography all of the negative things mentioned by al-Dhahabī in the *Mīzān* and adds to them much more negative material. He first cites a detailed report by "a scholar" (*baʿḍ al-ʿulamāʾ*) who said that Tawḥīdī was an upright man until he forged the epistle about the Saqīfa incident. This scholar then went on to attack particular sentences in that epistle, which exposed Tawḥīdī as one ignorant of the companions' demeanour and correct speech, and as one given to philosophy. Other general and conflicting citations from earlier authorities follow, including some of his poetry. But then Ibn Ḥajar gets back to the issue of Tawḥīdī's unreliability and bad faith, this time citing sentences from Tawḥīdī's own words in his books, which he says he has read. Ibn Ḥajar finds an anecdote in Tawḥīdī's *Mathālib al-wazīrayn* to be disrespectful of God; he finds another anecdote in his *Taqrīẓ al-Jāḥiẓ* to be excessive in praise and bordering on lifting men to the position of prophets; and, more importantly, he finds Tawḥīdī's transmission of two *ḥadīth*s, which he identifies, to be corrupt (*taḥrīfāt*). By so doing, Ibn Ḥajar leaves no room for any doubt about Tawḥīdī's unreliability in *ḥadīth* transmission, like all the other transmitters who inhabit his dictionary.

Tawḥīdī's biography in Junayd-i Shīrāzī's *Shadd al-izār fī ḥaṭṭ al-awzār ʿan zuwwār al-mazār*[80] goes very well also with that book's area of interest. It is a biographical dictionary on the people associated with the mausoleum of Shīrāz, many of whom were Ṣūfīs. Tawḥīdī's biography there gives general information about Tawḥīdī, but then concentrates on two points. The first is Tawḥīdī's Ṣūfism. There Tawḥīdī is portrayed as an excessively pious person who had lived for a while near the sanctuary in Mecca (*jāwara*), accompanied several Ṣūfī *shaykhs*, and narrated the esoteric words of a Ṣūfī master. Furthermore, Tawḥīdī authored pious verses, some of which are cited; they are quite different from the verses attributed to him in other biographies. The second is the circumstances surrounding Tawḥīdī's death and burial in the mausoleum of Shīrāz. We are told that Tawḥīdī was not on good terms with the Ṣūfī Abū al-Ḥusayn Ibn Sālbeh, the *shaykh al-shuyūkh* among Ṣūfīs. When Tawḥīdī died, Ibn Sālbeh saw him in a dream and learned from him that God had forgiven him despite Ibn Sālbeh. The next morning, Ibn

[80] Junayd-i Shīrāzī, *Shadd al-izār fī ḥaṭṭ al-awzār ʿan zuwwār al-mazār*, ed. Muḥammad Qazwīnī and ʿAbbās Iqbāl (Tehran, 1950), 53–55.

Sālbeh asked his disciples to take him to Tawḥīdī's grave in order to offer a prayer on his behalf. He was carried there on a litter, and he ordered that a marker be put on the grave with the inscription: "This is the grave of Abū Ḥayyān al-Tawḥīdī." He was thereafter buried next to him.

When we come to the last biographical dictionary, Yāqūt's *Muʿjam al-udabāʾ*,[81] we find the correspondence between the dictionary's interests and Tawḥīdī's biography not only good but stunningly great. This dictionary is devoted to litterateurs who authored books. Four things strike the reader of Tawḥīdī's biography there: it is very long (24 pages), almost as long as all of his biographies in other dictionaries put together: this is an indication of the author's appreciation of Tawḥīdī's importance as an author-litterateur; it has by far the fullest record of the titles of Tawḥīdī's books and epistles, which is what the author is keen on listing in all of the biographies of his dictionary; it is packed with extensive, sometimes pages-long citations from those books and epistles: this is an indication of the author's realization of Tawḥīdī's versatility as a prose stylist; and it has nothing to say other than a passing remark about Tawḥīdī's creed (*wa-l-nāsu yaqūlūna fī dīnihi*): this is simply a matter that falls outside of the book's sphere of interest. But there are two more things that make Yāqūt's biography of Tawḥīdī unique. The first is that it insinuates right from the beginning that Tawḥīdī's expertise was difficult to pin down to one field since he was conversant in many fields: he was "the *shaykh* of the Ṣūfīs, the philosopher of the litterateurs, the litterateur of the philosophers, the investigator of speech, the speaker of investigators, the *imām* of the eloquent ones, and the prop of the beggars (*ʿumdatun li-Banī Sāsān*) . . ." (5:1924). This statement lends support to the author's admiration of Tawḥīdī and provides justification for his dedicating so many pages to his biography. The second thing is that this is the only biography that cites in full (in over four pages) Tawḥīdī's letter justifying his burning of his books when he was in his eighties. This gesture speaks of the author's interest in his subjects as compilers of books; it may also explain the author's interest in citing long sections from Tawḥīdī's works—to which he clearly had access—for fear that others might

[81] Yāqūt al-Ḥamawī, *Muʿjam al-udabāʾ*, ed. Iḥsān ʿAbbās (Beirut: Dār al-Gharb al-Islāmī, 1993), 5:1923–1947.

have been deprived of such access due to Tawḥīdī's burning of his books.

Overall, Yāqūt's biography of Tawḥīdī is a monumental biographical achievement. More importantly, it is a shining proof that the biographies of Arabic Islamic biographical dictionaries are far from presenting their subjects as unreal "types" or as inane copies of each other. It, together with most of the above mentioned biographies, also provides strong evidence that there is a direct relationship between the items contained in biographies and the specific interests of authors of biographical dictionaries and the discipline to which the subjects in these dictionaries belong.

III

Before closing this discussion, I would like to mention some features in late biographical dictionaries and interpret them in light of the scholars' attempt, through biographical dictionaries, to write an alternative history of the Muslim community.

Late biographical dictionaries exhibit four main features: greater tendency to structure dictionaries alphabetically rather than according to *ṭabaqāt*; the start of compiling general dictionaries that are not limited to any specific field, place, or time period; the proliferation of mixing chronicles with biographies; and the emergence of abridgements of earlier, long biographical dictionaries.[82] The common denominator between all these features is that they make using the dictionaries much easier, thus allowing their readers greater access to them. The scholars surely had the members of their own ranks in mind when they undertook such "smoothing" steps in writing their dictionaries: the compilers of *ḥadīth* biographical dictionaries, for example, wanted the students of *ḥadīth* to access more easily such dictionaries; and perhaps it is inevitable, in a way, that a genre of writing should become smoother with its development over time. But such "smoothing" features can be seen as serving another purpose from the point of view of the scholars: to make their biographical dictionaries open

[82] To these main features can be appended the addition of titles of biographies in the margins of manuscripts, and the tendency of the authors' introductions to their works to be more elaborate. Both such features are attested, for example, in Ṣafadī's *al-Wāfī bi-l-wafayāt*.

to the community at large. For, by taking steps to provide wider access to their dictionaries, the scholars were assuming that the persons accessing these dictionaries needed greater assistance in so doing, and this applies to non-specialists much more than to specialists. This means that the scholars wanted their "history" of the Muslim community to be wide open to the members of the community at large, not only to the scholars among them, so that those members witness their own collective achievement in the contributions of their scholars to knowledge. Let us see how this is portrayed in each of the four features mentioned above.

III 1

There is no doubt that structuring biographical dictionaries alphabetically makes them much easier to access than structuring them according to classes, or *ṭabaqāt.* Ibn Khallikān, among others, mentioned the "ease factor" in his introduction to his alphabetically arranged *Wafayāt al-aʿyān,*[83] and the enormous difficulty of determining where the biography of a certain *ḥadīth* transmitter would fall in Ibn Saʿd's class-organized *ṭabaqāt* has been mentioned by several modern scholars. Now, structuring biographical dictionaries alphabetically is very old in Islamic civilization, and dates back to the middle of the third/ninth century. Its beginnings were rather crude, as we see it in Ibn Ḥibbān al-Bustī's (254/868) *Kitāb al-majrūḥīn* and Bukhārī's (256/870) *al-Tāʾrīkh al-kabīr.* There the structure is alphabetical only in the sense that the biographies are arranged according to the (oriental) order of the letters of the alphabet—but no more than that. Thus, the biographies of all the subjects whose first names start with the letter *alif,* for example, occur, in clusters of single first names, under the letter *alif,* but the order of the name-clusters within the letter *alif* is not alphabetical (the "Ismāʿīls" occur before the "Isḥāqs," for example, in Bukhārī), and although the subjects with the same name are grouped together, the sequence of their biographies does not take into consideration their fathers' names ("Ismāʿīl b. Yaḥyā b. ʿUbayd" occurs before "Ismāʿīl b. Qays b. Saʿd," for

[83] Since Ibn Khallikān considered his *Wafayāt* as a work of history, he stated (1:20) that the alphabetical arrangement is "easier" than the annalistic one (*fa-raʾaytuhu ʿalā ḥurūf al-muʿjam aysara minhu ʿalā l-sinīn*).

example, in Bustī); in addition, the biographies of all the "Muḥammads" in Bukhārī are placed at the beginning of the book before the biographies of all the rest of the subjects. The alphabetical order, however, developed quickly and became smoother in the following century, as we can see in Ibn Abī Ḥātim al-Rāzī's (327/938) *al-Jarḥ wa-l-taʿdīl*, and it covered not only dictionaries of scholars of a single field, as in Ibn Abī Ḥātim's book, but also in dictionaries of scholars of the same place, as in al-Khaṭīb al-Baghdādī's *Tāʾrīkh Baghdād*. But such dictionaries existed side by side with dictionaries arranged according to *ṭabaqāt* in the early period. In the late period, however, certainly by Mamlūk times, the alphabetical structure becomes by far the most dominant, and the *ṭabaqāt* structure becomes confined to few dictionaries, like the *Siyar aʿlām al-nubalāʾ* of al-Dhahabī; even the dictionaries of Shīʿī scholars become alphabetically arranged instead of being *imām*-based, as we see it in Najāshī's (d. 450/1058) *Kitāb al-rijāl* and Ibn Shahr-Āshūb's (d. 588/1192) *Maʿālim al-ʿulamāʾ*. Indeed, the biographical dictionaries that are specialized in specific time periods, the centennial dictionaries—all of which are late—are all structured alphabetically.

III 2

Compiling general biographical dictionaries rather than specialized ones is also a feature that demonstrates even more the scholars' desire to serve the larger community of the Muslims than the scholars of their own ranks. The tradition of writing general dictionaries did not take off seriously until the late seventh/thirteenth century, with Ibn Khallikān's (681/1282) *Wafayāt al-aʿyān*, as has been noted by several modern scholars. And what biographies did Ibn Khallikān include in his biographical dictionary? According to his own introduction, he included "those who possess some fame among people and about whom questions may be asked," (1:20, *kull man lahū shuhra bayna l-nās wa-yaqaʿ al-suʾāl ʿanhu*)—with some exceptions he specified. Now "among people" certainly does not refer to fellow scholars of Ibn Khallikān but rather to querying Muslims in general, i.e., to the community of whom the scholars are but a minority. And clearly the book is not of real use to the *ḥadīth* scholar or the jurist or the poet or the political historian, since the number of biographies of the scholars of each of these fields is relatively small, and much is left to the discretion of the author regarding what to include in each biography. Even when general dictionaries became large reference works—much larger than Ibn Khallikān's—as, for example in Ṣafadī's encyclopaedic *al-Wāfī bi-l-wafayāt*, the usefulness of such dictionaries for specialists remained limited, since biographies normally include general information about subjects which is insufficient for specialists, and since the subjects in each field have to share the space with subjects in other fields, or even with non-scholars altogether, from caliphs and sultans to jokers and singers. This made the general biographical dictionaries, in effect, open to a wide audience of the community at large, providing its members with informative reading material on those who achieved some renown among its ranks—not even among the ranks of the scholars alone.

III 3

This brings us to the third feature of late biographical dictionaries, namely the proliferation of mixing chronicles with biographies. This feature was mentioned above under II 1c, in connection with the writings that prepared the way for the rise of the centennial biographical dictionary. What concerns us of this feature here is that, like the general biographical dictionaries, it points to the broadening of the scope of the biographical dictionaries in such a way that many people other than scholars are chosen as subjects of biographies in them. For, when scholars such as Ibn al-Jawzī in his *Muntaẓam* or al-Dhahabī in his *Tā'rīkh al-Islām* first mention in the year/decade under discussion the political history of that year/decade, then they record the biographies of some people who died in that year/decade, they invariably broaden the pool of selection for biographical entries, if for nothing other than to create a kind of homogeneity between the narrative and biographical parts of their works. This means that, as in the case of general biographical dictionaries, the ratio of scholars of particular fields to the entire body of biographies is not inordinately high. More importantly, however, it means the audience for these works are not primarily specialized scholars but rather the members of the wider community. In addition, the fact that such works were written by people who were primarily religious scholars, not chroniclers (Ibn al-Jawzī, Ibn Kathīr, Dhahabī), points to the narrowing of the gap between the chronicle and the biographical dictionary in late Islamic society, after those scholars had made their peace with the state; but it also points to the interest of the scholars in opening up their mixed historical-biographical works to the Muslim community at large, in a manner which perhaps exceeds that of the general biographical dictionaries.

III 4

Finally, the later periods in Islamic civilization witnessed the emergence of abridgements of earlier, long biographical dictionaries, like the abridgement of al-Khaṭīb al-Baghdādī's huge *Tā'rīkh Baghdād*, which has not survived[84] and Ibn Ḥajar's abridgement of al-Mizzī's massive *Tahdhīb al-kamāl* with his *Tahdhīb al-Tahdīb*, which has survived.[85] Such abridgements were certainly intended for the students specializing in specific disciplines, it is true. But it is also true that they served as reference works for a body of the community larger than that of the specialized scholars. As such, they can be considered one of the ways in which the scholars made their works much more accessible to the wider community of the Muslims. Until now, we, as general Islamicists, use Ibn Ḥajar's *Tahdhīb* as a highly accessible and useful reference biographical work, and only rarely do we go to Mizzī's *Tahdhīb* in search of general information about *ḥadīth* transmitters.

* * *

In the above, I have suggested that the emergence of biographical dictionaries at the beginning of third/ninth century Islamic civilization is connected with the moment in which the scholars of the Muslim community recognized that they, along with most of the community, were marginalized in the histories of that community, the chronicles. Their choice of biographical dictionaries as the vehicle to record an alternative history of the Muslim community proved

---

[84] Ḥājji Khalīfa 1:288. This abridgement is by a certain Abū l-Yumn Mas'ūd b. Muḥammad al-Bukhārī. Ḥājji Khalīfa says that he died in 461/[1068]. But this makes his death date *before* al-Khaṭīb's two years later, which is very unlikely. Errors in death dates in Ḥājji Khalīfa are quite common.

[85] See also above, nn. 75 and 78, for Dimyāṭī's abridgement of Ibn al-Najjār's *Dhayl tā'rīkh baghdād*. For other examples of abridgements, see Ḥājji Khalīfa, 1:514, under al-Nawawī's (d. 676/12) *tahdhīb al-asmā' wa-l-lughāt*, and 2: 2018, under Ibn Khallikān's *Wafayāt al-a'yān*, for which three abridgements are cited. Al-Suyūṭī (d. 911/1505) was famous for making abridgements of earlier works.

to be successful, and biographical dictionaries became the most pervasive genre of historical writing in pre-modern Islamic civilization. In making this choice, however, the scholars made two assumptions, both of which made them face two major problems. The first assumption is that the real achievement of the Muslim community resides in the scholars' contribution to knowledge—which meant that non-scholars of the community do not play a role in the making of the history of that community; this made them look exclusivist. And the second is that knowledge resides in individual scholars; this made them place knowledge in an amorphous body that lacks the continuity and institutionalization needed for the historicization of any entity. The attempt of the scholars to overcome those two problems led to the appearance of four specific features in biographical dictionaries, all of which are related to various aspects of their understanding of knowledge. The first, which deals with the dictionaries' alignment, consists of grouping the scholars of their dictionaries in groups which share common factors, like fields, places, and time periods, thereby making these groups act like institutions; this feature is connected with the scholars' vision of the organization of knowledge. The second, which deals with the scope of biographical dictionaries, consists of the scholars' broadening of the parameters of inclusion in their dictionaries; this feature is connected with their vision of the pervasiveness of knowledge. The third, which deals with the structure of biographical dictionaries, consists of the scholars' arranging biographies in a chronologically hierarchical way that gives the scholars of particular fields a kind of institutional existence; this is connected with their vision of the configuration of knowledge. And the fourth, which deals with style, consists of selecting the information to be included in biographies such that it reflects both the general, stereotypical and specific, individual aspects of the subjects; this is connected with their attempt at channelling knowledge. In the last paragraphs, I suggested that, in late pre-modern Islamic civilization, the scholars showed increased interest in granting the broad Muslim community wide access to their biographical dictionaries. This interest resulted in the emergence or proliferation of structuring dictionaries alphabetically rather than according to *ṭabaqāt*, compiling general dictionaries, mixing chronicles with biographies, and making abridgements of earlier dictionaries.

There is no doubt that, when the scholars undertook to write the history of the Muslim community through biographical dictionaries, as an alternative to the chronicle, they were undertaking a major project with epistemological and practical implications, with both positive and negative results. Fundamentally changing the landscape of historical documentation, they proposed to move the centre of making history from the hands of powerful institutionalized groups, who actually effect change in society with the dominant machinery of the state, into the hands of an amorphous body of uninstitutionalized individuals, the reach of whose power hardly ever exceeds the control of the minds and hearts of some sectors of society. The basis of their project was not totally wrong, in that the chronicles had indeed departed from what they should have ideally done—to write the history of the entire community rather than the history of only the powerful of it. In that sense, the scholars' project was not only valuable but also necessary, for it is only through the additional information provided by the biographical dictionaries that any Islamic historical event, period, dynasty, idea, ideology, etc. can be understood. It is more difficult, however, to assess the value of the scholars' biographical dictionaries when they are taken in isolation. Their value in writing the intellectual history of the Muslim community is certainly great, as many modern scholars have pointed out;[86] but in other aspects of the history of that community, their value is only supplementary,[87] and there are areas of that history to which they can make hardly any contribution at all. The concept on which they are founded a series of biographies organized in a particular fashion about a particular group of scholars—was easy and quite free of methodological and other non-self-imposed strictures; but because

[86] Gibb, in his "Islamic Biographical Literature," 58, says: "To the historian of Islamic civilization in its broader aspects the dictionaries are obviously of capital importance, but with certain limitations . . . [I]t is evident that they provide the fullest and most complete detail for the religious and intellectual life of the Muslim community throughout its history, including educational and . . . scientific activities. Without these works, indeed, no detailed study of Islamic culture would be possible." Young, 176, considers biographical dictionaries as "essential for the study of Islamic civilization . . . Their potential contribution to narrative history is clear, but perhaps more important is the cumulative value of these thousands of life histories in reconstructing a picture of Islamic medieval society." See also Humphreys, *Islamic History*, 192; Robinson, 71.

[87] See Gibb, "Islamic Biographical Literature," 58, where he says that the data provided by biographical dictionaries "have often to be combined with other sources to become fully intelligible," adding on the same page that "[i]t is . . . unsafe to draw conclusions from the anecdotes of the biographical works, unless sustaining data can be adduced." See also Humphreys, *Islamic History*, 191–192.

of that, it allowed scholars of greatly varying degrees of competence to write dictionaries, with many of them being far less illuminating than they could have been, especially that the genre by its very nature did not discourage the copying-and-pasting many scholars indulged in.[88] Again, despite the efforts of the scholars to be as inclusive as possible, they could not, by the very nature of their project, but exclude from their history very large sectors of the community, thereby ending up being, not unlike their nemeses, the chroniclers, restrictive and to some extent elitist. And despite their efforts to endow their biographical dictionaries with the aura of institutionalization and continuity, they could not restructure the fundamental concept that knowledge lies in the individual. Such a concept, which made biographical dictionaries proliferate in Islamic civilization, prevented the development of a parallel proliferation of works on genuine institutions with which the scholars were closely involved, like schools, colleges, libraries, courts, mosques, and so forth. In fact, the scholars seemed to perceive those institutions as secondary, at best, in the role they can play in writing the history of the Muslim community.

The major contribution that the scholars' project made to the history of Muslim community is to indicate the inadequacy of the chronicle to write the history of that community. The community's alternative history, i.e. the scholars' biographical dictionaries, amended the situation and broadened the base from which knowledge of the history of the community is drawn. What it could not do, however, was to propose to write a history of Islamic *civilization*. Such a project was beyond the reach of the scholars when they began their project in the third/ninth century and continued to develop it successfully in later centuries until today. For that not only a different form of writing was needed, but also a more fundamentally inclusive and institutionalized one. And this is what did not happen until one scholar, Ibn Khaldūn (d. 808/1406), realized that the community is made up of more than politicians and scholars, that civilization lies in institutions as much as in individuals, and that, in addition, there is a powerful natural movement of history which is beyond the reach of

[88] Gibb, in "Islamic Biographical Literature," 57, notes the growth of biographies "into 20, 30, or even 50 pages," from Ibn Saʿd to al-Murādī, but says that this growth, while it indicates an "elaboration of the basic scheme," its purpose is often "simply to transmit all information which the writer has been able to collect on the biographies." See also above, n. 70.

politicians and scholars alike. His work could have produced a conceptual and epistemological revolution in the ranks of the scholars, the creators of biographical dictionaries. But it did not. Long after Ibn Khaldūn was dead and buried, the scholars continued to write—and pride themselves on—biographical dictionaries, all the way until today, not realizing how less and less relevant this form of writing had become, especially today, in a world of consolidated institutions and altered civilizational hegemonies.[89]

[89] R. Stephen Humphreys, *Islamic History*, 192: "for no other group in Islamic society can we construct such a systematic and comprehensive profile."

ENCYCLOPÆDIC ACTIVITIES IN ISLAMIC JURISPRUDENCE

Ridwan al-Sayyid
The Lebanese University, Beirut

I

The Authority of the Jurist

Not much is known about the emergence of the jurist in the early Islamic period, nor the development of his teaching and authority. As is known, Islamic Jurisprudence emerged in an environment of struggle between judges and jurists. If the judge derived his authority from the state or the ruler who appointed him, then from whom did the first jurists derive their authority that entitled them to produce legal pronouncement (*fatwā*) and, more importantly, the authority to systematize jurisprudence in manuals of law?

We do not know exactly the difference between the education of Saʿīd b. al-Musayyab, who was called a jurist, and the education of Ḥasan al-Baṣrī, renowned for his Arabic rhetoric, known as a theologian and as a Zāhid, who also produced legal pronouncements. If the jurist, it is said, depended on the religious tradition or the customary law of Medina or Kufa, inherited form the period of the Prophet or his companions, the Umayyad Caliphs used to do that as well. It is mentioned that ʿAbd al-Malik b. Marwān ordered the people to adhere to the traditions of the Medinan community in every respect, because these traditions were the essentials that united the community around ʿUthmān b. ʿAffān, the unjustly assassinated Caliph Mālik b. Anas (d. 795/179) in his book, *al-Muwaṭṭaʾ*, cited the legal pronouncements and judgments of ʿAbd al-Malik b. Marwān and his father, Marwān b. al-Ḥakam, who were considered jurists from al-Madīna. We know from the *History* of Abū Zurʿa al-Dimashqī that a controversy over legal authority started under the rule of ʿAbd al-Malik when Ghuḍaif b. al-Ḥārith al-Thumālī (d. 699/80) considered that some acts which ʿAbd al-Malik performed while praying were an uncalled-for innovation which contradicted the Prophetic

Traditions.[1] According to the text of Aḥmad b. Ḥanbal's book *al-Musnad*, Traditions (*Sunna*) transmitted what the community of al-Madīna inherited from the period of ʿUmar b. al-Khaṭṭāb. If ʿAbd al-Malik knew jurisprudence and traditions, why then did he ask Ghuḍayf, and whence had Ghuḍayf the authority to oppose the Caliph? From another text, we know that Saʿīd b. al-Musayyab (d. 712/94) gained his reputation and, perhaps, his authority in al-Madīna because of his knowledge of the rulings of ʿUmar b. al-Khaṭṭāb.

Consequently, we have two sources for this ambiguous authority of the jurist during the Umayyad period: customary practice, and Traditions inherited from the period of ʿUmar. The jurist is the custodian of such customs and judgments, and the initiator of legal pronouncements in accordance with this knowledge.

There is similar evidence on the meaning of *Sunna* in the beginning of the Umayyad period. However, the question over authority and power remains: what is the authority of the Caliph over religious issues—and what is the authority of the newly established jurists? It is said that the Umayyads recognized, besides adjudication, only the traditions of storytellers (*quṣṣāṣ*). However, Abū Zurʿa al-Dimashqī again provides a narrative which conveys two indications: he says that al-Wālid b. ʿAbd al-Malik (regn. 705/86–715/96) wanted people at the mosque to recite the Qurʾān in groups. In terms of jurisprudence, he wanted the judges to agree upon the legal rulings of his judge, Khālid b. Maʿdan (died 722/104).[2] It seems, however, that al-Walīd failed in carrying through this policy. This was followed up during the reign of ʿUmar b. ʿAbd al-ʿAzīz (717–20/99–101) who wanted people and regions to unite under one form of adjudication. But he shied away from this eventually, or his idea was not accepted by the people who were used to different forms of justice in their regions inherited from the time of the rightly guided Caliphs. What is important in another narrative on ʿUmar b. Abd al-ʿAzīz is the limitation of his legislative power. As the ruler, he must rule primarily according to the Qurʾān and Sunna. The opinion of the Caliph comes in as a third source only. We find the same line of thought over the legislative authority of the Caliph in

[1] Abū Zurʿa al-Dimashqī, *Tārīkh*, ed. Shukr-Allāh b. Niʿmat-Allāh al-Qūjānī (Damascus, 1980), 603f.

[2] *Tārīkh Ibn Zurʿa*, 351 § 723, 601 § 1701.

Ibn al-Muqaffaʿ's (756/139) treatise on the companions, *Risāla fī l-Ṣaḥāba*: his authority was to come after that of the Qurʾān and the prophetic Sunna. But Ibn al-Muqaffaʿ doubts the legislative authority of the so-called Sunna and attributes that view to the opinions of the Umayyad princes. However, he agrees with the idea of unifying the system of justice whereby judges should rule according to one text, integrating the rulings indicated in the Qurʾān and the Sunna, as also the Caliph's views considered as obligatory. We do not know to which Caliph the epistle was submitted. If it was Abū Jaʿfar al-Manṣūr (754–775/136–58), his attempt failed. Indeed, we have a famous report saying that Abū Jaʿfar al-Manṣūr wanted to impose the *Muwaṭṭaʾ* of Mālik b. Anas (d. 795/179) as a canon for the judges to base their rulings on. But Mālik opposed that and upheld the principle of ʿUmar b. ʿAbd al-ʿAzīz, namely that people in different regions had inherited various legislative traditions and it was better for them to keep with those traditions.

We have an ambiguous text on a difference between the Caliph al-Mahdī (regn. 775/158–785/169) and the judge ʿUbayd Allah b. Ḥasan al-ʿAnbarī of Basra over the issue of land taxation, which eventually led to the removal of the judge. Therefore, even at this early period, there were judges who had opinions that were independent from political authority although they were employed by the state. Therefore, what is the authority of the judge, and whence is it derived? Various sources mention that al-ʿAnbarī was one of the elders of the tribe of Banū Tamīm, but his Arab descent does not suffice to justify the power he had, and the authority in writing on taxation in opposition to the views of the state. It is known that the issues and problems of taxation and finance were the domain of the state chancellery, not the jurists or judges. However, the struggle over principles of jurisprudence, and especially over the sources of authority for interpreting the text in view of actual practice, became clear when Harūn al-Rashīd (786–809/170–193) appointed Abū Yūsuf (d. 790/182) chief judge, and entrusted him with writing a treatise on land taxation and the financial organization of the state on the basis of the practice initiated by ʿUmar b. al-Khaṭṭāb. We do not know how much the state benefited from his treatise. Nonetheless, this kind of financial writing attracted the interests of jurists for a short time only, resulting in the book on land taxation by Yaḥyā b. Ādam (d. 821/206) and a book on financial administration by Abū ʿUbayd al-Qāsim b. Sallām (d. 838/224). It seems that these two works were also commissioned by the state. Henceforth, the jurists' legitimacy started to crystallize in its double dependency on historical precedence and the Sunna tradition: that is, experience and history. Experience is based on the practice of state administration, history is based on transmission of the solutions which had been proposed to resolve administrative and financial problems since the period of the Rightly Guided Caliphs.

The controversy between al-Maʾmūn (813–833/189–218) and the legal scholars has nothing to do with jurisprudence, or the trespassing of the jurists into the domain of the state, but it is the other way around. The Caliph wanted to force the scholars of his age, especially those paid by the state, to adopt certain religious doctrines regarded as orthodox, and an authentic view of history as part of that creed. A few scholars, including Aḥmad b. Ḥanbal (d. 855/241) stood up against the Caliph. They accepted his authority in the public domain but claimed to themselves the role of custodians of the religious text and its interpretation. It is ironic that the group that challenged the Caliph called themselves *Ahl al-Sunna wa-l-Jamāʿa*, that is the followers of Prophetic tradition and consensus. This group was not known for its legal pronouncements or as working for the state, but consisted of transmitters of traditions and collectors of evidence concerning the transmission and its witnesses. In this way, a third group, in addition to the jurists and the readers and interpreters of the Qurʾān, was added to the circle of scholars (*al-ʿulamāʾ*), that is, the transmitters of traditions (*muḥaddithūn, ahl al-ḥadīth*).

I think that the period between 849/235 and 893/280 witnessed the separation of the religious sphere from the political—as it were, a division of labour between the political powers and the religious scholars. The Caliph lost his legislative authority, but, at the same time, encouraged the jurists as well as the new ideologists to work for the state. During this period in particular, Abū Bakr al-Khallāl (d. 923/311) wrote his treatise on Commanding Right and Forbidding Wrong, which gave the Sultan (the Caliph) the right to be obeyed and the scholar the right to interpret and observe state activity. He based this on his understanding that the concept of *ūlū l-amr* (those in charge) included both the princes and the scholars.

II

The Jurists' Vision and Vocation

Al-Karkhī (d. 952/340) said in his book *al-Qawāʿid* that the world constitutes one space (dār wāḥida). This seems contradictory given the obvious division of the world into the abode of Islam and the abode of war. But let us reflect on what took place at an earlier period, at the inception of juristic writing, i.e. around the middle of the second century of the Hijra. At that time, the jurists had already started to emerge as a distinct group which argued and struggled against the political authority and its judges, on the one hand, and with the traditionists and theologians, on the other. The first genre of writing was legal pronouncements (*fatāwā*) and short treatises on specific issues. It also included books classified according to the chapters of law (*al-muṣannafāt*) and books of Traditions (*sunan*) as well as specific treatments of the legal matter involving relations between Muslims and non-Muslims in war and peace (*siyar*) and land taxation (*kharāj*).

There were three main genres of juristic writing until late in the second century. (1) First, there were papers and documents containing responses to religious questions (which were added to the treatise) on specific cases of ritual or legal practice such as prayers, fasting or inheritance. (2) The second form makes the sources of its opinions the traditions, customs, and historical precedents based on the sayings of the companions and their followers. While the books on Traditions and history such as *al-Muwaṭṭaʾ* of Mālik and *al-Āthār* of Abū Yūsuf were concerned with proper behaviour and its rules, 'classified' (*muṣannaf*) books of legal traditions, such as those by ʿAbd al-Razzāq (d. 827/211) and Ibn Abī Shayba (d. 849/235) were interested in juristic topics in general in accordance with the systematic arrangement observed in the books on Traditions (*Sunan*). (3) Thirdly, books on *siyar* were concerned with the issues of war and peace. They started usually with an introduction on *jihād* and its laudability, followed by chapters concerning the dead and the injured on the battle field, and the distribution of booty among the different sorts of fighters, articles on land conquered by the Muslims, and the manner of dealing with hostages and the population of the conquered land. Chapters on truce, and dealing with non-Muslims during war and peace, sometimes were followed by expositions on contracts with non-Muslims. While we find rulings on apostasy, chapters on rebels—that is, on those Muslims who carry arms against the state—are missing. What is remarkable is that while various treatments of legal pronouncements, traditions, and classified cases continued to appear after the end of the third century, writings on war ended in the late second century. While books on general jurisprudence spread, war and *jihād* became chapters only, and ceased to be the subject of independent treatments.

Why would the jurist involve himself with chapters on war and peace, given the fact such affairs were the proper concerns of the Islamic state since its inception? It seems that the jurist considered himself to be a participant in the affairs of the state because of the religious nature of *jihād* in the wars of expansion and in view of the Qur'ānic verses on *jihād* and war. Consequently, the jurist viewed the traditions in a general sense, or customs and Traditions, as part of the sources to be used and to infer from. This is why he was concerned with history, as the venue of guidance for the community's dynamics. The inception of Islamic history is linked to the conquests and the *jihād* of the Prophet. The objective of the project of universal guidance is to expand the community of the guided to all of the world. This is why the jurist was linked, by choice or necessity, with the state which carried out the project of guidance through a long line of guides and monitors. The jurist who was interested in the teaching of faithful worship, and dealing with the religious law, was also concerned with the general mission of Islam through writing on issues of worship and legal dealings. This seems to be the cause for the jurist's early interest in war and peace. Indeed, N. Calder is not justified in evincing surprise at al-Māwardī's introduction of politics and the state in his book, *al-Aḥkām al-Sulṭāniyya*. In this context, the division of the world into a world of Islam, or peace, and the world of war became a legal division that necessitated the development of legal rules. However, this division could not be dissolved by uniting the world, since this is an exceptional event taking place only if all of mankind were to be guided by the religion of innate nature (*fiṭra*). This is why war was to stay as a part of the project of guidance, but not its basis, for guidance is a divine plan and is not the result of exemplary human effort. Consequently, the jurists viewed the cause of war as being solely aggression or fear of aggression (except al-Shāfiʿī who considered that unbelief might be a cause for war). In fact, the universalist view of religion in the world necessitated a view of the world not fitting in with the notion of a world of eternal unbelief that the believers had to fight indefinitely. Behind al-Shāfiʿī's view might be his separation of the prophetic traditions, covering specific legal rulings, from the prophetic biography that is a paradigm of universal guidance. He viewed the Prophetic traditions as having a legislative nature, and upholding his prophetic functions beyond his lifetime. Accordingly, the Muslim creed and the recealed law of Islam became two unique features that could not be repeated or routinized ouside the realm of Islam, and in this way, relations with the world turned into a struggle for uniqueness.

Thus, there were two visions of Islam and its function in history and the world. The vision upheld by the jurists and some historians viewed Islam as a universal mission, and as part of the divine guidance of mankind, and held that the Islamic state should have the responsibility of carrying it out. This project had to be continued through reasoning, criticism and redirection in order to succeed. This is clear in the juristic literature that was of an encyclopædic nature because the project itself covered all of humankind and because it affected the private and public spheres.

The other vision is led by the upholders of Traditions who viewed the prophetic traditions and sayings as a basis of ritual and legislation, functions that were unique and particular. It viewed *jihād* as a ritualistic function, a way of worship proceeding from the devotion of his performer, and eventually leading to his death, in order to spread the word of God. For them, the writing down of the Traditions was an assimilation of these rituals and observances so that nothing was to be lost or ignored because of their consequences on belief and unbelief.

III

The Jurist and Encyclopaedic Writing

The jurist's vision is then a vision of the project of salvation. Because the project comprehends all aspects of life, the jurist supervises the progress as well as the problems of the project. He attempts to resolve the problems through *ijtihād*. While the jurists shared the responsibility for the project with the Caliphal administration, responsible for the implementation of the project, they multiplied their interventions with the rise of the central emirate and the provincial sultanate at the expense of the Caliphate. The dignity and deep-rooted authority of the Caliphate as well as its lineage descending from the rightly-guided Caliphate of the *Salaf* provided it with a power which the jurists, even in the face of decline, could not ignore. Al-Māwardī's (d. 1055/450) works *al-Ḥāwī* and *al-Aḥkām al-Sulṭāniyya* indicate the division between the two phases of the jurists' function: as holder of a vision, and as instigator of a project.

It is known that juristic encyclopædias, concerned with the jurisprudence of different legal schools, were divided into three main sections: the first is concerned with the pillars of Islam such as prayer, fasting, *zakāt* and pilgrimage; the second is concerned with human interaction in society; the third is concerned with the common issues between the individual and the state. Therefore, there were (1) the issues of ritual and the religious; (2) the rules pertaining to the family, the functions of society, and the economy, based on contracts, and (3) finally, the intervention of the state in public life, which included the handling of crimes, legal means of deterrence, aggression, *jihād*, as also the supervision of inheritance and legacies. This does not mean that the state did not interfere in the first two, but the jurists divided the corpus of law in that way in an attempt to separate the different domains, namely in order to specify his own functions versus those of the state. The state appears in Friday prayer at the *jāmiʿ* mosque, where the *imām* leading the prayer represents the Sultan, and preaching the Friday sermon (*khuṭba*) is his original right. The state interferes as well in the implementation of the *zakāt*, whether through collection or distribution. At least this is what the state claimed until, at the beginning of the ʿAbbāsid caliphate, the state refrained from intervention. The state further intervenes in contracts and endowments, but only if there is a conflict. The jurists normally devoted a chapter to such cases of jurisdiction in the books on general jurisprudence. Here al-Māwardī's procedure in his twenty-volume book, *al-Ḥāwī*, represents a crucial phase, for he does not concern himself much with the third division: one third of the book is focused on worship and ritual, thirty percent on social dealings and contracts, and the rest of the book, less than a third, is focused on interaction between the state and the individuals. The largest part of this chapter is on legal judgements. Therefore, while al-Māwardī expands the domain of the jurists in regulating the daily life of the community, he does not show as much interest in the actions of the state, or the domains where the state plays an important role, with the exception of issues relating to the administration of justice. In his *al-Aḥkām al-Sulṭāniyya*, a book on 'constitutional' institutions, al-Māwardī focuses on the functions and the legal authorities of the state, but without diminishing the role of the legal establishment of the jurists. After the fifth century A.H., the sections on public functions of the state are extended in legal texts, not because of any need to increase the authority of the state but because the jurist became engaged in all these matters, with the exception of *jihād*. The division of functions between the state and the jurists collapsed due to the weakness of the Caliphate, and then, its downfall. The only way to save the body politic was by doubling the efforts of jurists in order to maintain legitimacy. This is what al-Juwaynī, al-Ghazālī, al-Rāfiʿī and al-Nawawī do in their legal encyclopædias. If the last period of strength of the Caliphal state is the period of *al-Aḥkām al-Sulṭāniyya*, the period of the Sultanate state is the period of legal politics, *al-Siyāsa al-Sharʿiyya*, that is, the effort to legitimize the behaviour of the state in order to maintain the project and to prevent the public from disregarding the religious law and therefore its legitimacy, as the jurists kept declaring until the day of the historian and jurist al-Maqrīzī.

*

What are the working mechanisms in the encyclopaedias of jurisprudence of the legal schools? The Mālikiyya and the Shāfiʿiyya dispose of a formative text inherited from the Shaykh of the school: *al-Muwaṭṭaʾ* by Mālik ibn Anas (d. 795/179) and *al-Umm* by al-Shāfiʿī (d. 819/204). However, the Ḥanafiyya and the Ḥanbaliyya do not have such a text. Nonetheless, this did not change the working mechanisms. The *Mudawanna* of Saḥnūn ('Abd al-Salām b. Saʿīd al-Tanūkhī, d. 854/240), a vast compilation going back to the third generation of the school, is said to have been transmitted from his Shaykh, Ibn al-Qāsim al-ʿUtaqī (d. 807/191) who read it with Mālik, although it does not precisely follow the order of *al-Muwaṭṭaʾ*. Nonetheless, the late Mālikī tradition was not based on that book, even though it was frequently quoted. It was based instead on *al-Risāla* or *al-Mukhtaṣar* by Ibn Abī Zayd al-Qayrawāni (d. 996/386), manuals on which dozens of commentaries were written, then on *al-Mukhtaṣar* by Khalīl ibn Isḥāq (d. 1365/767 or 1374/776), which received more than sixty commentaries.

The same holds for the Shāfiʿiyya. Ismāʿīl b. Yaḥyā al-Muzanī (d. 877/264) abbreviated the draft of the book, *al-Umm*, which al-Shāfiʿī had left in blueprint shape. Generation after another worked out commentaries on this *Muḫtaṣar*. Al-Māwardī's *al-Ḥāwī* is an expanded exposition of al-Muzanī's summary. The encyclopaedic *Rawḍat al-ṭālibīn* by al-Nawawī (d. 1278/676) from the seventh century of the Hijra is an explanation of *Fatḥ al-ʿazīz* by ʿAbd al-Karīm al-Rāfiʿī (d. 1226/623); al-Rāfiʿī's work, in its turn, is an explanation of Ghazālī's *Wajīz*, which—on the basis of his own extensive works, *al-Basīṭ* and *al-Wasīṭ*—epitomized the books of al-Muzanī, Abū Isḥāq al-Shīrazī (d. 1083/476) and al-Juwaynī (1085/478). The *Bayān* by Abū l-Ḥasan Yaḥyā b. Abī l-Khayr al-ʿImrāni al-Yamanī (d. 1163/558) is a commentary on an abbreviated version of *al-Muhaḏḏab* by Abū Isḥāq al-Shirāzī, which is in itself based on the *Muḫtaṣar* of al-Muzanī. The manuals of Ḥanafī and Ḥanbalī jurisprudence bore as well a rich literature of abridgements. It is true that Abū Ḥanīfa did not leave an authoritative text, but Muḥammad b. al-Ḥasan al-Shaybāni (d. 904/189) completed six shorter works on various aspects of the teaching of the school; these were given the title *Ẓāhir al-riwāya* 'The Books of the External Tradition' by the third generation of the Ḥanafī school. But the scholars of the school did not directly depend on these but on the manual by al-Ḥākim al-Shahīd al-Marwazī (d. 945/334), then al-Sarakhsī (d. 1090/483) gave a summary of al-Marwazī manual in his book, *al-Mabsūṭ fī l-furūʿ*, which is the largest encyclopædia of Ḥanafī jurisprudence written until the seventh century of Hijra.

The Ḥanbalīs did not depend on what was collected by Abū Bakr al-Khallāl (d. 923/311) from the jurisprudence of Aḥmad ibn Ḥanbal, but on the *Muḫtaṣar* of Abū l-Qāsim al-Khiraqī (d. 946/334), commented upon by Muwaffaq-al-Dīn Ibn Qudāma (d. 1223/620) in his *Mughnī*.

Therefore, the school text of any legal school did not develop in a linear way. It started with a short exposition, which grew into a comprehensive 'encyclopaedia', developing through explanations and commentaries up to a point where another abridgement was found useful. Then the same process started again. However, the encyclopædias would be supplemented with marginal notes and commentaries in order to explain issues under discussion. It should be kept in mind that all abridgements remained connected, even if only nominally, with the basic text. But there is no real connection between Khalīl's abridgement of the *Muwaṭṭā'* and the treatise by Ibn Abī Zayd, except the management of the chapters. The multiplicity of the abridgements is due to multiplicity of environments where the schools spread. Al-Qudūrī's (d. 1037/428) 'Abridgement', or summary, of Ḥanafite law, *al-Mukhtaṣar*, appeared in Baghdad where he stayed and wrote his commentaries. Al-Ṭaḥāwī's (d. 933/321) 'Abridgement', *al-Mukhtaṣar fī l-fiqh*, was quoted by others, but the weakness of the Ḥanafī school in Egypt until the Mamluk period precluded it from becoming the subject of commentaries and other expositions. The Hanafī jurists of Egypt did not use the famous writings of al-Shaybānī on war and peace (*Siyar*) in their books; they used instead the texts current in their region with minor exceptions. Therefore, and contrary to the general impression about the openness and elasticity of the legal schools, they were very tight in using one text almost exclusively for centuries. By this I mean that a vast encyclopædic work like al-Sarakhsī's *Mabsūṭ* or al-Nawawī's *Rawḍat al-ṭālibīn* would mention the views of all the jurists, and of all schools on every issue, but, in the end, the view prevailing in one's country was the view of this or that scholar. Indeed, the views of the jurists of the four early generations prevailed, but in most cases, the dominating view depended on the first and third generations.

One might think that a clear innovation appears in the books on legal pronouncements, *Nawāzil*, as the Mālikīs call the *fatāwā* manuals. But I noticed on two occasions that most of these pronouncements are copied almost verbatim from one of the abridgements or accepted commentaries.

Maybe this is the reason for the displeasure that Ibn ʿAqīl, Najm-al-Dīn al-Ṭūfī and Ibn Taymiyya had encountered. For they would declare that on one or more issues, they could not find an answer in Ḥanbalī teaching. However, the Ḥanafīs kept interpreting and re-interpreting topics such as rent and endowment while disregarding the views of the first two generations except in the issues they could attribute their views to al-Shaybānī or al-Luʾluʾī.

This does not mean that renewal was not possible or did not take place. Otherwise, how did the summaries become encyclopaedias? However, renewal was always kept within the confines of the school. That is, a jurist had to attribute his view to the writer of the formative text, or a summary of the first generation. From this, *furūʿ*

manuals of the next period would form a new basis of authority in the school, which in their turn would be condensed into epitomes and summaries to serve as a basis of teaching and reference for the next generation, whence the process starts again in a similar fashion. I do not find a convincing reason for this.

THE IRANIAN AND GREEK TRADITIONS

THE GREEK AND PERSIAN BACKGROUND OF EARLY ARABIC ENCYCLOPEDISM

Dimitri Gutas
Yale University

Early Arabic encyclopedism[1] expressed itself in at least three distinct genres of writings, the different forms and functions of which betray their different sources. The first is what can be called *inventories* of the sciences, rather than encyclopedias, insofar as these included not so much exhaustive treatments of the subjects covered but descriptions of them of varying brevity. In this group, two tendencies can be identified, though admittedly the distinction may not be always easily maintained. On the one hand there are those works which offer merely a classification of the sciences, for the most part as received from the Greek tradition, with additions of sciences indigenous to the Islamic tradition, and on the other there are those which go beyond the brief description and classification of a selected set of sciences to include all sciences and offer more substantial discussion of them. In the former category belong the works of al-Kindī, al-Khawarizmī, Ibn Sīnā, Abū Sahl al-Masīḥī, Abū l-Faraj Ibn al-Ṭayyib, Ibn al-Akfānī, and in the latter works by al-Fārābī, the Ikhwān al-Ṣafā', al-ʿĀmirī, Ibn Fārighūn, Abū Ḥayyān al-Tawḥīdī, Ibn Ḥazm, Fakhr al-Dīn al-Rāzī, and of course Ibn Khaldūn.[2]

The second genre is constituted by what could be roughly called mirrors for princes, writings offering advice of mostly a political and

[1] I prefer to speak of "encyclopedism" rather than "encyclopedias" both in order to express the attitude of encompassing all branches of knowledge that can be observed in the early Arabic literature under discussion, and to avoid calling these works "encyclopedias", a term that is not precisely enough defined with reference to them.

[2] For a somewhat different distribution of these works on related criteria, and for full bibliographical references to pertinent literature, see H. H. Biesterfeldt, 'Arabisch-islamische Enzyklopädien: Formen und Funktionen', in Christel Meier, ed., *Die Enzyklopädie im Mittelalter vom Hochmittelalter bis zur frühen Neuzeit* (München: Wilhelm Fink, 2002), pp. 43–83. Cf. also his 'Medieval Arabic Encyclopedias of Science and Philosophy', in Steven Harvey, ed., *The Medieval Hebrew Encyclopedias of Science and Philosophy* (Boston: Kluwer, 2000), pp. 77–98.

ethical nature, in form purporting to be letters by a wise person to a ruler.

The third is the well-known genre of Arabic *adab* works, the most representative specimens of which, Ibn Qutayba's *ʿUyūn al-akhbār* and Ibn ʿAbd Rabbihi's *al-ʿIqd al-farīd*, are veritable collections of entertaining and instructive information on various subjects each of which is treated individually in a dedicated chapter.

The sources of these genres of writings go back to pre-Islamic Greek and Persian works whose translations into Arabic began during the last decades of the Umayyad dynasty and blossomed during the grand epoch of the early ʿAbbāsid translation movement. In what follows this Greek and Persian background will be briefly presented.

I. *Inventories of the Sciences*

The first genre mentioned above, the inventories of the sciences, derives directly from Greek prototypes. The story has often been told before, but it is worth the while to review the essential facts and emphasize certain aspects of this development that are on occasion overlooked.

The organization of knowledge and education in ancient Greece began with the sophists in the fifth century B.C., during which time we already see the rudiments of what was later to become the *trivium* (grammar, rhetoric, dialectic) and the *quadrivium* (arithmetic, geometry, astronomy, music). The *quadrivium*, as a matter of fact, was already in place through the adoption of Pythagorean teachings and their emphasis on mathematical subjects by the fifth-century sophist Hippias. Aristotle, writing in the wake of these developments in classical Athens, produced work that in itself is encyclopedic insofar as it covered, in discrete treatises and other kinds of writings, most subjects then cultivated. The Peripatetic school that he founded was well aware of the significance of his achievement and accordingly Aristotle's successors effected a conscious systematization of all knowledge.[3] Much of this early Peripatetic literature has not survived, just

[3] For a brief orientation on these developments in ancient Greece see the articles in *Der Neue Pauly* on "Enkyklios Paideia" and "Enzyklopädie", with references to the basic literature.

as almost all of Aristotle's own works, other than the school treatises, have not; but in a strange twist of scholarly fate, the reappearance and publication of his surviving treatises constituted the basis for subsequent encyclopedism in late Greek antiquity and beyond, in both the Arabic and Latin Middle ages.

The story of the chance survival of Aristotle's school treatises—the so-called "esoteric" treatises, i.e., intended for consumption within the Peripatetic school and not for publication—is intriguing and relevant to the whole subject of the classification of the sciences.

According to the fullest version of the story, as told by the famous polygraph of the second century A.D., Plutarch (d. 120†), in his biography *Parallel Lives* (of the Roman dictator Sulla), and as also supplemented by other sources, Aristotle's lecture notes, which had passed upon his death into the possession of his student and executor of his will, Theophrastus, were bequeathed by the latter to a man named Neleus, who was a member of Aristotle's school in Athens. Neleus took the whole collection to his home town, Skepsis, a city in Western Asia Minor, near the straights of the Dardanelles. The collection apparently remained there for generations, unused and unappreciated, until it was found by a gentleman called Apellicon, a book collector and admirer of Aristotle, who brought it back to Athens; this must have happened at the end of the second century B.C. Subsequently, the Roman dictator Sulla seized the library from Apellicon and carried it to Rome in 83 B.C. In 71 B.C. Tyrannio, a famous Greek grammarian, was brought as a prisoner to Rome, where he was eventually freed, doubtless because of his education. Tyrannio gained access to Aristotle's library in Sulla's house by "cultivating the librarian", as a source tells us, and was able to put the manuscripts in order. He made copies of them and passed them on to Andronicus of Rhodes, who edited them for publication and made a catalogue of the writings. We have no exact date for this but it must have been around 50 B.C. In this fashion Aristotle's major works, that is, the school treatises that we know today, were finally published and made available to the scholarly world approximately 275 years after his death.[4]

[4] For full documentation of this account see P. Moraux, *Der Aristotelismus bei den Griechen*, vol. I, *Von Andronikos bis Alexander von Aphrodisias* (Berlin: De Gruyter, 1973), pp. 58–94, with references to earlier literature.

In his work, Andronicus solved the problem faced by all editors, namely, that of deciding on the order in which to put his material, by having recourse to Aristotle himself. As briefly hinted above, Aristotle was well aware of the need to have a theoretical position on the interrelatedness of all the sciences that make up human knowledge, and in a number of places in the works which were edited by Andronicus he divided all sciences into three categories, practical, productive, and theoretical, and the theoretical further into mathematical, physical, and theological.[5] Andronicus followed this classification and under each heading he included the works corresponding to it; at the head of the collection he put the logical treatises as methodological prolegomena. His classification of Aristotle's surviving school treatises, as it can be best reconstructed from all available evidence, was as follows:[6]

1. Logic: *Categories, On Interpretation, Analytics (Prior Analytics), Topics, Demonstration (Posterior Analytics), Sophistical Refutations*
2. Practical sciences (ethics and politics): (a) *Nicomachean Ethics, Magna Moralia, Eudemian Ethics*; (b) *Politics*
3. Productive sciences: *Poetics, Rhetoric*
4. Theoretical sciences:
   (a) *Physics, On the Heavens, On Coming to Be and Passing Away, Meteorology, On the Soul, On Sense Perception and Its Objects, On Memory and On Sleep, Movement of Animals, History of Animals, Parts of Animals, Generation of Animals, Progression of Animals, On Length and Shortness of Life, On Life and Death, On Plants*
   (b) *Metaphysics*

Andronicus' classification of Aristotle's works became canonical and had lasting consequences on education and philosophy. In particular, the Neoplatonist scholars of late antiquity amplified the Andronican classification with various modifications and additions. Specifically, they effected one major change in the classification of the books on logic. Whereas Andronicus had counted only six works under logic

[5] *Topics* 145a14–18, 157a9–11; *Metaphysics* E1 and K7. Cf. C. Hein, *Definition und Einteilung der Philosophie. Von der spätantiken Einleitungsliteratur zur arabischen Enzyklopädie* (Frankfurt: Peter Lang, 1985), pp. 25–28.

[6] Given in concise form by Hein, *Definition und Einteilung*, p. 414. I list below the English equivalents of the familiar titles.

and relegated the *Rhetoric* and the *Poetics* to another category, the productive, the Neoplatonists viewed these two works also as part of logic, or the Organon, on the basis that these works also dealt with statements—rhetorical and poetical statements—upon whose truth value we could express ourselves. In this way the number of the logical books of Aristotle was raised to eight, three of which—*Categories, On Interpretation, Prior Analytics*—were considered to be preparatory for demonstration, the fourth, *Posterior Analytics*, taught demonstration itself, and the remaining four—*Topics, Sophistical Refutations, Rhetoric,* and *Poetics*—protected demonstration by showing how dialectical, sophistical, rhetorical, and poetic statements and syllogisms fell short of demonstration. The revised logical curriculum now included all these eight works plus eventually the Introduction to them written by Plotinus' pupil, Porphyry, the famous *Eisagoge*.

It is interesting to note that this late antique development would appear to have been partly inspired by Galen's theories on language and logical propositions. In a number of places in his *On the Opinions of Hippocrates and Plato*, Galen identifies four classes of propositions or premisses (*lēmmata*) used in scientific discourse. These are, the scientific (i.e., the demonstrative), the dialectical, the rhetorical, and the sophistic, in descending order of truth value.[7] It is clear that except for the poetic propositions, which Galen does not mention, the remaining are identical with the kinds and numbers of propositions elaborated by the Neoplatonists in late antiquity. The significance of Galen for the philosophical developments in late antiquity in Alexandria is also related to his increasing importance in the higher education curriculum in the final decades before the rise of Islam. It was during this period that the abridgments of sixteen of his works known as the *Summaria Alexandrinorum* (*Jawāmiʿ al-Iskandarāniyyīn*) came into being in connection with the restructuring of medical higher education that also included logic.[8] It would thus appear that Galenic theories of language that were consonant with the general paedagogic tendencies of later Neoplatonists found their way into the curriculum

[7] See H. von Staden, "Science as Text, Science as History: Galen on Metaphor", in Ph. J. van der Eijk et al., eds, *Ancient Medicine in Its Socio-Cultural Context* (Amsterdam: Rodopi, 1995), vol. II, pp. 499–518, at 514 and note 45.

[8] See D. Gutas, "The 'Alexandria to Baghdad' Complex of Narratives. A Contribution to the Study of Philosophical and Medical Historiography among the Arabs", *Documenti e Studi sulla Tradizione Filosofica Medievale*, 10 (1999): 155–193, at 169–174.

and helped shape the final form of the classification of the sciences before the rise of Islam.

As a result of such developments the late Neoplatonists erected an elaborate schema of classification of Aristotle's works in which individual treatises corresponded to a field of study. The result of this process was that the classification of Aristotle's works became, in effect, a classification of all the sciences, and hence of all human knowledge. The progressively more substantive function of this classification must be emphasized. In Andronicus, its function was editorial; in the earlier commentators it became preponderantly descriptive and pedagogical, as the authors tried to teach their audience the arrangement of Aristotle's works and the order in which they were to be read for a proper philosophical education; and finally, with the scholars of late antiquity in Alexandria, the function of classification acquired normative value on the assumption that it reflected ontological reality as well: in other words, all knowledge was so divided because inherently and by its very essence knowledge could only be classified in this manner.[9] The theoretical justification of the classification thus became part and parcel of the philosophy that was taught and Aristotle was elevated to the status of the one human who possessed this knowledge to perfection.

This classification of the sciences became standard in the centuries to come and it re-appears, with slight modifications in each age and place, in the medieval Arabic and Latin worlds.

II. *Mirrors for Princes*

The mirror for princes literature in Arabic is the product of the confluence and integration of primarily three traditions: Arabic, Persian, and Greek. Indian elements and ideas, especially as portrayed in the Sanskrit works that appeared in Arabic under the titles of *Kalīla wa-Dimna* and *Bilawhar wa-B(Y)ūdāsaf*, also played a significant role, but because these works gained entry into Arabic from Middle

[9] For a full discussion of these points and the attendant charts see D. Gutas, "Paul the Persian on the Classification of the Parts of Aristotle's Philosophy: A Milestone between Alexandria and Baġdād", *Der Islam*, 60 (1983): 231–267, at pp. 255–267.

Persian (Pehlevi) translations, they can be counted as part of the Persian background of the mirrors.

The origins of the Arabic mirror for princes literature are to be sought, and its core certainly lies, in pre- and early Islamic wisdom literature together with the speeches, reports, and correspondence of the early Arab rulers and their functionaries. But what made this genre of literature encyclopedic in its scope is the expansion it experienced in the hands of the administrative elite of both the Umayyad and ʿAbbāsid courts. The initiative for compositions of counsel more comprehensive in their coverage and more sustained in their extent than the occasional pieces of political wisdom among the early Muslim Arabs came from the Umayyad chancellery secretaries, who were themselves the immediate successors of their Byzantine colleagues in Damascus.

The person credited with initiating the genre as well as the Arabic prose style appropriate to it is ʿAbd al-Ḥamīd b. Yaḥyā (d. 750), secretary to the last Umayyad caliphs, among whose extant correspondence there exists a famous letter, giving counsel to his fellow secretaries, and other incidental pieces addressed to the last Umayyad caliph Marwān b. Muḥammad.[10] More important for the ultimate influence they were to exert, however, seem to be the activities of ʿAbd al-Ḥamīd's brother (or father) in-law and senior colleague, Sālim Abū l-ʿAlāʾ, secretary to the caliph Hishām b. ʿAbd al-Malik (724–743). It appears that Sālim was responsible for instigating the translation, apparently from the Greek, of a series of pseudo-Aristotelian letters to Alexander on the general subjects of politics and the craft of government.[11] These letters, one of which has been claimed by S. M. Stern as authentic,[12] derive primarily from Byzantine manuals on administration and warfare (the *Tactica*), with accretions from Greek material from the classical and Hellenistic periods, and from so-called Hermetic material deriving from sundry sources.[13] Significant

[10] On ʿAbd al-Ḥamīd see the comprehensive article, with full bibliographical references, by W. al-Qāḍī, "Early Islamic State Letters: The Question of Authenticity", in A. Cameron and L. I. Conrad, *The Byzantine and Early Islamic Near East* (Princeton: The Darwin Press, 1992), pp. 215–275.

[11] This is the thesis of M. Grignaschi, defended in particular in "Les 'Rasāʾil Arisṭāṭālīsa ilā l-Iskandar' de Sālim Abū-l-ʿAlāʾ et l'activité culturelle à l'époque Omayyade", *Bulletin d'Etudes Orientales*, 19 (1965–66): 7–83.

[12] S. M. Stern, *Aristotle and the World State* (Oxford: Cassirer, 1970).

[13] See M. Manzalaoui, "The Pseudo-Aristotelian *Kitāb Sirr al-asrār*", *Oriens*, 23–24 (1974): 147–257, at 194–219.

portions of the contents of these letters were re-worked and augmented in Arabic with the addition of further material from Persian sources until, by the end of the 10th century, they appeared under the title *Sirr al-asrār* (*Secret of Secrets*), an encyclopedic mirror for princes of immense influence both in Islam and, in its European translations (the famous *Secretum Secretorum*), in the medieval and early modern West.[14] In its fullest recension, the Arabic *Sirr al-asrār* contains in ten chapters a veritable encyclopedia of information on all subjects that a ruler would conceivably need to know, as follows: Chapter 1, kinds of kings; 2, conduct of kings and proper behavior; defense of astrology; physical and spiritual health and its preservation; physiognomy and its uses; 3, justice; 4, ministers; 5, secretaries; 6, ambassadors; 7, governors; 8, generals; 9, wars; 10, occult sciences.

III. *Wisdom Literature and* adab *Works*

The story of the mirror for princes, however, is best continued under a discussion of the sources and development of the Arabic genre of works on *adab*. These are also both Greek and Persian. The Greek sources consist primarily of the sayings of the philosophers which appear in Arabic in such well-known collections as the famous *Ṣiwān al-Ḥikma* (*Depository of Wisdom Literature*) or al-Mubashshir b. Fātik's *Mukhtār al-Ḥikam* (*Choice Sayings*). I have dealt with these works extensively elsewhere and there is no need to go into them here beyond the mere mention of their significant presence in and influence on Arabic *adab*.[15] But it appears that what gave the Arabic *adab* collec-

[14] See the collection of articles edited by W. F. Ryan and C. B. Schmitt, *Pseudo-Aristotle, The Secret of Secrets. Sources and Influences* (London: The Warburg Institute, 1982). On the Persian background of this work see M. Grignaschi, "La '*as-Siyāsatu-l-ʿāmmiyah*' et l'influence iranienne sur la pensée politique islamique", in *Monumentum Nyberg* III (Leiden: Brill, 1975) (= *Acta Iranica* 6), pp. 33–287. The question of the Pehlevi background of some of this material has still not been treated with the fullness it deserves. See the preliminary sketch of the Pehlevi background of the contents of the gnomological MS Istanbul, Köprülü 1608, as well as of the gnomologium normally attributed to Ḥunayn b. Isḥāq, *Ādāb al-falāsifa*, by M. Zakeri in "*Ādāb al-falāsifa*: The Persian Content of an Arabic Collection of Aphorisms," *Mélanges de l'Université Saint-Joseph*, 57 (2004): 173–190.

[15] See, in particular, my "Pre-Plotinian Philosophy in Arabic (Other than Platonism and Aristotelianism): A Review of the Sources", in W. Haase and H. Temporini, eds, *Aufstieg und Niedergang der Römischen Welt* (Berlin/New York: De Gruyter, 1994),

tions their vast range and encyclopedic nature was primarily Sasanian wisdom literature and *adab*, the extensive *andarz* literature and books of etiquette in Pehlevi which were translated into Arabic in an equally fundamental Perso-Arabic translation movement that ran parallel to the Graeco-Arabic one during the early ʿAbbāsid period.[16] To gain an idea of the wide range of subjects treated in Sasanian *adab* I will list the kinds of knowledge that an educated young man was supposed to have according to the Pehlevi book *Xusraw ud rēdak* (a short treatise on the education of the Sasanian nobility) as these appear in Arabic translation in al-Thaʿālibī's *Ghurar al-siyar*:

> Knowledge of religion; literary composition, calligraphy, history, philosophy; clothes; beds and bedcloths; sports: horsemanship, archery, spearsmanship, polo, hammer throwing; music, singing, poetry, instrument playing, musical modes and melodies; stars; games: chess, backgammon, and others; cooking and the development of elegant taste; fruit; wines; water; flowers, perfumes; women; of their moral virtues and physical beauty; mounts; riding and pack animals.[17]

If the Umayyad bureaucracy, because of its immediate links with Byzantine administration, was responsible for the transmission of many Greek ideas into the Arabic mirrors for princes, Persian functionaries in similar positions under both the late Umayyads and especially the early ʿAbbāsids formed their counterpart with regard to Sasanian material translated from Pehlevi. Ibn al-Muqaffaʿ stands unrivalled as the translator of Sasanian wisdom and related texts into Arabic, and as the author, based on these, of an independent mirror for princes *al-Adab al-kabīr* (*The Great Adab Book*), and of an advisory epistle to the ʿAbbāsid caliph al-Manṣūr, *Fī l-Ṣaḥāba* (*On the*

Part II, Vol. 36.7 (reprinted in my *Greek Philosophers in the Arabic Tradition* [Variorum Collected Studies Series], Aldershot 2000, no. I), pp. 4949–4954, with references to all the pertinent literature.

[16] The Perso-Arabic translation movement has yet to be studied in depth. A preliminary assessment is given by C. E. Bosworth, "The Persian Impact on Arabic Literature", in A. F. L. Beeston et al., eds, *Arabic Literature to the End of the Umayyad Period* [*Cambridge History of Arabic Literature*] (Cambridge: University Press, 1983), pp. 483–496, at 486–492. A paradigmatic and detailed first study of a participant in this movement, other than ibn al-Muqaffaʿ, is given by M. Zakeri, "ʿAlī ibn ʿUbayda ar-Raiḥānī. A Forgotten Belletrist (*adīb*) and Pahlavi Translator", *Oriens*, 34 (1994): 76–102. For the *andarz* literature see the article in the *Encyclopaedia Iranica*, Vol. II, 11–22 (S. Shaked, Z. Safa).

[17] See the article on *adab* in the *Encyclopaedia Iranica*, vol. I:434–435 (Dj. Khaleghi-Motlagh).

[Caliph's] Entourage), in which he advocated the centralized authority of the caliph over all governmental institutions and the enforcement of an "orthodox" religious code. With the continuous translation of Pehlevi texts into Arabic after Ibn al-Muqaffaʿ, like the *Kitāb at-Tāj* (*Book of the Crown*), which became available in Arabic between 847 and 861, Sasanian material in the mirrors for princes literature tended to predominate. This situation eventually led, after the re-emergence of Persian as a literary language in the 11th century, to the composition of mirrors for princes in Persian. Within a period of less than thirty years during the rise of the Seljuks in Iraq and Iran, there were written in Persian *three* such works: *Qābūsnāma* (*The Book for Qābūs*), composed in 1082 by Kay Kā'ūs, the Ziyārid prince of Ṭabaristān, for his son and heir, Gīlānshāh; *Siyāsatnāma* (*The Book of Government*), written for the Seljuk sultan Malikshāh by his famous vizier Niẓāmulmulk shortly before his assassination in 1092; and *Naṣīḥatu l-mulūk* (*Counsel for Kings*) by none other than al-Ghazālī himself, addressed to the Seljuk ruler Muḥammad b. Malikshāh.[18] These works eventually occupied a central position among Islamic mirrors for princes and determined to a large extent the later development of the genre. The first was translated into Ottoman Turkish, while the third was translated both into Arabic and Turkish. Al-Ghazālī's work also prompted a similar effort on the part of the Andalusian al-Ṭurṭūshī (d. 1126 or 1131), whose *Sirāj al-mulūk* (*Lamp for Kings*) was studied by Ibn Khaldūn. Al-Ṭurṭūshī's intention was to surpass al-Ghazālī; as it turned out, however, he fell quite short of the mark, but it was precisely his failures that gave Ibn Khaldūn much food for thought. The ideas implicit in the long series of encyclopedic mirrors for princes and *adab* works about the nature of government, the qualities, duties, and conduct of the ruler, and the causes of the rise and fall of dynasties found their theoretical formulation, like so many other concepts constitutive of the fabric of Islamic civilization, in Ibn Khaldūn's masterpiece, the *Muqaddima* (the introduction to his historical work, *Kitāb al-ʿIbar, Book of Examples*). Ibn Khaldūn himself tells us in his preliminary remarks that it was works such as

[18] Though it appears that only the first part of the work, consisting of a treatise on faith, is by al-Ghazālī, and not the second part, which is the mirror for princes proper; see P. Crone, 'Did al-Ghazālī Write a Mirror for Princes? On the Authorship of *Naṣīḥat al-mulūk*', *Jerusalem Studies in Arabic and Islam*, 10 (1987): 167ff.

these that he considered to have been the predecessors of his own research: he mentions among them the statements of the Sasanian rulers and dignitaries, the *Secret of Secrets* which is "ascribed to Aristotle and has wide circulation", the *adab* books of Ibn al-Muqaffa', and the *Lamp for Kings* of al-Ṭurṭūshī. In this way the encyclopedism that was based on Greek and Persian sources, and as it developed in medieval Islamic civilization, became one of the sources that inspired Ibn Khaldūn.[19]

[19] See D. Gutas, 'Ethische Schriften im Islam' in W. Heinrichs, ed., *Neues Handbuch der Literaturwissenschaft: Orientalisches Mittelalter* (Wiesbaden: Aula, 1990), pp. 346–365, for a fuller exposition of aspects of the subjects treated in sections II and III, above, and for references to the literature cited.

THE CYCLE OF KNOWLEDGE: INTELLECTUAL TRADITIONS AND ENCYCLOPÆDIAS OF THE RATIONAL SCIENCES IN ARABIC ISLAMIC HELLENISM

Gerhard Endress
Ruhr-Universität Bochum, Germany

1. *Knowledge on its Way to Power*

Knowledge is power. It was Francis Bacon who in the early 17th century put into words his insight into the power of human reason over the workings of nature: "parendo imperare", i.e. dominating nature by obeying the laws of nature, detected by induction. Such power would yield means for the practical exploitation of the natural forces. This attitude is the signature of modernity.[1] The Middle Ages were far from weighing such considerations. Only gradually, and tentatively, the scholars and teachers approached a comparable concept of knowledge. Knowledge, in the Middle Ages, was on its way to power. A recent book by the historian Martin Kintzinger under the title 'Knowledge *becoming* power' thus aptly describes the signature of the Middle Ages. The cultural techniques of managing and imparting knowledge form a central factor within the structures of authority and control in mediæval society. This knowledge includes hermeneutical knowledge and pragmatical knowledge. Communication in the mediæval knowledge society functions between the poles of textual tradition and the personal authority of the teacher. Mediæval Islamic society is probably the most impressive paradigm of an epistemic community based on the authoritative interpretation of a corpus of texts. The procedures of knowledge management in the Latin West were preceded by a rich variety and intensity of knowledge transfer and knowledge production in Islam.[2] In Arabic-Islamic civilization,

[1] Martin Kinzinger, *Wissen wird Macht: Bildung im Mittelalter* (Ostfilder: Thorbecke, 2003); and review by Johannes Fried, in: *Frankfurter Allgemeine*, no. 256 (Nov 4, 2003), p. L-10, referring to Hans Blumenberg a. o.

[2] Illustrated by Olga Weijers in her book on 'intellectual practices in the age of

not only do the clerical traditions of courteous-administrative and of legal-theological expertise concur, and compete for primacy, but both are challenged by the traditions of professional science, and are confronted with the claims of philosophy as the science of sciences, *epistêmê epistêmôn*: the science of demonstration and the ideology of the rational soul, claiming supreme knowledge and supreme authority.

Documenting constructions of identity in the schools of knowledge, we perceive new systems of knowledge organisation: first in a tradition of classificatory outlines, and then in comprehensive expositions which we have been accustomed to call encyclopædias, based on, but not used in the same sense as the ancient etymon of the word.

2. *Multiple Traditions*

It is true that pre-modern societies did not know the narrow professionalism typical of the modern division of labour. Nevertheless it is true that since early Hellenism, philosophy itself competed with the individual sciences for recognition of a professional status in society, and sought to found its claim on the unconditioned knowledge (*epistêmê anhypothetos*) of the principles. On the one hand, the philosophical schools assumed competence, and took charge of education, in the mathematical sciences. The conception of philosophy in Aristotle and the old Peripatetic school had embraced, ideally at least, the applied sciences—these in turn being regarded as elements of *paideia* in the sense of propaedeutics to philosophy: a stage in philosophical education leading the way to the advanced level of dialectic, the 'science of sciences.'[3] Neither in the Hellenistic nor in the Roman/Byzantine period, on the other hand, did mathematical studies form part of a general education. Outside the ἐγκύλιος παιδεία, 'encyclopædia' in its original sense of a general, 'all-round' education of the rhetor, jurist and physician in philosophy and letters, such studies

the first universities in 13th–14th century Europe': *Le maniement du savoir: pratiques intellectuelles à l'époque des premières universités (XIIe–XIVe siècles)*, Studia Artistorum: Subsidia, 3 (Turnhout: Brepols, 1996).

[3] See Ilsetraut Hadot, 'Les aspects sociaux et institutionels des sciences et de la médecine dans l'Antiquité tardive', *Antiquité tardive*, 6 (Turnhout, 1998): 233–50; *ead.*, *Arts libéraux et philosophie dans la pensée antique* (Paris: Études Augustiniennes, 1984).

were linked up with, and restricted to, the professional training of engineers, architects, geometers, and musicians.[4] But here, even in the individual and practical sciences, the teaching of the leading authorities and their basic texts maintained the intimate connection between applied mathematics and its epistemological and metaphysical background. Beyond the decline of the philosophical schools in the civilization of late Hellenism, the philosophical doctrine of the principles and of the cosmos survived in the gnostic Platonism of the natural sciences, in the Neoplatonism of the mathematicians, in the Peripatetic cosmology of Ptolemy, as also—but this is a matter different and apart—in the elementary logic reading of the Christian schools. The earliest translations of Aristotelian logic were commissioned to scholars of the Syriac churches, who had kept up the teaching of logic, and of the isagogic tradition of the Alexandrian school. This is how Greek philosophy entered the urban and courtly society of Islam: as methodology and ideology of the professional sciences, notably of mathematics and astronomy on the one hand, of medicine on the other. It is a philosophy neither pagan nor Christian nor Islamic, but universal: a rational religion for the intellectuals of Greek erudition, giving an ulterior sense to their activity.

Each scientific tradition carried its own philosophical discourse: a choice of authorities, a methodology, a classification and hierarchy of the sciences, and a general orientation of cosmology and ethics. With the physicians we find Galen's Platonism as also Galen's own logic, anthropology and ethics, competing with philosophy in pretending to teach an *ars vitae*. (In consequence, the philosophic or non-philosophic character of medicine, being *technê* 'art', Arabic *ṣināʿa*, or *epistêmê* 'science', Arabic *ʿilm*, was under dispute in apology and polemic from both sides.)[5] The mathematician and astronomer, and the professional astrologer or geometer, pretended to a universal competence no less than the physician, but on a different scale: on the authority of a time-honoured tradition, and of an eminent ancestry, in the history of philosophy itself. The mathematicians were

[4] Hadot, *ibid.*, 242–4.

[5] Cf. Albrecht Dihle, *Philosophie als Lebenskunst*, Rheinisch-Westfälische Akademie der Wissenschaften, Vorträge, G 304 (Opladen, 1990); *id.*, *Philosophie—Fachwissenschaft—Allgemeinbildung*, in *Aspects de la philosophie hellénistique*, Entretiens sur l'Antiquité classique, 32 (Vandœuvres-Genève: Fondation Hardt, 1986), 188–232.

Platonists and Pythagoreans in the tradition of Nicomachus, Proclus and Iamblichus. But the Astronomers cherished the Aristotelian propædeutic and, above all, the Aristotelian cosmology conjoined with the authority of Ptolemy. Hence it was Aristotle who came to dominate the system of the physical world, and it was a Peripatetic structure which, since being adopted by Ptolemy, prevailed in the method and epistemology of professional science.

Thus we find not one tradition, but multiple traditions in competition, documented in reports, and remarks on transmission found in our manuscript sources. The self-view, the definition, and the fundamentals of positive knowledge in the sciences, are found in classifications, and—after a period of reception, consolidation and integration—in comprehensive handbooks, and encyclopædic *summae.*

In the face of a somewhat loose and inconsistent usage in the scholarly literature, the meaning of *encyclopædia*, as an ideal standard of erudition ('Bildungsideal', to use a German word oriented towards the standard of classical education)—and of 'enyclopædias', in the sense of book sketching, and exposing, or giving the full content, of the essential knowledge, needs to be defined, and to be refined in the face of a multifarious development:

- Greek *enkyklios paideia*, bound up with the educational canon of the study of rhetoric in the law school, means a general, 'all-round' education encompassing the fields of knowledge preparing the way to higher learning.
- While the ancient cycle of knowledge, alive in late Hellenism even after the rise of the Christian empire, had become obsolete long before the rise of Islam, the old canons of learning were to be replaced, in the urban civilization of Islam, by a new rule of behaviour, and a new canon of useful and elegant knowledge. In Arabic, this would be called *adab*, especially in the sense of the *adab al-kātib*, the erudition required of the experts of administration and the chancery.

In forming this cycle of knowledge, several literary and intellectual traditions compete for the prerogative of definition:

- Early Iranian Hellenism provided models of political ethics and manuals of the ruling art and its ancillaries: the etiquette of state craft, the science and practice of astrology, and early manuals of logical and isagogic method in philosophy.

- Arabism, as a counter-movement of the Iranian emancipatory Shuʿūbiyya, joined Greek Hellenism in establishing the foundations of professional science, and—based on the Platonism and Gnosticism of the mathematicians—a religion for intellectuals (*vide* the work of the philosopher-scientist al-Kindī).
- In the erudition of higher administration and the courts, a first process of integrating Arabic, Iranian and Hellenistic elements joined literary *adab* (mastery of the *ʿArabiyya*) with Greek gnomologia, religious hermeneutics with practical science (*n.b.* geometry, algebra and astrology)—excluding the philosophical paradigms in world-view and demonstrative method, and creating the first draft of 'encylopædic' erudition: the *adab al-kātib* (*vide* Ibn Qutayba, Qudāma ibn Jaʿfar).
- On the other hand, in the same milieus of the Arabic-Islamic administration, disciples of the pioneer philosopher-scientists around al-Kindī and his competitors, created the first draft of a dual canon of learning where the secretarial arts of the Arabic-Islamic community and the philosophical and scientific heritage of Greek Hellenism entered a harmonious symbiosis (*vide* Abū Zayd al-Balkhī and his school spreading from Baghdad to the Iranian East).
- Then, a movement led by professional scientists, philosophers, astronomers, and physicians, within and without the court and courteous administration, and gradually including and informing the *kuttāb*, assumed competence in the Islamic disciplines while subordinating the latter to universal rationality—confining the philosophical encyclopædia to the syllabus of theoretical, demonstrative science.
- In a final development, philosopher-jurists, teaching law at the *madrasa*, and including—first outside, and then inside the law college—the rational sciences into their teaching, transformed the old encyclopædia into a curriculum of religious learning.

3. *The System of the Sciences: Encyclopædia and Classification*

The philosophical 'encyclopædia' follows both in arrangement and in the designation of its parts—of logic, physics, and metaphysics—the traditional division and sequence of the Corpus Aristotelicum and its companion syllabus of auxiliary writings (where the question of 'where to start', πόθεν ἀρκτέον, had become a routine topic as well), adding the mathematical *Quadrivium*. In the beginning, the genre of classification precedes the encyclopædic genre as a framework and blueprint.

The Alexandrian Commentators of the works of Aristotle opened their lectures on Porphyry's *Isagoge* with introductory chapters on the definition, scope, and classification of philosophy. Within the same curriculum, the commentaries on Aristotle's *Categories* began with a special introduction into the philosophy of Aristotle, the sequence and method of study, adding a list of his writings. Lists of his works were also transmitted separately in connection with biographical notices, as for example the so-called *Pinax* of Aristotle, which is preserved in Arabic only and attributed to a certain Ptolemy (called in Arabic 'the Stranger', *al-Gharīb*, in distinction from the famous astronomer); another one, providing detailed summaries of the contents of the individual works, is found in a report on pre-Islamic Greek science by the historian Ibn Wāḍiḥ al-Yaʿqūbī (second half of the 3rd/9th century). The late Hellenistic biographies, available to the Arabic authors in various recensions, presented through the curriculum of the Master the ideal cursus of the sciences—if you want, an encyclopædia.[6] Arabic translations of commentaries and scholia, mostly transmitted through Syriac versions and compendia, presented this material as a summary *Isagoge* of philosophical studies. Such introductions came to the Islamic-Arabic centers of learning firstly through the Iranian tradition; here we find not only the compendium of logic by Paul the Persian in a Syriac version; also his division of philosophy, part of the Alexandrian prolegomena, became available, and is known through quotations in a treatise of the 10th century historian and philosopher Miskawayh (m. 421/1030)—a common source both of Miskawayh's treatise and of al-Fārābī's earlier *Enumeration of the Sciences*.[7] On the other side, the same system is propagated in Miskawayh's ethical handbook, 'The Refinement of Character' (*Tahdhīb al-akhlāq*), as an ideal school of the sciences, paving the way to happiness. A complete version of the traditional Alexandrian prolegomena is extant in the Arabic commentaries by

[6] D. Gutas, 'The Spurious and the Authentic in the Arabic Lives of Aristotle,' in: *Pseudo-Aristotle in the Middle Ages* (London: Warburg Institute, 1986).
[7] *V. infra*, p. 115.

Abū l-Faraj Ibn al-Ṭayyib (m. 435/1043) on Porphyry's *Isagoge* and Aristotle's *Categories*, compiled from Syriac versions of the Greek commentaries available to the Christian translators. But apart from the Arabic adaptations of the Alexandrian commentary lectures on the works of Aristotle, both the course of studies and the individual topics of the definition and division of philosophy were treated separately since the beginnings of Arabic writing on the rational sciences.[8]

Particular topics, especially of the logical *Isagoge*, were treated by the teachers of logic on the basis of their Greek sources in introductory texts, as for example the Four Questions of philosophical inquiry proposed by Aristotle in the first chapter of book II of the *Posterior Analytics*: asking for the fact, the why, if a thing is, and what it is; also the Eight Chapters preceding the Alexandrian commentaries on the particular writings of Aristotle (starting with the scope and the usefulness of each book), and the questions of the aim and profit of philosophy in general.

The division of philosophy grew particularly important, and was treated apart from the routine of the old *Prolegomena*. The expansion, reduction and segmentation, respectively, of its components is part of the programmes and views of the diverse traditions of philosophers and professional scientists. In underlining the rank and importance of the sciences, the genre itself comes to be part of a general discourse—of 'cultural politics'.[9]

Definitions and divisions of philosophy are found in the oldest Arabic introductions to logic, viz. the compendium of Ibn al-Muqaffaʿ and the 'Definitions of Logic' by the Nestorian Christian Ibn Bihrīz. One of the points treated in the school is the question: was logic a part of philosophy—as held by the Platonists (quoting Xenocrates): that is to say logic in the sense of an ontological dialectic of ideas as treated in the early Academy—or was it just a tool, the *Organon* of the Aristotelian syllogism, forming the introduction to philosophy in the Peripatetic course of studies. The topic figured in the traditional prologues to Aristotle's *Analytics*, and in most later treatments

[8] See the comprehensive treatment of the genre by Christel Hein, *Definition und Einteilung der Philosophie: von der spätantiken Einteilungsliteratur zur arabischen Enzyklopädie*, Europäische Hochschulschriften. Reihe 20: Philosophie. Bd. 177 (Frankfurt am Main: Lang, 1985).

[9] See the comprehensive treatment of the genre by Ch. Hein, *op. cit.* [preceding note].

was reduced to the description of logic as a tool or as a balance and straightedge for distinguishing between right and wrong. Treated by the Christian translators and teachers of logic, as in the famous discussion of 938 C.E. between the Nestorian translator Matthew (Abū Bishr Mattā) and the Arab grammarian Abū Saʿīd al-Sīrāfī, and in a monograph by the Jacobite Yaḥyā ibn ʿAdī (m. 363/974), the question was taken up on the side of Islamic *falsafa* by al-Fārābī (m. 339/950), and again by Ibn Sīnā (Avicenna, m. 428/1037) in the *Isagoge* of his philosophical *summa, al-Shifāʾ*.[10]

The first full, though sketchy attempts at systematic classification are encountered in the isagogical writings of the philosopher-scientist al-Kindī (m. after 252/866). These reflect the interference of several traditions and sources in the first half of the 9th century, the blossoming of Græco-Arabic reception and translation. A propædeutical treatise entitled 'On the Quiddity of Science and its Divisions' (*Kitāb Māʾiyyat al-ʿilm wa-aqsāmihī*), according to a fragment extant in a 11th century quotation, contained a division of the rational sciences into physics, mathematics and theology based on the respective objects of knowledge. The same principles are applied to the mathematicals in his treatise 'On the String Instruments Producing Sound' (*K. al-Muṣawwitāt al-watariyya*): introducing *musikē* as a discipline of mathematics, he expounds the position of the mathematical sciences as intermediate between physics and metaphysics.[11] On the other hand, al-Kindī's well-known epistle on the 'Number of the books of Aristotle and what is necessary for the attainment of philosophy' (*Risāla fī kammiyyat kutub Arisṭūṭālīs wa-mā yuḥtāj ilayhi fī taḥṣīl al-falsafa*)[12] is based on the Hellenistic introductions to Aristotle in the context of the Alexandrian lecture course; this contains expositions of the scope of each of the books and supplementary details concerning the classification of the philosophical sciences in general. The treatment of mathematics as an introduction to philosophy and the place given to psychology as an intermediary part of the theoretical disciplines

[10] Gerhard Endress, 'Grammatik und Logik: arabische Philologie und griechische Philosophie im Widerstreit,' in: *Sprachphilosophie in Antike und Mittelalter*, Bochumer Studien zur Philosophie, 3 (Amsterdam: Grüner, 1986), 163–299.

[11] Ed. by Zakariyyā Yūsuf, *Muʾallafāt al-Kindī al-mūsīqiyya* (Baghdād: al-Majmaʿ al-ʿIlmī al-ʿIrāqī, 1962), 67–92; cf. Amnon Shiloah, *The theory of music in Arabic writings (c. 900–1900)* (München: Henle, 1979), 254f.

[12] M. Guidi, R. Walzer, *Studi su al-Kindī, I: Uno scritto introduttivo allo studio di Aristotele* (Roma: Accademia Nazionale dei Lincei, 1940).

point to his Neoplatonic models, common to the mathematical tradition of the mathematical quadrivium. For the rest al-Kindī follows—as also Avicenna and later authors—the Peripatetical consensus in arranging the mathematical disciplines, according to their degree of abstraction, between physics and metaphysics and divides the quadrivium according to the Pythagorean tradition, which again is represented in early Arabic translations from Nicomachus of Gerasa's 'Introduction to Arithmetic'. Parallels, but also some differences point to a different line of reception in a treatise on the division of the sciences of al-Kindī's younger contemporary Qusṭā ibn Lūqā (m. 300/912).[13] The traditional definitions of philosophy, finally, are listed by al-Kindī, along with the definitions of further philosophical concepts, in his 'Epistle on the Definitions and Descriptions of Things' (*Risāla fī ḥudūd al-ašyā' wa-rusūmihā*),[14] an important testimony to his pioneer achievement in elaborating an Arabic teminology, continued and enlarged by his pupil Isḥāq al-Isrā'īlī[15]—an effort taken up and refounded by al-Fārābī and Ibn Sīnā.

Al-Kindī's introductory writings represented not only a program behind the encyclopædic wealth of his œuvre but also a specific legitimization of philosophy with regard to the revealed law and the Muslim teaching of religious and legal hermeneutic: notwithstanding the universal and absolute validity of rational knowledge, revelation is necessary for imparting this knowledge to all of mankind. Once detached from the routine of the introductions and commentaries from the Alexandrian teaching of Aristotle, the development of classification and systematization mirrors the subsequent stages of conflict and integration between religious and rational studies. In the context of the applied sciences, put into the service of Islamic administration, the school of al-Kindī, a school uniting encyclopædic scope and professional scientific competence with the Platonic ethics of knowledge, is followed by the *kuttāb*, the secretaries of the caliphal vizierate and the provincial administrations of the Iranian East.

---

13 Hans Daiber, 'Qosṭā ibn Lūqā (9. Jh.) über die Einteilung der Wissenschaften,' in: *Zeitschrift für Geschichte der arabisch-islamischen Wissenschaften*, 6 (1990): 93–129.

14 Samuel M. Stern, 'Notes on al-Kindī's Treatise on Definitions', *Journal of the Royal Asiatic Society* (1959): 32–43.

15 Alexander Altmann, and S. M. Stern, *Isaac Israeli, a Neoplatonic philosopher of the early tenth century: his works, translated with comments and an outline of his philosophy*, Scripta Judaica, 1 (London: Oxford University Press, 1958).

Among the professional scientists attached to the courts, but also the learned administrators from the milieu of the *kuttāb* and the less fortunate who earned their living on the *Sūq al-Warraqīn*, al-Kindī's programme of philosophy as a rational way of life in coexistence with the schools of Islam remained the most successful. The continuity of his teaching can be followed up until the time of Avicenna and beyond the Oxus, among a group of scholars who studied with himself or with his immediate pupils. From Balkh in Transoxania, Abū Zayd al-Balkhī (m. 322/934) came to Baghdad in order to study with al-Kindī, acquiring a broad competence in the natural sciences, in astronomy and geography, but also in the religious disciplines of Islam, and thus realizing, and transcending the ideal of the *adab al-kātib* drafted by his contemporary Ibn Qutayba.[16] Balkhī defined a two-part encyclopædic programme in a classificatory framework, but without writing an encyclopædic manual comprising the substance of knowledge. His outline of the 'Divisions of the Sciences' (*Tartīb al-ʿulūm*) is now lost, but may be followed up in further treatments of the topic, elaborated in the next generation of his school in Transoxania. Here Ibn Farīghūn of Chaghaniyan (fl. 330–40 H.) included the religious studies and the expertise of the *adab al-kātib* into his somewhat eccentrical 'Summary of the Sciences' (*Jawamiʿ al-ʿulūm*),[17] a rare form of didactically organized outline, presenting systematic relations through ordered graphs, similar to a pedigree (*tashjīr*). Ibn Farīghūn's graphical paradigm had only a few predecessors; it appears in the early introductions to logic by Ibn Bihrīz, then in the medical compendia of Ḥunayn ibn Isḥāq (m. 264/877, where it may be a later adaptation of the original work) and of Ibn Māsawayh (m. 243/857). In a similar vein, another pupil of al-Balkhī, Abū Ḥayyān al-Tawḥīdī, displays the interests of the Muslim jurist and theologian in his 'Epistle on the Sciences' (*Risāla fī l-ʿulūm*).[18] In Balkh, the meet-

[16] Everett K. Rowson, 'The philosopher as littérateur', in: *Zeitschrift für Geschichte der arabisch-islamichen Wissenschaften*, 6 (1990): 50–92.

[17] See Hans Hinrich Biesterfeldt, 'Medieval Arabic encyclopædias of science and philosophy', in: *The medieval Hebrew encyclopedias of science and philosophy*, ed. by Steven Harvey (Dordrecht: Kluwer, 2000), 77–98; *idem*, 'Arabisch-islamische Enzyklopädien: Formen und Funktionen', in: *Die Enzyklopädie im Mittelalter: vom Hochmittelalter bis zur frühen Neuzeit*, hrsg. von Christel Maier (Paderborn: Fink, 2002), 43–83.

[18] Marc Bergé, 'Épître sur les sciences (*Risāla fī l-ʿulūm*) d'Abū Ḥayyān at-Tawḥīdī', in: *Bulletin d'études orientales*, 18 (1963–4): 241–300, 21 (1968): 313–46.

ing place of trade routes from Central Asia, Transoxania and Iran, the tradition of the *Faylasūf al-ʿArab* was passed on to Abū l-Ḥasan al-ʿĀmirī who spent some time in Baghdad at the Būyid court in Rayy before returning to Nishapur (where he died in 381/992), and finally—through al-ʿĀmirī—to Abū l-Faraj ibn Hindū (m. 420/1029) who after his studies in Nishapur was a *kātib* in Rayy.

A common trait of this 'school' is the catholic treatment of the encyclopædia of the sciences. We can observe a growing tendency to include disciplines of the *ʿulūm al-sharʿiyya*. Tawḥīdī's *Risala fī l-ʿUlūm* was written as a reply to scholars who maintained "that logic had no place in jurisprudence, philosophy no connection with religion, wisdom (*ḥikma*, philosophical ethics) no influence on the laws." He starts with jurisprudence, the Koran, Tradition, legal method, theology, and philology; he explains at length and with emphasis the object and benefit of logic, then treats more briefly medicine, astronomy, arithmetic and geometry, presents rhetoric in some detail, and then—what is most remarkable—closes with *taṣawwuf*. Greek rationalism is not seen as transcending the revelation and its traditional exegesis, but as serving sound argument and valid reasoning.

The most detailed attempt to determine the relation of the religious and the philosophic cycles of knowledge in a harmonious symmetry is al-ʿAmirī's *Iʿlām bi-manāqib al-Islām*. The very title is an apologetic programme: the rational sciences (*al-ʿulūm al-ḥikmiyya*) are put into the service of Islam, the absolute religion, and of the religious sciences (*al-ʿulūm al-milliyya*). Both spheres "are based on tenets which agree with pure reason (*al-ʿaql al-sarīḥ*) and are supported by valid demonstration (*al-burhān al-sarīḥ*)." Insight into the true essences (*ḥaqāʾiq al-mawjūdāt*, the scope of philosophy in al-Kindī's traditional definition of philosophy) will show the way to perfect human virtue, and will reveal the wisdom of the Creator. But the ultimate superiority of prophecy over philosophy is uncontested: "Every prophet is a *ḥakīm*, but not every *ḥakīm* is a prophet."[19]

[19] G. Endress, 'The defense of reason: the plea for philosophy in the religious community', in: *Zeitschrift für Geschichte der arabisch-islamischen Wissenschaften*, 6 (1990): 1–49; Everett K. Rowson, *An Islamic philosopher on death and the afterlife: Abū l-Ḥasan al-ʿĀmirī's Kitāb al-Amad ʿalā l-abad*, edited, and translated with a commentary (New Haven, Conn.: American Oriental Society, 1987), containing a detailed worklist and a general assessment of this author's philosophical attitude.

The ethical component of this *ḥikma*, the autonomous ethics of the philosopher who finds in the encyclopædia of sciences the instruction for educating his soul toward purity and ultimate bliss, is found again in the *Tahdhīb al-akhlāq* of Abū ʿAlī Miskawayh (m. 421/1030). The way to intellectual perfection is outlined in the encyclopædia of the sciences, sketched by Miskawayh in the tradition of his predecessors under the programmatic title *Tartīb al-ʿulum wa-tartīb al-saʿādāt* 'The Grades of the Sciences and the Grades of Happiness'.[20]

The same Miskawayh, in his obituary of the Būyid vizier Abū l-Faḍl Ibn al-ʿAmīd, whom he served as a librarian at the Būyid residence of Rayy, depicted his master as a man who had been encompassing the twofold encyclopædia, the religious-hermeneutical disciplines, and the applied sciences of the Greek tradition:[21] his learning is depicted as a living example of the education commended in his ethics. It was al-Kindī's concept of philosophy as an autonomous way of thought and way of life—albeit in the service of the Muslim community and compatible with the Koranic revelation—which stayed alive in the circles of the *ḥukamāʾ*: of scientists, of learned courtiers, and of physicians who in the spirit of both Galenism and Stoicism revered in philosophy the healing art of the soul: the same who in the following century reached eagerly for Ibn Sīnā's new system of being, of knowledge, and of the sciences.

In the Andalus, the gradual convergence of philosophical learning and the disciplines of the professional jurists, while never leading to a full integration, is instigated by a professional jurist: the versatile and brilliant Ibn Ḥazm (m. 456/1064), who in his 'Ranks of the sciences' (*Marātib al-ʿulūm*) starts with the *ʿulūm al-šarʿiyya*, specific to each politico-religious community, and goes on to the sciences common to all, of mathematical and medical knowledge, arriving in the end at the most universal: philosophy.[22]

---

[20] Mohammed Arkoun, *Contribution à l'étude de l'humanisme arabe au IVe/Xe siècle: Miskawayh (320/325–421 = 932/936–1030), philosophe et historien*, Études musulmanes, 13 (Paris: Vrin, 1970, ²1982).

[21] Miskawayh, *Tajārib al-umam*, ed. H. F. Amedroz and D. S. Margoliouth, *The Eclipse of the ʿAbbasid Caliphate* (Oxford 1920–1), 2:275ff.

[22] Biesterfeldt, 'Arabisch-islamische Enzyklopädien' [as quoted above, n. 17], 75f.

4. *The Dual World of Learning: from Manual to Encyclopædia*

Hitherto we have looked at concise treatments, outlines and systems of the sciences in the context of the traditions and professions who took all or parts of their knowledge from the Greek tradition of philosophy—offering frameworks, but not the core and substance of functional theory and useful knowledge. The content management, to use an expression from present-day informatical science, was taken care of in different genres: in catalogues of books, in lexica of terms, and in comprehensive manuals of the individual sciences of medicine, astronomy, and philosophy. A true encyclopædia, in the sense of a handbook comprising the matters of all the cycles of knowledge in the rational and natural sciences, did not come into being in the early period of Hellenistic learning (like it did in the bulky *adab* encyclopædias of literary knowledge for the *kātib* and chancery official, from the *ʿIqd al-farīd* of Ibn ʿAbd-Rabbih, m. 328/940, to the *Nihāyat al-Arab* of al-Nuwayrī, m. 733/1333, and the *Ṣubḥ al-aʿshā* of al-Qalqashandī, m. 821/1418). There was no institution to demand such encyclopædias and to support them by the living practice of a curriculum of learning.

The first attempt at an 'additive' encylopædia is a fairly early one, but does not presuppose an epistemic system, nor an educational institution: the first comprehensive 'Catalogue', *Fihrist*, of books of all disciplines compiled by the learned Baghdadi bookseller Ibn al-Nadīm (m. 380/990), is systematic in dividing its matter according to the demands of his various clientele.[23] He devoted the seventh chapter of his Catalogue to "philosophy and the ancient sciences" (*al-falāsifa wa-l-ʿulūm al-qadīma*)—philosophy, mathematical sciences, medicine, whereas in the first part of his work, he lists books on the philological and religious disciplines. Similarly, his Iranian contemporary Muḥammad ibn Aḥmad al-Khwārizmī, in the 'Keys of the Sciences', *Mafātīḥ al-ʿulūm*, written for a vizier of the Sāmānid Nūḥ ibn Manṣūr (regn. 976–97), explained the technical terms of the dual

[23] On the state of research, see Stefan Leder et al. eds., *Ibn an-Nadīm und die mittelalterliche arabische Literatur: Beiträge zum 1. Johann-Fück-Kolloquium (Halle 1987)* (Wiesbaden: Harrassowitz, 1996).

world of learning in an 'encyclopædic' lexicon: first those of the "sciences of religion and those of the Arabic sciences connected with them" (*al-ʿulūm al-sharʿiyya wa-mā yaqtarin bihā min al-ʿulūm al-ʿarabiyya*), then "the sciences of the non-Arabs, the Greeks and other peoples" (*ʿulūm al-ʿajam min al-Yūnāniyyīn wa-ghayrihim min al-umam*) in the second part of his work.[24] The bipartition of the world of learning persisted as long as the *madrasa*, as an institution, remained confined to the teaching of the law and its ancillaries. Ibn Khaldūn (m. 808/1406) continues to divide the sixth chapter of his 'Introduction' (an introduction to history as being the science of human culture), the chapter on the sciences, into two basic classes, the philosophical disciplines (*al-ʿulūm al-ḥikmiyya al-falsafiyya*)—a treatment not sparing with criticism of metaphysics and some of speculative sciences—and the "traditional-conventional disciplines" (*al-ʿulūm al-naqliyya al-waḍʿiyya*).[25]

Only in a very late period, the rational sciences joined the Islamic disciplines in the curriculum of the *madrasa*; only gradually, from the period of Fakhr-al-Dīn al-Rāzī (m. 606/1209), of Sayf-al-Dīn al-Āmidī (m. 631/1233) and above all of the Iranian Shīʿite school of Naṣīr-al-Dīn al-Ṭūsī (m. 672/1274), classifications and encyclopædias of the sciences added philosophy and the mathematical sciences to the classical curriculum studiorum (*taʿlīqa*) of the law school.[26] Even then, the diverse traditions were not united in literary treatment, but were dealt with separately. We shall confine ourselves to pursue the further development of the rational sciences in the schools of philosophy—'schools' which only in a later period were to be integrated into institutions of scholarly learning.

5. *The Rational Sciences in the Philosophical Encylopædia*

One century after al-Kindī, the whole range of the Greek sciences, the methods and models of philosophy had become available in Arabic. On this basis, a new programme was drafted by al-Fārābī

[24] Clifford E. Bosworth, 'A pioneer Arabic encylopaedia of the sciences: al-Khwārizmī's Keys of the Sciences', in: *Isis*, 54 (1963): 97–111.

[25] Ibn Khaldûn, *The Muqaddimah: an introduction to history*, translated by F. Rosenthal (New York, London, 1958), vol. 2, p. 409–vol. 3, p. 480.

[26] See George Makdisi, *The rise of college: institutions of learning in Islam and the West* (Edinburgh: Edinburgh University Press, 1981), ch. 2, II: 'Organization of learning', pp. 80–98. See also *infra*, p. 125ff.

(m. 339/950): the system of the theoretical and practical sciences accompanies the emancipation of philosophy as being a universal science of demonstration. The introduction to the canon of writings by Plato and Aristotle (presumably based on a late Hellenistic Greek source) is presented as leading to 'The Acquisition of Happiness', *Taḥṣīl al-saʿāda*.[27] The 'Concordance between the two sages Plato and Aristotle' (*al-Jamʿ bayna raʾyay al-ḥakīmayn*) is not only meant to demonstrate the unity of philosophical truth, but—like in his interpretation of Aristotle's *Rhetoric*, like in his writings on philosophical language (*ḥurūf, alfāẓ*)—is presented to degrade practical philosophy, using rhetoric in view of informing the community of the virtual city, while the demonstrative science of Aristotle is available to the true philosopher only.[28] The minor, practical and empirical arts of medicine and astrology on the other hand are eliminated from the circle of the theoretical sciences. Al-Fārābī's introduction to the scope of metaphysics, in defining the First Philosophy as the Science of Being *qua* Being is proposing the universal claim of metaphysics, subordinating theology and practical ethics.[29] Avicenna, in his autobiography, evokes his discovery of the small treatise as a significant experience in his own way towards philosophy. But then, in his 'Enumeration of the Sciences' (*Iḥṣāʾ al-ʿulūm*),[30] al-Fārābī went further in constructing a dual system of the sciences: the limited hermeneutics and applications of the religious disciplines are subordinated under the theoretical sciences, that is to say the particulars of grammar, theology and jurisprudence are being assigned to the universals of logic, metaphysics and ethics—arts of a comprehensive normative system. In his book on the 'Words of Philosophy' (*Kitāb al-Ḥurūf*), as also in his expositions of the Aristotelian *Rhetoric*, al-Fārābī gives an historical

[27] Muhsin Mahdi, 'Remarks on Alfarabi's *Attainment of Happiness*,' *Essays on Islamic Philosophy and Science*, ed. George F. Hourani (Albany, N.Y.: SUNY Press, 1975), 47–66.

[28] Cf. G. Endress, 'L'Aristote arabe: réception, autorité et transformation du Premier Maître,' *Medioevo: rivista di storia della filosofia medievale*, 23 (1997): 1–42; cf. Maroun Aouad, 'Les fondements de la *Rhétorique* d'Aristote reconsidérés par Fārābī, ou le concept de point de vue immédiat et commun,' *Arabic Sciences and Philosophy*, 2 (1992): 133–80.

[29] Thérèse-Anne Druart, 'Le traité d'al-Farabi sur les buts de la Métaphysique d'Aristote', *Bulletin de philosophie médiévale*, 24 (1982) 38–43.

[30] See Muhsin Mahdi, 'Science, philosophy and religion in Alfarabi's Enumeration of the Sciences,' in *The Cultural context of medieval learning*, ed. J. E. Murdoch, E. D. Sylla (Dordrecht, Boston, 1975), 113–47.

perspective upon the same system of universal science and the particulars of the linguistic and religious community: before Plato, rhetoric, poetics, and grammar were founded, and then the mathematical and physical sciences, followed by the minor logical procedures of sophistics and dialectics; Plato in his turn founded political science upon principles of ethical conduct using didactical methods—dialectic and rhetoric which in his hands attained merely but not fully the level of apodictical certainty. Aristotle finally provided the criteria of rational knowledge in his science of demonstration, but only after Aristotle did true religion, based on true philosophy, provide criteria of action for the perfect city, crowning the historical development of rational activity. Similarly, the 'Harmony between Plato and Aristotle' drives home the difference in method, while pointing out the unity of philosophical truth: the precedance of the Aristotelian *burhān* over the Platonic politics, that is to say: certainty based on demonstrable knowledge is a condition for the perfection of the political science as well.[31]

The further development of the definition, classification and encyclopædic presentation of the sciences is dominated, not by those of the *kuttāb* who were ready to integrate *ḥikma* into *adab*, but by the professional representatives of the Hellenistic sciences: physicians, mathematicians, astronomers. The *falāsifa* kept strictly to the Hellenistic canon, and continued using a classification based on the ancient cursus of philosophy, treating logic, physics and metaphysics under the titles and according to the division of the Aristotelian text books. The methodology of hermeneutics and logic is followed by the universals of physics and metaphysics, and accompanied by the 'middle sciences' (coming between physics and metaphysics) of mathematics: geometry, arithmetic, astronomy and musicology. The basics of mathematics are supplemented by optics and mechanics. Even though some of the catalogues of the sciences were written by physicians, mathematicians or astronomers by profession, the empirical arts of astrology, medicine, agriculture and alchemy, however, are excluded from the canon of the pure theoretical sciences, as also practical phi-

[31] Wolfhart Heinrichs, 'Die antike Verknüpfung von *phantasia* und Dichtung bei den Arabern,' in: *ZDMG*, 128 (1978): 252–298; Dimitri Gutas, 'Paul the Persian on the classification of the parts of Aristotle's philosophy: a milestone between Alexandria and Baghdād,' in: *Der Islam*, 60 (1983): 231–267; G. Endress, 'L'Aristote arabe' [*v. supra*, n. 28].

losophy—ethics, economics, politics which are relegated into the forecourt of propædeutics. A characteristical specimen of this genre is the 'Book of Classes of the Philosophical Sciences' (*Aṣnāf al-ʿulūm al-ḥikmiyya*) by the Christian physician, Abū Sahl ʿĪsā ibn Yaḥyā al-Masīḥī (m. 401/1010); this, however, starts with the heights of universal theology and ends with the elements of logical method and ethical education.[32] This is not only the precursor but also a likely model for the 'Divisions of the Sciences' (*Aqsām al-ʿulūm*) of Ibn Sīnā, who as a physician was al-Masīḥī's student.[33]

Ibn Sīnā's small treatise drafts the programme and the arrangement of his oeuvre, truly encyclopædic if taken as a whole. Whereas Abū Sahl al-Masīḥī mentioned the basic texts and the commentaries for each of the sciences, Avicenna—after doing the same in his *Aqsām*—undertook to refound and to rewrite the whole encyclopædia of the sciences in his 'Book of Healing', *Kitāb al-Shifāʾ*.

A second draft was sketched by Avicenna in the logical part of his 'philosophy of the Easterners', *Kitāb al-Mashriqiyyīn* (written c. 418–20/1027–9, lost except for its inlogic),[34] a philosophy emancipated from the traditional Peripatetic Hellenism of the Christian commentators. This second draft reached farther in its influence on later divisions and encyclopædias of philosophy in late mediaeval scholasticism. The *Aqsām*, as also the *Isagoge* of the *Shifaʾ*,[35] start with the treatment of logic and physical science; and then, in a comprehensive treatment of *First Philosophy*, deal with the universals (*al-maʿānī l-ʿāmma*) and the principles of the sciences (*mabādiʾ al-ʿulūm*), going on to philosophical theology in the chapter on *Ilāhiyyat*: the essence, emanation and activity of the divine First Cause (*al-mabdaʾ al-awwal, al-wājib al-wujūd*), followed by the doctrine of revelation and the 'return' of the soul to its origin. The prolegomena of the *Kitāb al-Mashriqiyyīn*, on the other hand, allot the doctrine of universals and of theology proper

---

[32] See Biesterfeldt, 'Arabisch-islamische Enzyzlopädien' [as quoted above, n. 17], pp. 55–60.

[33] Jean Michot, 'Les sciences physiques et métaphysiques selon la *Risālah fī Aqsām al-ʿulūm* d'Avicenne: essai de traduction critique,' *Bulletin de philosophie médiévale*, 22 (1980): 62–73.

[34] On the identity and title of this work, see Dimitri Gutas, *Avicenna and the Aristotelian tradition* (Leiden: Brill, 1988), 115–30; *idem*, 'Ibn Ṭufayl on Ibn Sīnā's Eastern Philosophy', *Oriens*, 34 (1994): 222–41.

[35] See Michael E. Marmura, 'Avicenna on the division of the sciences in the Isagoge of his *Shifāʾ*', *Journal of the History of Arabic Science*, 4 (1980): 239–51.

to separate sections of theoretical science (*ʿilm naẓarī*, followed by the divisions of practical philosophy), yielding a fourfold division into naturalia, mathematica, divina and universalia which became the general framework for the integration of Islamic theology into the system of the theoretical sciences.

While the system of the rational sciences was first drafted in introductory classifications at a very early time of the translation and reception of the Greek sources, the content and doctrine of these sources was presented in commentaries, paraphrases and epitomes of the basic texts by Aristotle for philosophy, by Hippocrates and Galen for medicine, by Euclid, Archimedes and Apollonius for mathematics and by Ptolemy for astronomy. After the first phase of original reinterpretation and research on the subject matter of the sciences, the commentaries were superseded by new, comprehensive summaries of theoretical and practical sciences: general 'encyclopædias' in the sense of summary expositions of a province of learning as well as specific manuals of the individual disciplines.

A fundamental influence on this development, as on the systems of classification, had been exercised by Abū Naṣr al-Fārābī. It is true that his 'Principles of the Opinions of the Inhabitants of the Virtuous City' (*Mabādiʾ ārāʾ ahl al-madīna al-fāḍila*)[36] is yet far from a complete summary of the Hellenistic cycle of knowledge; this is to be found, up to the time of al-Fārābī, and most impressively in his own work, in the corpus of commentaries on the fundamental Greek manuals of logic, of the parts of philosophy—ethics, physics and metaphysics—and of the mathematical quadrivium. Seen in the light of the 'Enumeration of the Sciences' and the systematic remarks preceding his individual works, the sum of his work may be perceived as a encyclopædic whole, where philosophy, emancipated from the escort of the professional and practical sciences (medicine, geometry, astronomy) provided the principles of demonstrative science and of the cosmological *Weltbild*. The *Mabādiʾ* define both the theological-cosmological and the religious-political frame of this concept: the principles of the world order founded by the divine intellect, and intelligible to rational insight, reflected through macro-microcosmical analogy

[36] Richard Walzer, *Al-Farabi on the perfect state: Abū Naṣr al-Fārābī's Mabādiʾ ārāʾ ahl al-madīna al-fāḍila. A revised edition with introduction, translation and commentary* (Oxford: Clarendon Press, 1985).

in the sublunary world, revealed to the Prophet in religious symbols, and translated by the philosopher-king into precepts which will show the 'Inhabitants of the Virtual City' the way to true felicity and ultimate knowledge. The philosophical interpretation of the religious community, revelation and divine law serves to justify philosophy and the sciences as guarantors and safeguards for the Orthodox interpretation of the revealed law.

6. *The* Summa *of Demonstrative Science*

Although influenced by al-Fārābī's concept of the philosopher-*imām*, the first Arabic *summa* of the philosophical canon of learning which also forms a literary unit goes back to the Neoplatonic and Neopythagorean background of early Arabic science, first found in al-Kindī, and then, in a different context, in the 'Science of the Balance' of the Jābirian corpus.[37] I am speaking of the *Book of the Sincere Brethren*, in Arabic *Kitāb Ikhwān al-Safā'*, written in the sixties or seventies of the 10th century by a man named Abū Sulaymān al-Maqdisī, addressed to, and perhaps written in collaboration with, a group of Ismāʿīlī scholars styled as the community of the true faith.[38] Going beyond an encyclopædic summary, the book presents knowledge as being the highway to rational illumination: the gnosis of the initiate. True to the Neopythagorean tradition, the series of 52 treatises or epistles starts with Philosophy (the truly/essentially philosophical sciences, *al-ʿulūm al-falsafiyya al-ḥaqīqiyya*) and the mathematical quadrivium, forming the propædeutics of philosophy in the tradition of the Platonic Academy (as also in al-Kindī's introduction to Aristotle), and demonstrating the cosmic sympathy between the upper and lower worlds through Pythagorean number theory and arithmetical speculation (going back to the *Introduction to Arithmetic* by the Neopythagorean Nicomachus of Gerasa). This is followed by Logic,

[37] Cf. G. Endress, 'Mathematics and philosophy in medieval Islam,' in *The enterprise of science in Islam: new perspectives*, ed. by Jan P. Hogendijk and Abdelhamid I. Sabra, Dibner Institute Studies in the History of Science and Technology (Cambridge, Mass.: The MIT Press), 2003, 121–76.

[38] Useful synopsis by Alessandro Bausani, *L'enciclopedia dei Fratelli della Purità: riassunto, con introduzione e breve commento, dei 52 trattati o epistole degli Ikhwān aṣ-Ṣafā'*, Istituto Universitario Orientale, Seminario di Studi Asiatici, series minor, 4 (Napoli, 1978).

introducing the cursus and method of demonstrative science. The next part, Physics, presents a physical doctrine imbued by the gnostical concept of the World of the Intellect and depending heavily on astrology, alchemy and the occult sciences within the general framework of the peripatetic theory of physical motion. Last comes Theology, depicting the processus of the divine intellect through the cosmic hypostases of the neoplatonic system. The world view of the *cognoscenti* is the master plan of the *Nāmūs*, the spiritual empire founded by divine law and established by the Imām; here, as in the 'Principles' of al-Fārābī politics and ethics are practical interpretations and applications of theoretical knowledge as realised by the revelation, subordinated under the chapter on theology, and concluding with the doctrine of redemption, the 'return' (*al-Maʿād*) of the soul to its divine origin. The epistles of the *Ikhwān* remained influential in the popular philosophy of the occult sciences (having drawn themselves upon the older traditions of hermetism), were spread by the Ismāʿīlī Shīʿa and were still read by the teachers of the Safavid schools of philosophical *kalām*. But they were not only eliminated from the orthodox Sunnī schools, but fiercely attacked for their heretical affiliations, and left no trace in the teaching of Avicenna's school, nor in the philosophical encyclopædia of Sunni *kalām* drafted by Fakhr-al-Dīn al-Razī and his continuators from the end of the 12th century.

Ibn Sīnā continued, but also refounded the transmission of the *ʿulūm al-awāʾil*. Departing from al-Fārābī's paradigm of demonstrative science, he renewed the philosophical basis of rational scientific theory and practice, and set out to develop philosophy—*ḥikma*—as a metaphor of religious knowledge. Departing from the encyclopædic, courteous and administrative tradition of al-Kindī's science and Abū Zayd al-Balkhī's *adab*, he reviewed the old canon of the theoretical sciences, and created a new encyclopædia of the method and matter of philosophy.

The far-reaching influence of the *Shifāʾ*, both as a manual of the Peripatetic paradigm of philosophy, *falsafa*, in Islam, and as a model of all philosophical *summae* for the seven centuries to come, its influenced remained unimpaired. It is true that the authority of Avicenna the physician did much to strengthen his authority as a philosopher in the scientific community, all the more so since his philosophy provided a philosophic interpretation of revealed law not provided by the early schools of *falsafa*—a religion for intellectuals not in open conflict with the religion of the *jamāʿa*. But it was also the systematic economy of his œuvre which contributed to its success, a success so overwhelming that the Arabic translation and early commentaries of the ancient sources fell into near-oblivion. The classical cursus studiorum is maintained as a standard system and sequence: logic followed by physics, the mathematicals taking the place of 'middle sciences',[39] followed and crowned by the *Ilāhiyyāt* in the sense of metaphysics and covering both aspects of the Aristotelian work: ontology, investigating being *qua* being, and theology, inquiring after the Necessary Being and First Cause, and also solving the apory of transcendence vs. immanence of the Divine in a Neoplatonic model of πρόοδος—ἐπιστροφή, reconciling the immanence of the transcendent and the way of the rational soul towards knowing the Beyond. The chapters of the *Shifā'* bear the titles of the basic texts of philosophy and the theoretical sciences, maintaining the normative tradition of the ancient canon, and with an impressive coherence and systematic unity of presentation, integrate the various levels of cognition into the framework of demonstrative science, still put under the aegis of ontological and cosmological orthodoxy.

Following the same tradition, and in keeping with al-Fārābī's *Iḥṣā'*, Avicenna delegated the nether regions of practical and applied science to numerous parerga; it is only for medicine—his own profession—that he wrote a comprehensive manual, a 'medical encyclopædia' on its own, covering both theory and practice: the 'Canon of Medicine' *Qānūn fī l ṭibb*; in this, he had predecessors, as ʿAlī ibn al-ʿAbbās al-Majūsī, whose *Kitāb al-Malakī* (dedicated to the Būyid *malik al-mulūk*, ʿAḍud al-Dawla, regn. 338/949–372/982) competed with his own work for a long time before being replaced by the *Qānūn*.[40] But other fields he covered in concise introductory manuals—as the mathematical sciences (*taʿlīmiyyāt*) in the third part of the *Shifā'*—while leaving the elaboration of full-fledged applications to his professional predecessors and contemporaries.

[39] See Roshdi Rashed, 'Metaphysics and mathematics in classical Islamic culture: Avicenna and his successors', in *God, Life and Cosmos*, ed. by Ted Peters, Muzaffar Iqbal and Syed Nomanul Haq (Aldershot: Ashgate, 2002), 173–193.

[40] See G. Endress, 'Die wissenschaftliche Literatur', *Grundriss der arabischen Literatur*, vol. 3 (Wiesbaden: Reichert, 1992), 121–5.

For mathematical astronomy, geodesy and astrology, Abū l-Rayḥān al-Bīrūnī (m. 440/1048) was the most prominent and the one Ibn Sīnā respected most. Just in passing, I may refer to his *Qānūn al-Masʿūdī* in order to point out the difference between professional manual and general encyclopædia: The *Qānūn* (written in 421/1030) is a *summa* of all the mathematical and astronomical knowledge (but not of cosmological theory) required for the 'science of the stars': chronology, trigonometry, gnomonics, geodesy, calculus of planetary and other celestial motions, and presented in tables (*zījāt*) for the purposes of the practical astronomer and astrologer.

In Ibn Sīnā's First Philosophy, the primacy of philosophy is not safeguarded through advocating a political model, contrary to al-Fārābī's *Mabādiʾ ārāʾ ahl al-madīna al-fāḍila*, where the truth is maintained in a dual system of demonstrative and poetical-rhetorical discourse; the identity of universal, demonstrative philosophy and the particular symbols of revelation is not presupposed, but exposed through hermeneutical procedures; the world of the *imām*-ruler is relegated to an ethical-political discipline, but rooted in the same cosmological plan as the principles of metaphysics. Prophecy, the doctrine of *imāma*, and the political order, are treated in an appendix of the final part of the *Ilāhiyyat*, the doctrine of resurrection, *maʿād*, and eschatology; political language—at the same time, the discourse of the religious community, in the Rhetoric taught by al-Fārābī.

For his monumental and original work, Ibn Sīnā created a sophisticated hierarchy of subdivisions. The four main parts of the *Shifāʾ*, called *jumla* 'summa', are each divided into subdivisions of *fann* 'class', *maqāla* 'treatise', and *faṣl* 'section'. The *Qānūn*, a special manual of medicine, is divided, in a somewhat different manner, and at the same time, even more deeply layered, into *fann* 'disciplina', *taʿlīm* 'lesson', *jumla* 'summa', then (in some of the more lengthy chapters), *faṣl* 'section', while some of the units have only *funūn* and *maqālāt*. In the designation of *taʿlīm*, Avicenna takes up the lecture unit of the Alexandrian commentary, the πρᾶγμα, translated by *taʿlīm* in some Arabic adaptations of Greek commentaries, mainly known from the commentaries of Abū l-Faraj ibn al-Ṭayyib (m. 435/1043) on Porphyry's *Isagoge* and Aristotle's *Categories*, and a few other texts stemming from this school.[41] Ibn Sīnā's *jumal* and *funūn*, as also many variations of such *schemata*, were also used by his epigones who taught philosophy and the sciences in the *madrasa*. A remarkable example is an important Persian encyclopædia modelled on the *Shifāʾ*, the *Durrat at-tāj li-ghurrat al-Dubāj*

[41] See G. Endress, *ibid.*, vol. 2 (1987): 461f.

of Ṭūsī's master pupil, Quṭb-al-Dīn al-Shīrāzī (m. 710/1311), to be mentioned presently.[42] Similar, but even more complex divisions are a distinctive trait of the philosophical-theological manuals of the later Middle Ages.[43]

More concise than the *Shifā'*, easier in approach and less demanding as to the level of theoretical discussion, are Ibn Sīnā's shorter compendia of the rational encyclopædia:[44] the *Kitāb al-Najāt* (written in 418/1027) in Arabic, and the *Dānishnāma-i 'Alā'ī* (some time after 414/1023) in Persian;[45] both served the rapid dissemination of his philosophy and his system of scientific knowledge in method and content, so successfully that the reading of the basic Greek sources and the earlier manuals was superseded. The ancient authorities were to be recovered from oblivion only by those who in professing open disgust of Avicenna's religion for intellectuals, returned to the authentic text and the true interpretation of Aristotle (or, in the case of medicine, of Hippocrates and Galen). 'Abd-al-Laṭīf al-Baghdādī (m. 629/1231),[46] the most versatile and most anti-Avicennian mind of the period commanded by Kamāl-al-Dīn ibn Yūnus (m. 639/1242) in the *'aqliyyāt*, and by Fakhr-al-Dīn al-Rāzī (m. 606/1209) in *Kalām*, confined himself to a compendium of 'Metaphysics' (*Mā ba'd al-Ṭabī'a*) based on Aristotle and the Neoplatonic texts known under his name. But in the Muslim West, we may perceive in the great project of Ibn Rushd (Averroes, m. 595/1198), not only an alternative philosophy, but—seen in this context—the project to found an alternative encyclopædia, in returning to the text of Aristotle, and in exposing his true doctrine in a series of multi-levelled commentaries to the whole of his œuvre, restituting a firm and irrefutable basis to the encyclopædia of knowledge for all of society.[47]

---

[42] *V. infra*, p. 129.
[43] See G. Endress, *loc. cit.*, vol. 2 (1987): 468–71.
[44] See D. Gutas, *Avicenna and the Aristotelian tradition* [as quoted *supra*, n. 34], 112–14.
[45] Cf. Jules Janssens, 'Le Dânesh-nâmeh d'Ibn Sînâ: un texte à revoir?', *Bulletin de philosophie médiévale*, 28 (1986): 163–77.
[46] Summary and partial translation of his autobiography in George Makdisi, *The Rise of Colleges* (Edinburgh: Edinburgh University Press, 1981), 84–91, esp. 86, 87; partial ed. and trans. of his *Kitāb Mā ba'd al-ṭabī'a*: Angelika Neuwirth, *'Abd al-Laṭīf al-Baġdādī's Bearbeitung von Buch Lambda der aristotelischen Metaphysik* (Wiesbaden: Harrassowitz, 1976).
[47] Jamāl-al-Dīn al-'Alawī, *al-Matn al-rushdī: madkhal li-qirā'a jadīda* (Casablanca: Tūbqāl, 1986).

The philosophical encyclopædia after Avicenna bears his mark.[48] Not only does the *Taḥṣīl* of his immediate disciple, Bahmanyār ibn al-Marzubān (m. 548/1067) follow the great model. But also the *Kitāb al-Muʿtabar* of Abū l-Barakāt al-Baghdādī (m. pp. 560/1164), notwithstanding many differences in doctrine found in the thought of this highly original mind—as in the theory of principles, in the physical theory of motion, in psychology and the doctrine of creation—is in its systematical organisation modelled on the *Shifāʾ* and the *Najāt*. On the other hand, the theologians among Avicenna's followers transformed the horizon of the readers' expectations. Avicenna's immediate public, his readers and interpreters, were members of the scientific professions: physicians (who adopted his *Shifāʾ* as eagerly as they read his medical *Qānūn*) and astronomers, Muslims and non-Muslims, who found the principles of their science explained in the frame of his philosophic encyclopædia. They made his philosophy their *credo*, and read the Koran in the light of his philosophical exegesis. But his influence went beyond the closed circles of experts trained in the disciplines of the Greek tradition, and engaged in the higher échelons of the central and provincial administrations. The clear-cut division between non-Arab and non-Muslim transmitters of the sciences on the one hand and the representatives of the Islamic schools had long since been blurred, and soon ceased to exist (albeit the presence and prestige of Jews and Christians in the medical professions continued to be acknowledged—and also to be resented). The scientists themselves had put their knowledge in the service of religion, such as the astronomers working as time-keepers of the *jāmiʿ* mosques. A growing number of educated Muslims, not a few of them judges and professors of law already in the generation of Avicenna's immediate pupils, felt attracted by his work which promised a comprehensive explanation of the world, a view of demonstrable truth in the dilemma between of schism and traditionist reaction, and a view of cosmic order in the face of chaos.

Among the eminent continuators of Avicenna we find philosophers who were at the same time followers of al-Ghazālī, the jurist and theologian who studied philosophy before turning against it, and who

[48] An overview was given by Francis E. Peters, *Aristotle and the Arabs: the Aristotelian tradition in Islam*, New York University Studies in Near Eastern Civilization, 10 (New York, 1968).

in his compendium of *manṭiq, ilāhiyyāt* and *ṭabīʿiyyāt* (in this order) summarized the scopes of the philosophers, *Maqāṣid al-falāsifa*, following Ibn Sīnā's *Najāt* and *Dānishnāma* so closely as to raise doubts over the authenticity of his own work.[49]

In the wake of al-Ghazālī's criticism, using the instruments of demonstrative science in order to denounce invalid reasoning on the side of the Peripatetic canon of doctrines, theologians employed systematically the method and the system of the rational sciences in order to redefine theological concepts in terms of philosophical physics and metaphysics, to refound analogical reasoning in law by means of the syllogism, and to defend religious doctrines by means of philosophical reasoning.

In consequence, the defense of philosophy—of a philosophy to be further developed, refined and made immune—was undertaken by members of the same community who regarded rational demonstration indispensable as a firm basis of sound argument in the service of Islam, and prepared the way for an Islamic scholasticism, adopted as propædeutics and methodology by the teachers of theology and law. At first outside rather than inside the religious community, but increasingly inside the colleges of law—in Mongol and post-Mongol Iran, and then in late empires of the Ottomans and of Mughal India—the rational sciences joined the Islamic disciplines of the Sharīʿa, and in building a theology made scientific, paved the way to a philosophy made religious.

The social background of this development is the rise of a rank of scholars assuming a general competence: the philosopher-scientist, and at the same time philosopher-theologian, at home in the courts as well as in the *madrasa*. Until the first half of the 12th century, teaching of the *ʿaqliyyāt* was kept out of the *madrasa*, and restricted to the libraries, observatories, hospitals, and to the private circles of professional scholars, men like Kamāl-al-Dīn ibn Yūnus (551/1156–639/1242) who divided his time between the teaching of law at the *madrasa* and the teaching of mathematics at home. While such learning began to spread more widely among Muslim scholars who as a

[49] See Janssen, 'Le Dânesh-nâmeh' [as quoted *supra*, n. 45]; cf. Marie Bernand, 'Al-Ghazālī, artisan de la fusion des systèmes de pensée', *Journal asiatique*, 278 (1990), 223–51, raising objections discussed by Janssen, *An annotated bibliography on Ibn Sīnā: first supplement (1990–1994)*, Textes et études du moyen âge, 12 (Louvain-la-Neuve, 1999), 120 no. 392.

matter of course had graduated from one of the law schools, more and more eminent representatives of logic, of medicine, of mathematics and of spherical astronomy are found among professors of the law colleges. Still, it took a long time before the teaching of these subjects was admitted into the traditional institutions of learning, confined to the cursus, *taʿlīqa*, of jurisprudence, and the *majālis al-baḥṯ*, disputations devoted to the *ikhtilāf al-fuqahāʾ*.

So while this leads to the development of a twofold discourse in intellectual discussion, a full integration of the *maʿqūl* and the *manqūl* in a common encyclopædia of the sciences was far from being accomplished. Even while the rational sciences begin to enter the *madrasa*, we cannot—not yet—observe an integration of hermeneutical and theological traditions from the one side, and logical-philosophical from the other, in a common encyclopædia. On the one hand, the same scholar might write extensive, separate manuals for each of the branches of learning, and keeping within the traditional system of method and of divison of each. On the other hand, comprehensive 'encyclopædias', when they were compiled, in the first instance were additive, not integrative. The first important example of this was worked out by Fakhr-al-Dīn al-Rāzī (m. 606/1209) in his *Jāmiʿ al-ʿulūm* (extant [and written originally?] in Persian), a truly catholic, and somewhat chaotic, survey of everything for everybody—and certainly not for philosopher-theologians and professional scientists. This starts with theology: *kalām*, goes on to the principles, methods and chapters of law (*uṣūl al-fiqh, jadal, khilāfiyyāt, maḏhab, farāʾiḍ, waṣāya*), the Koranic and hermeneutical sciences (*tafsīr, maʿānī, dalāʾil al-iʿjāz, qirāʾāt*) and the Sunna, *aḥādīṯ*—in this order—, accompanied by sundry historical and philological matters from the side of *adab*, then followed by an assortment of theoretical, practical and applied sciences from the Hellenistic tradition: logic, physics, oniromancy, physiognomy, medicine, surgery, pharmacology, occult sciences, geometry, geodesy, and in a final part, a motley sequence of mathematical, theological, occult, ethical and eschatological topics.[50]

[50] Extant in Persian versions: *Jāmiʿ (Jawāmiʿ) al-ʿulūm* containing 40 disciplines, and *Ḥadāyiq al-anwār fī ḥaqāyiq al-asrār* in sixty parts, hence also called *Kitāb-i Sittīnī*; see C. A. Storey, *Persian Literature*, II, 3 (London, Leiden, 1977), 351f.; the latter printed Teheran 1346 h.sh./1967; see H. H. Biesterfeldt, 'Arabisch-islamische Enzyklopädien' [v. *supra*, n. 17], 76–8.

> A later successor to Rāzī's *Jāmiʿ*, and truly encyclopædic in size and scope, was Shams-al-Dīn al-Āmulī's work *Nafā'is al-funūn fī ʿarā'is al-ʿuyūn*, written in Sulṭāniyya under Öljeytü's reign (703–16/1304–16). This covers 160 sciences, dealing first with the 'recent' disciplines of Islam (*ʿulūm-i awākhir*) and then with the 'sciences of the ancients'. Rāzī's and Āmulī's works were imitated, but not substantially renewed, by a number of 16th and 17th century Persian authors.[51]

It was Fakhr-al-Dīn al-Rāzī who on the other hand provided systematic treatments of the whole range of the cursus studiorum, in separate manuals, including a theology which in using logical method and Peripatetic concepts, defined and defended the stance of theology. For the philosophical encyclopædia of al-Rāzī and his successors as well as for the polymath scentists of Iran from al-Ṭūsī to the Safavid schools, both of Avicenna's divisions of philosophy serve as alternative models: the tripartite division of the classical canon beside the four-part division presented in the introduction of the *Kitāb al-Mashriqiyyīn*; logic in many cases is separately mentioned in the titles of such handbooks, or treated in separate manuals. Al-Rāzī gives both the *ḥikma* part of his *Mulakhkhaṣ fī l-ḥikma wa-l-manṭiq*[52] (written in 579/1184) and his *Mabāḥith al-mashriqiyya*[53] the same division (i.e. three-part, without the logic): he relegates the First Philosophy, the ontology and doctrine of principles of the old metaphysics to the beginning: the doctrine of the universals (*al-umūr al-ʿāmmiyya*); he goes on with the doctrine of substances and of natural processes of physics—categories (*aʿrāḍ*), and substances (*jawāhir*: body, soul, intellect)—a physical theory which in its principles of movement and causality eliminates the old stumbling-blocks of the philosophers' doctrine of the eternity of the world. In the final part, he crowns the cursus studiorum with the theology of the *Kalām* ('the pure divinalia', *al-ilāhiyyāt al-maḥḍa*).

Another example of such wide-ranging activity is the work of the Shāfiʿite Sayf-al-Dīn from Āmid on the upper Euphrates (b. 551/1156,

---

[51] Storey, *Persian literature* [*v.* n. 50], II 3:355; Ž. Vesel, 'Mawsūʿa, 2: In Persian', in *Encylopædia of Islam*, s.v.; *ibid.* on later works of this kind.

[52] See Rudolf Sellheim, *Materialien zur arabischien Literaturgeschichte*, Verzeichnis der Orientalischen Handschriften in Deutschland, Bd. 17, Reihe A (Wiesbaden: Steiner, 1976–1987), 1:141f.

[53] Detailed table of contents in Wilhelm Ahlwardt, *Verzeichniß der arabischen Handschriften*, Die Handschriften-Verzeichnisse der Königlichen Bibliothek zu Berlin, Bd. 17 (Berlin 1887–1899), 4:403–15 no. 5064.

m. 631/1233), who taught law, theology and philosophy in Egypt and Syria, and among whose considerable œuvre are three full treatments of *uṣūl al-fiqh* (the *Iḥkām al-ḥukkām fī usūl al-aḥkām*), of *uṣūl al-dīn* (under the title of *Abkār al-afkār fī uṣūl al-dīn*), and a treatment of *ḥikma*, philosophy, on the lines of Avicenna's system, *al-Nūr al-bāhir fī l-ḥikam al-zawāhir*, divided into logic, physics, and metaphysics. Each of the three manuals, we should add, has its own treatment of logic: the legal of *qiyās*, the methodology of theological *naẓar*, and the syllogistic logic of the Aristotelian *Analytics*.[54] But like Fakhr-al-Dīn al-Rāzī, al-Āmidī did not integrate all of the hermeneutical, and rational disciplines into one comprehensive and systematic 'enyclopædia'; he had to face public persecution, and fled Egypt, because of his propagating philosophy in his teaching of the *uṣūlān*. The reason for the lack of a scholastic encyclopædia is that there existed no one institution where all its components would be taught. This situation changed, if only in gradual stages, during the period of emergence of the great empires after the fall of the Caliphate—Mongol, Ottoman, Safavid, Mughal—of the Muslim East.

In the next generation, and following the Mongol invasion, Sunnī and Shīʿī scholars, mainly in the Iranian East, created the all-time bestsellers of the Hellenistic encyclopædia, many of them philosopher-theologians who at the same time were also highly competent mathematicians and astronomers. Aṯīr-al-Dīn al-Abharī (m. 663/1265?) treated logic not only in his popular *Īsāghūjī*, but also in the first part of his equally popular *Hidāyat al-ḥikma*,[55] keeping to the traditional tripartition: logic is followed by the naturalia (*ṭabīʿiyyāt*) in three disciplinae (*funūn*): 1. *mā yaʿumm al-ajsām* ('what is common to the bodies'), 2. *al-falakiyyāt* ('concerning the celestial spheres'), 3. *al-ʿunṣuriyyāt* ('concerning the sublunar elements'), then by the three parts (*funūn*) of the First Philosophy: 1. *taqāsīm al-wujūd* ('divisions of being'), 2. *al-ʿilm bi-l-ṣāniʿ wa-ṣifātihī* ('knowledge of the Maker and His attributes'), 3. *al-malāʾika wa-hiya l-ʿuqūl al-mujarrada* ('the angels and the separate intelligences'). A contemporary of al-Abharī's, and a co-student of his, and of the eminent Naṣīr-al-Dīn al-Ṭūsī, at

[54] See G. Endress, 'Die dreifache Ancilla: Hermeneutik und Logik im Werk des Sayf-al-Dīn al-Āmidī,' in *Logik und Theologie: das Organon im arabischen und im lateinischen Mittelalter*, ed. D. Perler, U. Rudolph (Leiden: Brill, 2005), 117–45.

[55] Ahlwardt [*v. supra*, n. 53], 4:415–22 no. 5065–75, on the structure of this work and its commentaries.

Mossul, was Sirāj-al-Dīn al-Urmawī (of Konya, m. 682/1283); his *Maṭāliʿ al-anwār*[56] divide philosophy into two 'sides' (*aṭrāf*): *manṭiq* (logic) and *ilāhiyyāt* (res divinae, metaphysics), the latter—as in Rāzī's *ḥikma*, albeit in a different arrangement and subdivision of its parts—into four aqsām, parts: 1. *al-umūr al-ʿāmmiyya* (universalia), 2. *al-aʿrāḍ* (categories/accidents), 3. *al-jawāhir* (substances), and 4. *al-ʿilm al-ilāhī* (theology). The *Hidāya* and its successors were explained in numerous commentaries, supercommentaries and glosses, vehicles of many an original observation and novel tendency while observing the conceptual and systematic structure of the Ibn Sīnā—Rāzī—Ṭūsī lineage of the rational encyclopaædia.

Philosophical theology is merged with the mystical philosophy of the *Shaykh al-ishrāq*, Shihāb-al-Dīn al-Suhrawardī (m. 587/1191) in the attitude of many of the later encyclopædists, interpreting Ibn Sīnā's allegory of the conjunction of the soul with the Active Intellect as a philosophical paradigm of Sūfī mysticism, and re-interpreting the concepts of demonstrative sciences as allegories of mystical illumination.[57] In Marāgha, center of the circle of astronomers around Naṣīr-al-Dīn al-Ṭūsī (m. 672/1274), Urmawī's *Maṭāliʿ* were commented by Rukn-al-Dīn al-Astarābādhī (m. 715/1315),[58] as also by the later philosopher-theologians of Iran: by the Sayyid al-Sharīf al-Jurjānī (m. 816/1416) and Jalāl-al-Dīn al-Dawanı (m. 908/1502). Also active in the circle of al-Ṭūsī was Najm-al-Dīn al-Kātibī al-Qazwīnī (m. 675/1276), who accompanied his popular logic *Risālat al-ʿAyn fī ʿilm al-manṭiq*[59] with an equally famous manual of scholastic theology, the *Ḥikmat ʿayn al-qawāʿid*,[60] in two parts, Metaphysics (*al-ʿilm al-ilāhī*) and Physics (*al-ʿilm al-ṭabīʿī*); the first has five sections, treating the traditional topics of metaphysics: 1. universalia (*al-umūr al-ʿāmma*), 2. causes and effects (*al-ʿilal wa-l-maʿlūlāt*), 3. principles of

---

[56] Ahlwardt, *ibid.* 4:428–32 no. 5087–95.

[57] Allegiance to al-Suhrawardī is paid prominently in the introduction to Quṭb-al-Dīn Shīrāzī's *Durra* and in Dawānī's œuvre. One of the better known glosses of al-Abharī's *Hidāya* is the *ḥāshiya* written in 880/1475 by Mīr Ḥusayn al-Maybudī, who in his concluding words refers the reader to the study of the *shaykhān*, Ibn Sīnā and Shihāb-al-Dīn al-Suhrawardī.

[58] Sellheim, *Materialien* [*v. supra*, n. 52], 1:153–7. On Ṭūsī's school, see also G. Endress, 'Die wissenschaftliche Literatur', *Grundriss* [*v. supra*, n. 43], 2:438f., 495.

[59] On this and other manuals of logic see G. Endress, *ibid.*, 56f.

[60] Ahlwardt [*v. supra*, n. 53], 4:423–8 no. 5080ff., with commentaries by Quṭb-al-Dīn al-Shīrāzī [*v. infra*], Saʿd-al-Dīn al-Taftazānī (m. 792/1390)—see Sellheim, *Materialien* [*v. supra*, n. 52]—and his rival at Timur's court, al-Sharīf al-Jurjānī.

substances and categories (*aḥkām al-jawāhir wa-l-aʿrāḍ*)—and of the *uṣūl* and *furūʿ* of theology proper: 4. proof of the Necessary Being (*ithbāt al-wājib*), 5. principles obtaining in the rational soul (*aḥkām al-nafs al-nāṭiqa*). Ṭūsī's most eminent disciple, Quṭb-al-Dīn al-Shīrāzī (m. 710/1311) annotated the *Ḥikmat al-ʿayn*, taught Ibn Sīnā's *Shifāʾ* at Damascus and commented upon his *Ishārāt*; his own treatment of the philosophic-scientific encyclopædia is the most important work of its genre in the Persian language, the *Durrat al-tāj li-durrat al-Dubāj*, in 5 *jumal*: 1. logic (*manṭiq*), 2. first philosophy (*falsafa-i ūlā*), 3. natural philosophy (*ṭabīʿiyyāt*), 4. mathematical sciences (*riyāḍiyyāt*)—displaying the eminence in mathematics, astronomy and musical theory of Ṭūsī's master pupil—, 5. metaphysics (*ilāhiyyāt*); the disciplines of the *sharīʿa* are added in an appendix (*khātima*): legal methodology (*uṣūl-i dīn*), positive law (*furūʿ*), practical philosophy (*ḥikmat-i ʿamalī*), and political ethics (*sulūk*).

In Iran, the Ṣafavid 'renaissance' brought the most far-reaching renewal and re-interpretation of Ibn Sīnā's, Ṭūsī's and Suhrawardī's schools of *ḥikma*, philosophic 'wisdom'. Launched by Bahāʾ-al-Dīn al-ʿĀmilī (m. 1030/1621) and his successor Shaykh-al-Islām of Isfahan, Muḥammad Bāqir b. Muḥammad (Mīr-i Dāmād, m. 1040/1630—called the 'third teacher' after Aristotle and al-Fārābī!), it was brought to its culmination by Ṣadr-al-Dīn al-Shīrāzī (Mullā Ṣadrā, m. 1050/1640). In his *Asfār al-arbaʿa* we find the last great summa in Avicenna's tradition: four 'Journeys' to metaphysics, physics, theology and (as a *farʿ* of the latter) the doctrine of the soul, transforming the rationalism of Hellenistic philosophy to become a 'theosophy' amalgamating Ibn Sīnā's conceptual framework, the neoplatonism of the Pseudo-Aristotle and of Suhrawardī's *ishrāq*, and the hermeneutics of Shīʿite *kalām*.

In general, Arabic was to stay as principal language of philosophy and the rational sciences in the Iranian East as well as in Anatolia, where the traditions of learning and teaching of the Mongol period branched out—from Ṭūsī's Marāgha in the 12th/13th centuries and Ulugh-Bek's Samarqand in the 15th—well into the Ottoman period,[61] and were presented in encyclopædic manuals: organizing knowledge

[61] See Yaşar Sarıkaya, 'Osmanlı medreselerinde aklî ilimlerin ihmali meselesi üzerine bazı mülahazalar', in *Osmanlı dünyasında bilim ve eṯitim: milletlerarası kongresi, Istanbul 1999* (Istanbul: IRCICA, 2001), 145–58.

in a way representing the practice, breadth and scope of higher education in the great empires of later Islam. Representing the matters as well as the books which were taught in this framework, a number of late Mamluk and Ottoman scholars presented their 'encyclopædic' handbooks in the form of a detailed bibliography of basic texts. Best known is the manual of the Egyptian doctor Ibn al-Akfānī (m. 749/1348), *Iršād al-qāṣid ilā asnā l-maqāṣid*, which in its turn became the model of the 'Key of Happiness' (*Miftāḥ al-saʿāda*) by the Ottoman scholar ʿIṣam-al-Dīn Ṭāšköprüzāde (m. 968/1561); both present the 'highest aim', *al-maqṣad al-asnā*, attained by Muslim scholarship in the later Middle Ages in uniting both traditions, the Islamic and the Hellenistic.[62]

[62] Jan Just Witkam, *De egyptische arts Ibn al-Akfānī en zijn indeling van de wetenschappen* (Leiden, 1989); on Ṭāshköprüzāde pp. 269–76. On the influence of the *Irshād* on the bibliographical chapter in al-Qalqashandī's (m. 821/1418) chancery handbook *Ṣubḥ al-aʿshā* see Gaston Wiet, 'Les classiques du scribe égyptien au XVe siècle', *Studia Islamica*, 18 (1963): 43–80.

ORGANIZING SCIENTIFIC KNOWLEDGE: THE 'MIXED' SCIENCES IN EARLY CLASSIFICATIONS

Elaheh Kheirandish
Harvard University

Introduction

'Mixed' science is an expression most commonly associated with mathematical disciplines such as astronomy, harmonics, optics and mechanics following Aristotle's reference to the first three as "the more natural/physical of the mathematical sciences" (*ta physikôtera tôn mathématôn*), and the last three, as respective subordinates of arithmetic, and plane and solid geometry.[1] Such combined disciplines were, formulated in the Arabic literature, not only in the corresponding language of "mathematical sciences closer to natural science" (*taʿālīm aqrab ilā l-ʿilm al-ṭabīʿī*), or those literally falling "under another" (*aḥad al-ʿilmayn taht al-ākhar*), but also, the "sharing" (*mushtarak*) and "composite" (*murakkab*) nature of disciplines such as optics and mechanics.[2] While devoid of standard forms of expression or classification, these combined disciplines had distinct conceptions and places in the extant literature of the Islamic Middle Ages.[3] The present paper focuses on

---

[1] Aristotle, *Phys.* 194a7: *The Physics*, ed. E. H. Warmington, trans. Philip H. Wicksteed and Francis M. Cornford (Cambridge: Harvard University Press, London: William Heinemann Ltd., 1970), pp. 120–121; *Post.An.* 76a23–26; 78b36–39: *Posterior Analytics*, ed. G. P. Goold, trans. Hugh Tredennick (Cambridge: Harvard University Press, London: William Heinemann Ltd., 1976), pp. 67–69; 89–91; for reference to relevant passages, see also Jonathan Barnes, *Aristotle's Posterior Analytics*, trans. with notes (Oxford: Clarendon Press, 1975), pp. 151–152, where the wording of the *Physics* passage on astronomy, harmonics, optics is given as "the more mathematical of the natural sciences."

[2] For the first two formulations, see the Arabic version of Aristotle's *Physics*: *Arisṭūṭālīs, al-Ṭabīʿa*, ed. ʿAbd-al-Raḥmān Badawī (Cairo: al-Dār al-Qawmiyya, 1964), p. 92; and *Posterior Analytics* [Arabic version] = *Kitāb al-Burhān*, in *Manṭiq Arisṭū*, ed. ʿAbd-al-Raḥmān Badawī, *Islamica*, 7 (Cairo: Dār al-Kutub al-Miṣriyya, 1949), 2:309–465, p. 352; for the case of "sharing" and "composite", see App. I–II.

[3] Elaheh Kheirandish, "Mixed Mathematical Sciences: Optics and Mechanics in the Islamic Middle Ages", *The Cambridge History of Science*, 8 vols., vol. 2, eds. David C. Lindberg and Michael Shank, forthcoming; see also, Elaheh Kheirandish, *The Arabic Version of Euclid's Optics: Kitāb Uqlīdis fī Ikhtilāf al-manāẓir*, 2 vols., Sources in

early classifications, descriptions and distinctions of various formulations of the "mixed sciences", an expression coined only recently and applied initially to astronomy[4] through case studies of optics and mechanics, the two sciences with the closest historical associations and most distinct applications of "mathematical" and "natural" combinations in the scientific literature.[5]

The organization of *scientific* knowledge, an extension of the title of the present volume, may indeed be illuminated by the case of optics and mechanics, two of the more outstanding Islamic scientific traditions from this and other perspectives. An overall picture of premodern practices as referred to in the subtitle, may itself emerge not only through historical classifications and distinctions of optics and mechanics in their earliest and most critical phases, but also through their specific developments and fates in Islamic and European lands in the course of further transmissions and transformations. Through a close examination of the evidence, from both the early and late periods, and in both the Arabic and Persian languages, the various propositions are first enunciated (*v. infra* 'Outlines' I–III) and then demonstrated (*v.* 'Documentations' and Appendices I–III)—following historical models of scientific propositions[6]—as a contribution to a better understanding of themes around and beyond the scope of the present publication.

---

the History of Mathematics and Physical Sciences 16, ed. G. J. Toomer, (New York: Springer, 1999), and "The Many Aspects of Appearances: Arabic Optics to 950 AD," *The Enterprise of Science in Islam: New Perspectives*, eds. Jan P. Hogendijk and Abdelhamid I. Sabra, Dibner Institute Studies in the History of Science and Technology (Cambridge: MIT Press, 2003), pp. 55–83.

[4] F. J. Ragep, *Naṣīr al-Dīn al-Ṭūsī's Memoir on Astronomy*: *al-Tadhkira fī ʿilm al-hay'a*, edition, translation and commentary, 2 vols., Sources in the History of Mathematics and Physical Sciences 12, ed. G. J. Toomer, (New York: Springer, 1993), p. 38; A. I. Sabra, "Configuring the Universe: Aporetic, Problem Solving, and Kinematic Modeling as Themes of Arabic Astronomy," Review Article, Perspectives on Science: Historical, Philosophical, Social, 6, 3 (1998), 288–330, p. 288.

[5] A. I. Sabra, "The Physical and the Mathematical in Ibn al-Haytham's Theory of Light and Vision," reproduced with corrections from *The Commemoration Volume of Bīrūnī International Congress in Tehran* (Tehran: High Council of Culture and Arts, publication no. 38, 1976), reprinted in A. I. Sabra, *Optics, Astronomy and Logic: Studies in Arabic Science and Philosophy*, Collected Studies Series, CS 444 (London: Variorum, 1994), no. VII: 1–20; Sabra, "Ibn al-Haytham's Revolutionary Project in Optics: The Achievement and the Obstacle," *The Enterprise of Science in Islam: New Perspectives*, eds. Hogendijk and Sabra, pp. 85–118; the case of mechanics is awaiting close study from similar angles.

[6] Heath, T. L., "The Formal Division of a Euclidean Proposition," *The Thirteen Books of Euclid's Elements*, translated from the text of Heiberg with introduction and

Outline I. 'Mixed' Sciences: Historical Meaning and Distinctions

The 'mixed' or combined sciences of the Islamic Middle Ages were disciplines most explicitly formulated as "sharing" (*mushtarak*) and "composite" (*murakkab*) mathematical-natural sciences with specific reference to optics and mechanics (App. I–II). These disciplines were, despite non-standard designations and formulations, conceptually and linguistically distinct enough to be contrasted to at least three comparable sets: (b) mathematical or "intermediate" (*awsaṭ*) sciences (the "quadrivium" of arithmetic, geometry, astronomy and music and their subdivisions) (App. Ib); (c) inter-mathematical or "intermediary" (*mutawassiṭ*) sciences (several subjects, from algebra and spherical astronomy to optics and mechanics, studied intermediately between geometry and astronomy) (App. Ic); and (d) comprehensive or "collective" (*jāmiʿ*) sciences/crafts (*ṣināʿa*), a term which in its turn was used interchangeably with "sharing" (*mushtarik*) sciences/crafts (*ṣināʿa*) for cases not limited to two components or mathematical and natural combinations, as in the case of medicine (*ṭibb*), surveying (*misāḥa*), secretarial arts (*kitāba*) (App. I.d).

Outline II. Mathematical-Natural 'Mix': Formulations and Combinations

The earlier "sharing" (*mushtarak*) sciences, involving components within or beyond the fields of mathematics and natural philosophy, sc. of optics and mechanics (App. I.a,d; II.a), were themselves predecessors to the later "composite" (*murakkab*) sciences, an expression used in connection with the subset of mixed *mathematical* sciences and with reference to the combinations of mathematical and natural sciences in the same two disciplines. The latter formulation, while present in some form early on, finds full expression much later, in optics through Ibn al-Haytham (d. ca. 432/1040), and in mechanics, through al-Khāzinī (d. 593/1196), with more formulations and applications in the case of the former than are found in the latter (App. II.b–d and e respectively).

commentary, second edition, 3 vols. (Cambridge: Cambridge University Press, 1926; reprinted New York: Dover Publications, 1956). The Arabic forms: *khabar* (enunciation), and *burhān* (demonstration), appear along with their intermediate steps in Yaʿqūbī's *Taʾrīkh*, ed. M. Th. Houtsma, 2 vols. (Leiden: E. J. Brill, 1883), vol. I, p. 136.

Outline III. 'Mixed' Traditions: Organization and Transmission

A standard designation for 'mixed' or combined sciences is not often found in early Arabic classifications such as those by al-Fārābī (d. 339/950) or al-Khwārizmī (d. ca. 367/977), not even in the later Persian ones by Ṭūsī (d. 672/1274) or Shīrāzī (d. 711/1311). But the evidence, including the less known early treatises by Qusṭā ibn Lūqā (d. ca. 300/912)[7] indicates that: a) the relevant conceptions and distinctions are present in the early literature of science and its classification (App. II.a–b); and b) 'mixed' mathematical sciences such as optics and mechanics are themselves not always representing the same scholarly organization or transmission (App. III.c–d), apparently not without consequence.

Documentation I. 'Mixed' Sciences: Historical Meaning and Distinctions: What they are and what they are not in the light of historical formulations

In order to identify 'mixed' sciences according to their historical formulations and distinctions, it would not be enough to state what they *were* without stressing what they *were not*. Given their non-explicit Greek formulation on the one hand (as the physico-mathematical sciences of optics, mechanics, astronomy and harmonics), and non-standard Arabic expressions on the other hand (as "sharing", "composite" mathematical-natural sciences with reference to the first two), it may be best to first determine what the 'mixed' or combined sciences of the Islamic Middle Ages were *not*. From comparable cases alone it may be determined that, despite natural overlaps, 'mixed' mathematical sciences were *not* the same as "mathematical" (*riyāḍī*) disciplines,[8] also referred to as *ʿilm al-awsaṭ* (or *miyāngīn* in Persian)

[7] E. Ruth Harvey, "Qusṭā ibn Lūqā," *Dictionary of Scientific Biography*, XI, pp. 244–246; Elaheh Kheirandish, "Qusṭā ibn Lūqā," *Biographical Encyclopedia of Astronomers* (*BEA*, forthcoming).

[8] Some common designations are: *al-ʿulūm al-riyāḍiyya* (mathematical sciences), *al-ʿulūm al-taʿlīmiyya* or *taʿālīm* (instructional/pedagogical sciences), *riyāḍiyyāt* (mathematics); for general treatments, see Gerhard Endress, "Mathematische Wissenschaften," *Grundriss der arabischen Philologie*, vol. 3: Supplement (Wiesbaden: Ludwig Reichert Verlag, 1992), pp. 62–116; Roshdi Rashed, "Riyāḍiyyāt," *Encyclopaedia of Islam*, 2nd edition (EI²), 8 (1994), fasc. 139–140, pp. 549–562; J. L. Berggren, "The Mathematical Sciences," *History of Civilizations in Central Asia*, 4 volumes, vol. 4: *The Age of Achievement:*

in the ontological sense of being *positioned* intermediately between the lower (*asfal*) or natural/physical (*ṭabīʿī*) sciences, and the higher (*aʿlā*) or metaphysical (*ilāhī*) sciences, and often represented by the four mainstream disciplines of arithmetic, geometry, astronomy and music as subjects of the classical quadrivium (App. I.b); neither were they identical with inter-mathematical or "intermediary" (*mutawassiṭ*) sciences, the latter being the subjects of the "Intermediate/Middle Books" (*al-Kutub al-Mutawassiṭāt*)[9] in the *instructional* sense of being intermediately studied after Euclid's *Elements* and before Ptolemy's *Almagest* (specifically, Euclid's *Optika, Data*, and *Phaenomena*; Theodosius's and Menelaus's *Spherics*, and Autolycus's *Moving Sphere* and *Rising and Setting* (App. I.c). What was, rather, referred to, in the case of optics and mechanic at least, as "sharing" (*mushtarak*) and "composite" (*murakkab*) disciplines as early as the 3rd/9th and as late as the 6th/12th centuries respectively, was understood in the *methodological* sense of a mixed discipline: 'participating' not only in the topical sense of shared subjects (in this case, mathematics and natural philosophy), but also in the procedural sense of combined methods (App. I.a; II.a–d). As such, 'mixed' mathematical-physical sciences were further distinguished from the so-called "collective" sciences/crafts (*ṣināʿa jāmiʿa*) or "sharing" sciences/crafts (*ṣināʿā mushtaraka*), when associated with respect to more than two components, or disciplines other than mathematics and natural philosophy, as in the case of medicine, surveying and secretarial arts (App. I.d).

There is, in fact, more than one case of evidence indicating that at least the so-called "sharing" (*mushtarak*), *mathematical* sciences, had clear conceptions from early on. The evidence is as early as an optical composition by Ibn Lūqā, the translator and scholar of Greek origin working in Baghdad during the 3rd/9th century, where he states that "The best of the demonstrative sciences are those in which there is a sharing (*ishtirāk*) [i.e. combination] of natural science and

A.D. 750 to the End of the Fifteenth Century, part 2, eds. C. E. Bosworth, M. S. Asimov (Paris: UNESCO, 1992), pp. 182–193. The "ontological" sense of mathematical sciences (as distinct from instructional and methodological senses) benefits from the constructive remarks of Gerhard Endress during the conference preceding the present publication.

9 On the "Intermediate Works", see Moritz Steinschneider, "Die 'mittleren' Bücher der Araber und ihre Bearbeiter," *Zeitschrift für Mathematik und Physik, 10* (1865), 456–498.

geometrical science", before claiming that none is "better and more perfect than the science of rays (*ʿilm al-shuʿāʿāt*) [i.e. optics]" (App. I.a); in mechanics, an apparently early Arabic version of the pseudo-Aristotelian *Mechanics*, is where "mechanical problems" (*al-masāʾil al-ḥiyaliyya*) are said to be have "a share (*mushtaraka*) in both mathematical (*riyāḍiyya*) and natural (*ṭabīʿiya*) sciences, the how (*kayf*) in them belong[ing] to mathematical sciences, and the what (*mādhā*), to natural sciences" (App. II.a).

There is also evidence that such early formulations, anticipating the so-called "composite" (*murakkab*) *mathematical* sciences of the more celebrated periods of scientific synthesis (in optics, in three works by Ibn al-Haytham, and in mechanics, in at least one work by al-Khāzinī) (see Section II; App. II.a–e), were not just distinct, but *conscious* formulations. Strongest among such evidence is the formulation of several comparable, yet distinct, early expressions for the very conception of a 'mixed' science, not only by one and the same author, but also in one and the same work. An example of the first kind is the side-by-side appearance of such distinct expressions as "intermediate" (*awsaṭ*), "intermediary" (*mutawassiṭ*), "collective" (*jāmiʿ*), and "sharing" (*mushtarak*) sciences/crafts (*ṣināʿa*) in the work of an early author such as Ibn Lūqā [*Classes of Crafts* (*ṣināʿāt*): App. I.a–d]. An example of the second kind is the appearance of a term such as the "sharing" (*ishtirāk*) of the natural and mathematical sciences in his equally little known *Optics* (App. I.a), not only in a similar sense in other early works, as in the anonymous *Mechanical Problems* already quoted above (App. II.a), but also in a different sense in Ibn Lūqā's own works, as the "sharing" of crafts (*ṣināʿa mushtaraka*) such as linguistic (*kalāmiyya*), operative (*ʿamaliyya*), and productive (*fiʿliyya*), in sciences apart from optics and mechanics (App. I.d). All such early formulations are of great interest for the shift, however subtle, in a conception so central to the organization of scientific knowledge, the conceptual shift from a more neutral "participation" (*ishtirāk*) of a particular science in two or more disciplines (sc. mathematical and natural disciplines in the case of a 'mixed' *mathematical* science) (App. I.a; App. II.a), to a more active "combination" (*tarkīb*) of those or other components, applied this time, consciously and explicitly, to both subject *and* method (App. II.d).

Documentation II. Mathematical-Natural 'Mix', Formulations and Combinations: When and where they occur in historical sources and how they are formulated or combined

It is indeed in the sense of "sharing" or "participation" in two or more scientific disciplines or traditions that the conception of a 'mixed' science seems to have been initially expressed in the Arabic scientific literature. Qusṭā ibn Lūqā has, in fact, what is arguably, not just the earliest, but the closest expressions of such a conception: In his classification of the sciences, he refers directly to "sharing sciences/crafts" (*sināʿa mushtaraka*) as a class (*ṣinf*) of sciences/crafts, defined as "gathering" (*jamʿ*) a number of others, i.e. disciplines as diverse as medicine (*ṭibb*), surveying (*misāha*) and secretarial arts (*kitāba*) (App. I.d). In another rarely mentioned treatise on optics, Ibn Lūqā speaks more specifically—and indeed prophetically—of the best of the demonstrative sciences being those which participate (*ishtirāk*) in mathematics and natural philosophy, and the best form of such coming together (*jamʿ*) being that of the science of optics (App. I.a).

The evidence for the early association of these same expressions with the science of mechanics, is no less notable. This is not originating from the author who is credited, among other works on the subject, with the surviving Arabic translation of Heron of Alexandria's important *Mechanica*,[10] but from the anonymous Arabic author of the [pseudo-] Aristotelian *Problemata Mechanica*, talking about the subject matter of mechanics in the problematic and crucially important opening passage of the first book. He conveys the same sense of "[co-]participation" when he describes mechanical problems (*al-masāʾil al-ḥiyaliyya*) as "having a share" (*mushtarak*) in mathematical and physical problems (*al-masāʾil al-ṭabīʿiyya*), thereby making a clear and unmistakable distinction between *mechanical* and *physical* problems (App. II.a). It is, however, through a different expression, that of "composite" (*murakkab*) sciences, found as early as the Arabic versions of Aristotle's *Physics* (reportedly translated and commentated by none other than Ibn

[10] Qusṭā ibn Lūqā (tr.), *Book of Heron on the Lifting of Weighty Objects* (*Kitāb Īrun fī Rafʿ al-ashyāʾ al-thaqīlah*), edition and German translation: L. Nix und W. Schmidt, *Herons von Alexandria Mechanik und Katoptrik* (Leipzig: Teubner, 1900); on the content and importance and content of Heron's *Mechanics*, see A. G. Drachmann, *The Mechanical Technology of Greek and Roman Antiquity* (Copenhagen: Munksgaard, 1963).

Lūqā, among others),[11] that combinations of mathematical and physical entities find their fullest and best forms of expression in both optics and mechanics.

There are at least three explicit descriptions of the combination of mathematical and physical concepts in Ibn al-Haytham's optical works—descriptions that are all expressed in the terms of "composition" (*tarkīb*). The "Optics" (*Kitāb al-Manāẓir*) describes the combined nature of its subject, the study of vision, in terms of sight, being, as one of the senses, the *natural* component, and perceptible objects such as magnitudes with geometrical shapes, as being the *mathematical* component (App. II.b). The "Treatise on Light" (*Risāla fī l-ḍaw'*), written after the *Optics*, describes the combination as one between *physical natures* (of such matters as light, rays or transparent bodies) and *mathematical forms* (such as shapes, structures, and angles of radiation), adding questions of essence (what), of accident (how) and cause (why) (App. II.c); and "The Rainbow and Halo" (*Qaws quzaḥ wa-l-hāla*), written ten years before Ibn al-Haytham's death, goes further to describe the combination, no longer in terms of the respective involvement of subjects such as air (*natural*) and shapes such as circles and segments (*mathematical*), but also, the composite (*murakkab*) nature of inquiries (*naẓar*) required for composite subjects (App. II.d). Al-Khāzinī comes to extend the same expression to other subjects when he writes in his "Balance of Wisdom" [or "Philosophical Balance"] (*Mīzān al-ḥikma*): "Every science/craft (*ṣināʿa*) is combined (*murakkab*) of geometrical and natural crafts through the two complementary (*jāmiʿ*) categories of quantity (*kamm*) and quality (*kayf*)", before stating that the mechanical subject of his discussion (*al-mīzān al-ʿadl*) is "founded upon geometrical demonstrations (*al-barāhīn al-handasiyya*), and deduced from physical causes (*al-ʿilal al-ṭabīʿiyya*)" (App. II.e). Whereas the statements of Ibn al-Haytham in general, and their methodological consequences in particular, represent outstanding and irreversible transformations in the conceptions and applications of optics, the relevant statements of al-Khāzinī in his celebrated mechanical work seem to have been rather limited in scope,[12] and not going beyond

[11] On the Arabic versions and commentaries of Aristotle's *Physics*, including Ibn Lūqā's reported translation, see F. E. Peters, *Aristoteles Arabus*: The Oriental Translations and Commentaries on the Aristotelian Corpus (Leiden: E. J. Brill, 1968), pp. 30–34.

[12] See Robert E. Hall, "Al-Khāzinī, Abu'l-Fatḥ ʿAbd al-Raḥmān," *Dictionary of Scientific Biography*, VII: 335–351, pp. 336–337: "Al-Khāzinī's scientific accomplishments", esp. p. 337 on the limited impact of his important scientific work.

Ibn Lūqā's assertion in a much earlier work that optics "gets from natural philosophy, 'sense perception' (*idrāk ḥissī*), and from mathematics, 'geometric demonstrations' (*barāhīn khuṭūṭiyya*)" (App. I.a). In retrospective, no statement by al-Khāzinī or any one else before or after him, comes even close to the prophetic statements of the opening lines of Quṣṭā's treatise, one of the earliest and least known scientific compositions of the Islamic Middle Ages—that optics is the "best and most perfect" (*akhtharu ḥusnan wa-kamālan*) of such 'mixed' or combined sciences (ibid.).

Documentation III. 'Mixed' Traditions, Organization and Transmission: In what forms or divisions are 'mixed' traditions organized and transmitted

A moment's glance at the standard classifications of the sciences is enough to reveal that while there are several expressions such as "mathematical sciences" (*al-ʿulūm al-riyāḍiyah, taʿlīmiyyah, taʿālīm, riyāḍiyyāt*) or their cognates, "intermediate science" (*al-ʿilm al-awsat, ʿilm-i miyāngīn*)—usually under foreign, "non-Arab" (*al-ʿajam*) or "ancient" sciences (*ʿulūm al-awāʾil*) to distinguish them from native, "Arab" (*al-ʿarabiyya*), or "Islamic/legal sciences" (*al-ʿulūm al-sharʿīyya*) (App. III.f)—there is no terminology corresponding to the 'mixed' or 'mixed mathematical' sciences in such classifications, whether early or late, Arabic or Persian.[13] The closest case in the classification literature itself is that of Ibn Lūqā's "Classes of sciences/crafts" (*Aṣnāf al-ṣināʿāt*), where there are such categories as "sharing" (*mushtaraka*) and "gathering" (*jāmiʿa*) crafts/sciences (*ṣināʿa*) (App. I.d). But even there, it is clear from both the examples of such collective sciences (medicine, surveying, secretarial arts), and the components forming those disciplines

[13] On Greek and Latin classifications, see James A. Weisheipl, "The Nature, Scope, and Classification of the Sciences," *Science in the Middle Ages*, pp. 461–482; on the Islamic Middle Ages, see F. E. Peters, *Aristotle and the Arabs: The Aristotelian Tradition in Islam* (New York: New York University Press, London: University Press of London, 1968), pp. 104–120; A. Cortabarria Beitia, O.P., "La Classification des sciences chez al-Kindi," *Institut Dominicain d'Etudes Orientales: Mélanges* (Cairo: Dar al-Maaref), 11 (1972): 49–76; Franz Rosenthal, *The Classical Heritage in Islam*, translated by E. and J. Marmorstein (London: Routledge and Kegan Paul, 1975), pp. 52–73; Jean Jolivet, "Classification of the Sciences," in Roshdi Rashed, ed., *Encyclopedia of the History of Arabic Science*, 3 vols. (London: Routledge, 1996), vol. 3, pp. 1008–1025; and Mahdi Muhaqqiq, "The Classification of the Sciences," *The Different Aspects of Islamic Culture*, Volume Four: Science and Technology in Islam, part I: Science, editor, A. Y. al-Hassan, co-editors, M. Ahmed and A. Z. Iskandar (Paris: UNESCO publishing, 2002), pp. 111–131.

(linguistic, productive, operative sciences/crafts), that a 'mixed' mathematical subject such as optics and mechanics, would only fall under such a classification by extension. We have seen, on the other hand, that scientific writings, including those of Ibn Lūqā himself, contain a distinct formulation—if not a single expression—of mixed sciences such as optics and mechanics. It remains to be seen what other formulations of the concept there may be, and in what genre of literature they occur most frequently.

What is clear from the outset is that the terms encountered in the scientific literature, from "sharing" and "combining" to "composite" sciences, are not likely to be found as a standard division within the classification literature, neither in the earlier Arabic classifications of al-Kindī, al-Fārābī or al-Khwārizmī, nor in the later Persian classifications of Ibn Sīnā, Ṭūsī, or Shīrāzī (App. III.a–b). But at least one of these classifications—the rich and influential *Catalogue* of al-Fārābī—contains, if not a separate division, a clear formulation not only of the concept of a 'mixed' science, but also the nature of their mathematical and natural components, in the long entries under optics and mechanics, each with two divisions (App. III.c, d–e).

In the case of optics, the "science of aspects" (*ʿilm al-manāẓir*) or direct vision, distinguished from the "science of mirrors" (*ʿilm al-marāyā*) or indirect vision (i.e. mediated appearances), is described as a study of vision that involves a *natural* phenomenon, namely vision, and *mathematical* reasoning applied to it through "certain demonstrations" (*al-barāhīn al-yaqīniyya*) (App. III.c–d). The "science of mechanics" (*ʿilm al-ḥiyal*), on the other hand, itself distinguished from the "science of weights" (*ʿilm al-athqāl*), is described as "the knowledge of the procedure by which one applies *mathematical* statements and proofs (*barāhīn*) to natural (*ṭabīʿī*), perceptible (*maḥsūs*) bodies" (App. III.d). Such descriptions representing clear formulations and distinct conceptions even in the absence of standard classifications, reveal not only al-Farābī's atypical classification of mathematical sciences such as optics and mechanics as part of "mathematical science" (*ʿilm al-taʿālīm*), *along with* the four mainstream sciences of arithmetic, geometry, astronomy, and music (however different from each other, see below), but also, different mathematical and natural components being involved in two mathematical disciplines *both* classified as *sub-divisions* of geometry: optics involving the *natural* phenomenon of appearances undergoing *mathematical* demonstrations to explain appearances (*manāẓir*), and mechanics, involving *mathematical* ideas and *natural* bodies that need preparation to convey those ideas through devices/

contrivances (*ḥiyal*) (App. II.a–b). Close attention to the particular divisions and formulations of this rich and influential work, makes it clear that the classifications and conceptions of optics and mechanics, despite their common status of mathematical arts, and of dual-component disciplines (mathematics and natural philosophy), with two-fold subdivisions, are quite distinct when it comes to the exact components of their combined constitutions.

Even in cases such as the [pseudo]-Aristotelian *Mechanica*, where "mechanical problems" have a "share in both mathematical and natural speculations (the 'how' coming from mathematics, and the 'what' from natural philosophy)" (App. II.a), the 'what-how' combination of the mechanical tradition can be distinguished from the 'that-why' of the optical traditions: the latter is where the corresponding natural and mathematical components are *topically* distinct as the physical natures and mathematical shapes of entities such as optical rays, and also methodologically, as in the physical set-ups and mathematical tests of optical demonstrations.

The fields of optics, mechanics, harmonics, and astronomy may indeed all be considered 'mixed' mathematical sciences, for their integration of non-mathematical areas in general and natural philosophy in particular. But they cannot be considered as being analogous in their functional structure because they were not 'mixed' in the same sense, beginning with Aristotle. The Aristotelian description of optics, harmonics and astronomy as "the mathematical sciences closer to natural philosophy" points to the mixed nature of their subjects, while the subordination of mechanics, optics and harmonics to solid and plane geometry and arithmetic respectively, concerns the hierarchical division of their otherwise mixed methods. The subordinate vs. superior division of Aristotelian classification placed particularly strict limitations on the nature of such a mix: the distinction between knowledge of the fact (*to hoti*) and of the reason why (*to dioti*)—the observation of the *fact* that something is in a certain way and the reasoning *why* it is that way—, was not merely a distinction between the so-called "that" and "why" proofs, where the proof of a *fact* such as the circularity of the heavens came from observational astronomy, and the explanation of the reason why, as one involving nature of bodies, from natural philosophy.[14] As subordinate sciences

[14] On the knowledge of the fact (*to hoti*) and of the reason why (*to dioti*), see Aristotle, *An. post.* I.13, Arabic expressions (*anna al-shayʾ*, *lima al-shayʾ*): *Kitāb al-Burhān*,

were to demonstrate the "facts" (statements or observations), and superior sciences, the "reasoned facts" (proofs), only proofs from the superior sciences such as geometry or arithmetic could be applied to subordinate sciences such as optics and mechanics (in the case of geometry), and harmonics (in the case of arithmetic). Such principles were also applicable to further subdivisions, for example, demonstrations in optics were to be used in the study of rainbows, and those in astronomy, in the study of the phenomena,[15] before more open systems were to bring closer the methods of mathematical and natural sciences, in particular.

The Arabic traditions of optics, mechanics, astronomy and music[16] all had notable developments and breakthroughs, without representing similar or comparable cases in general, and of method in particular, even with the same authors working on more than one such 'mixed' science. Scholars engaged in one of the mixed sciences were typically involved with at least one other. Authors on the science of optics (*ʿilm al-manāẓir*) or heavenly configurations (*ʿilm al-hayʾa*), would also write, for example, on the sciences of mechanics (*ʿilm al-ḥiyal*) or weights (*ʿilm al-athqāl*), and occasionally, on all those subjects at once, as in the case of Qusṭā ibn Lūqā. Some of the best known names associated with weights and balances, Thābit ibn Qurra (d. ca. 289/901), Abū Rayḥan al-Bīrūnī (d. ca. 440/1048), and ʿAbd al-Raḥmān al-Khāzinī (fl. ca. 509–525/1115–1130), were among the great names of astronomy, just as the main authors on music (*ʿilm al-taʾlīf, ʿilm al-mūsīqī*), Yaʿqūb al-Kindī (d. ca. 257/870), Abū ʿAlī Ibn Sīnā (Avicenna, d. ca. 429/1037), Naṣīr al-Dīn al-Ṭūsī (d. 672/1274),

ed. Badawī, pp. 349–353 and p. 352); on "that" (*annī*) and "why" (*limī*) proofs in astronomy, see Ragep, Naṣīr al-Dīn al-Ṭūsī's *Memoir on Astronomy*, II.1, p. 386; on the Latin "*quia, propter* quid", see A. Crombie, Robert Grosseteste and the Origins of Experimental Science 1100–1700 (Oxford: Clarendon Press, 1962), pp. 25–26 and pp. 53–54.

[15] Aristotle, *An. Post.* 76a24, *An. Post.* 79a10, and *An. Post.* 78b39, Loeb ed., pp. 67–69, and 89–91 respectively; On the latter, see Berggren, J. L. and Robert S. D. Thomas, "Mathematical Astronomy in the Fourth Century B.C. as Found in Euclid's *Phaenomena*", *Physis*, 29 (Firenze, 1992): 7–33.

[16] See entries in *EI*[2] under "Manāẓir, 'Ilm al-manāẓir" (the science of optics); "mīzān" (balance); "'Ilm al-hay'a", "Nujūm" (astronomy), and "Mūsīqī" (music): A. I. Sabra, "Manāẓir, or 'Ilm al-Manāẓir," *EI*[2], VI (1987), fasc. 103–104, 376–377; Eilhard Wiedemann, "al-Mīzān," *EI*[2], VII (1991), fasc. 117–118, 195–204; David Pingree, "'Ilm al-hay'a," *EI*[2], III (1970), fasc. 57–58, 1135–1138; Paul Kunitzsch, "al-Nujūm," *EI*[2], VIII (1992), 97–105; O. Wright, "Mūsīqī, later Mūsīqā," *EI*[2], VII (1992), fasc. 125–126, 681–688.

and Quṭb al-Dīn al-Shīrāzī (d. 711/1311),[17] all covered optics from classification to theory.

Among the Aristotelian mixed sciences commonly classified as subdivisions of a mathematical science, it was optics that made particularly good use of such a mixed constitution in its subsequent transmission. A mixed science mentioned by Aristotle, not only repeatedly, but specifically with reference to both subject and method, the optics of Aristotle had a clearly mixed subject, as optical entities such as "visual-rays" were explicitly described in the *Physics* as "mathematical lines *qua* natural/physical, not *qua* mathematical." And the application of geometrical proofs to physico-mathematical lines for explanations of various appearances, clearly amounted to mixing a mathematical method with a natural phenomenon such as vision. But this was hardly an unqualified mix insofar as demonstrations of the *Posterior Analytics* were restricted to geometrical proofs for the study of optics, and to optical proofs for studies such as that of the rainbow.[18] The case of Arabic optics, however, may be distinguished from both the Greek traditions and the Arabic tradition of other mixed sciences, for the integration of natural methods—and not just subjects—into optical demonstrations, often in the form of a physical set-up next to geometrical proofs, in optical texts as early as the mid-3rd/9th century.

A comparison of optics to a mixed science such as mechanics is of particular interest in light of the fact that despite common features in their capacities as subdivisions of geometry (plane and solid, respectively), and subsets of the Aristotelian mixed sciences (alongside astronomy and music), the two disciplines were at times classified differently—if not inconsistently—in terms of hierarchical and lateral disciplinary positions. We can readily see, for example, that while optics is altogether missing from an early work of classification such as al-Khwārizmī's "Keys to the Sciences", where mechanics is represented in most of its early variations (App. III.f), the same may not be said of another uncommon treatment, that of al-Fārābī's "Enumeration of the Sciences," where optics occupies a prominent position (between the mainstream mathematical disciplines of geometry and astronomy)

[17] There are entries on these and other relevant figures in both the *Encyclopaedia of Islam (EI) and Dictionary of Scientific Biography (DSB)*.

[18] Aristotle, *An. Post.* 78b36, Loeb edn. pp. 66–67, Arabic: Badawi edn., p. 353.

and far ahead of mechanics (the last entry under mathematical sciences with its own two divisions) (App. III.c–d).

In the absence of studies devoted to the rather uncommon, and possibly consequential case of optics as compared to both mechanics and the other 'mixed' sciences, the most that may be presently noted is the particularly outstanding breakthrough of optics in both medieval and early modern Europe, where besides the "good fortune" of scientific works such as Ibn al-Haytham's *Optics*, the wide transmission of classifications such as Fārābī's *Catalogue*[19] may have itself played a decisive role. As such, the question of the relation between the organization, transmission, and indeed transformation, of scientific knowledge, may itself move beyond the realm of the *facts*, and unto the "how"s and "why"s.

Appendix I. 'Mixed' Sciences: Historical Meaning and Distinctions

a. Qusṭā ibn Lūqā (d. ca. 300/912–13), *Fī ʿIlal mā yaʿriḍu fī l-marāyā min ikhtilāf al-manāẓir*, MS. Mashhad: Āstān-i Quds, 392 (5593), 1: 1–31, 867H (French trans., R. Rashed, *Œuvres philosophiques et scientifiques d'al-Kindī*, Leiden: Brill, 1997, 571–645, 573; English trans., E. Kheirandish, "'Mixed' Mathematical Sciences: Optics and Mechanics in the Islamic Middle Ages," *Cambridge History of Science*, ed. David Lindberg and Michael Shank, v. 2, forthcoming).

> The best of the demonstrative sciences (*al-ʿulūm al-burhāniyya*) are those in which there is sharing (*ishtirāk*) of natural science (*al-ʿilm al-ṭabīʿī*) and geometrical science (*al-ʿilm al-handasī*), because it acquires from natural science (*al-ʿilm al-ṭabīʿī*), sense perception (*al-idrāk al-ḥissī*), and from geometrical science (*al-ʿilm al-handasī*), demonstrations through lines (*al-barāhīn al-khuṭūṭiyya*)" . . . and nothing in which these two sciences/crafts (*ṣināʿatān*) gather (*tajtamiʿ*) is found better and more perfect (*aktharu kamālan*) than in the science of rays (*ʿilm al-shuʿāʿāt*) [i.e. optics].

[19] Al-Fārābī, Abū Naṣr, *Iḥṣāʾ al-ʿulūm*, ed. ʿUthmān Amīn [= Osman Amine], (Cairo: Librairie Anglo-Égyptienne, 1968) [earlier editions, Cairo, 1931, 1949; Arabic edition from Escorial manuscript by A. González Palencia, *Alfarabi, Catálogo de las Sciencias* (ACLS), includes two medieval Latin and a modern Spanish translation (Madrid, 1932). On the wide transmission of the Optics of Alhazen, including two Latin versions, one Italian translation, and a printed edition, see Sabra, *The Optics of Ibn al-Haytham*.

b. Qusṭā ibn Lūqā (d. ca. 300/912–13), *Min kalām Qusṭā ibn Lūqā*, MS. Aya Sofya 4855, 78–81, ca. 1313H (German trans.: Hans Daiber, "Qosṭā ibn Lūqā (9. Jh.) über die Einteilung der Wissenschaften", Zeitschrift für Geschichte der arabisch-islamischen Wissenschaften, 6 [1990]: 93–129, 105):

> Philosophy (*falsafa*) is theoretical (*ʿilmī*) and practical (*ʿamalī*); theoretical (*ʿilmī*) [philosophy] has three divisions (*qism*): lower science (*al-ʿilm al-asfal*) or natural science (*al-ʿilm al-ṭabīʿī*) . . ., the intermediate science (*al-ʿilm al-awsaṭ*) or mathematical science (*al-ʿilm al-riyāḍī*) . . . and the third is the upper science (*al-ʿilm al-aʿlā*) or the science of metaphysics (*ʿilm mā baʿd al-ṭabīʿa*) . . .

c. Qusṭā ibn Lūqā (d. ca. 300/912–13) attributed with the translation of few of the Middle Books:

> The *Optica* (*Manāẓir*), *Data* (*Muʿṭiyāt*), and *Phaenomena* (*Ẓāhirāt*) of Euclid (Uqlīdis), *Spherics* (*Ukar*) of Theodosius (Thāwudūsiyūs) and Menelaus (Minālāwus), and the *Moving Sphere* (*Kura mutaḥarraka*), and *Rising and Setting* (*Ṭulūʿ wa-ghurūb*) of Autolycus (Uṭūlūqūs).

d. Qusṭā ibn Lūqā (d. ca. 300/912–13), *Min kalām Qusṭā ibn Lūqā*, MS. Aya Sofya 4855, 78–81, ca. 1313H (German trans.: Hans Daiber, "Qosṭā ibn Lūqā (9. Jh.) über die Einteilung der Wissenschaften", 1990, 102–104): Four Classes of crafts (*ṣinaʿat*):

> i. Linguistic (*kalāmiyya*): learnt through statements (*qawl*) only: the crafts of dialectic (*jadal*), rhetoric (*khiṭāba*), poetry (*shiʿr*), and grammer (*naḥw*)
>
> ii. Productive (*fiʿliyya*): production by instruments (*fiʿliyya āliyya*), operates (*ʿamal*) by hands and instruments (*ālāt*) on a subject (*mawḍūʿ*), as in the crafts of carpentry (*najjāra*), construction (*bannāʾ*), and goldsmithing (*ṣiyāgha*).
>
> iii. Operative (*ʿamaliyya*):
>
> [1] The craft of operation (*ʿamaliyya*) by hands: operates (*ʿamal*) by hand or body, without an instrument (*āla*), and not on a subject (*mawḍūʿ*) other than that of the practice (*fiʿl*), as in the craft of wrestling (*ṣirāʿ*), dance (*raqṣ*), and singing (*ghināʾ*).
>
> [2] The craft of operation (*ʿamal*) by hands, with an instrument (*āla*), such as arms (*silāḥ*) and subjects (*mawḍūʿ*) such as peoples' bodies, e.g. the craft of wars (*ḥurūb*), exercises (*riyāḍa*), and fencing (*muthāqafa*).
>
> [The distinction between the "productive" (*fiʿliyya*) crafts (II) and "operative" (*ʿamaliyya*) crafts (III) is that with the former, operation (*ʿamal*) remains with the cease (*bāṭil*) of its crafter (*ṣāniʿ*) as in building constructions, but not in the latter, as in body exercises].

iv. Collective (*jāmiʿ*): The craft having a share in (*ṣināʿa mushtaraka min*) all these [crafts], as in medicine (*ṭibb*), surveying (*misāḥa*) or secretarial (*kitāba*) crafts.

Appendix II. Mathematical-Natural 'Mix': Formulations and Combinations

a. Anonymous, *al-Masāʾil al-ḥiyaliyya* ("Mechanical Problems"), Greek ed. 847a24–847b in Aristotle, *Minor Works*, Loeb, p. 331 (English translation: M. Abattouy, in "*Nutaf min al-ḥiyal*: a partial Arabic version of Pseudo-Aristotle's *Problemata Mechanica*," *Early Science and Medicine*, 6, 2 (2001): 96–122, pp. 110–112):

> In every difficult action which happens contrary to nature, mechanical artifices (*al-ḥiyal al-ṣināʿatiyya*) are needed, and for this reason the lesser (*aṣāghir*) [things] overcome the greater (*akābir*). Mechanical problems (*al-masāʾil al-ḥiyaliyya*) are common to (*mushtaraka*) [i.e. have a share in] both mathematical (*riyāḍiyya*) and natural (*ṭabīʿiya*) sciences, for the how (*kayf*) in them belongs to mathematical sciences, and the what (*mādhā*), to natural sciences.

b. Ibn al-Haytham, *Kitāb al-Manāẓir* (ed. A. I. Sabra, Books I–II–III <*On Direct Vision*>, Kuwait: The National Council for Culture, Arts and Letters, 1983, p. 60, English translation, A. I. Sabra, in *The Optics of Ibn al-Haytham: Books I–III, On Direct Vision*, 2 vols., London, 1989, vol. I: 3–4):

> Our subject is obscure and the way leading to knowledge of its nature difficult; moreover, our inquiry requires a combination (murakkab) of the natural and mathematical sciences. It is dependent on the natural sciences because vision is one of the senses and these belong to natural (*ṭabīʿī*) things. It is dependent on the mathematical (*taʿlīmī*) sciences because sight perceives shape, position, magnitude, movement and rest, in addition to its being characterized by straight lines; and since it is the mathematical (*taʿlīmī*) sciences that investigate these things, the inquiry to our subject truly combines (*murakkab*) the natural and mathematical sciences . . .

c. Ibn al-Haytham, *Maqāla* (or *Qawl*) *fī al-Ḍawʾ* ("The Discourse on Light"), *Majmūʿ al-rasāʾil*, Hyderabad, 1357 (= 1938–39) (English translation: A. I. Sabra in "The Physical and the Mathematical in Ibn al-Haytham's Theory of Light and Vision," *The Commemoration Volume of Bīrūnī International Congress in Tehran*, Tehran: High Council of Culture and Arts, 1976: 439–478 [reprinted in Sabra, *Optics*,

Astronomy and Logic, 1994, VII: 1–20], p. 7, quoted in Sabra, *The Optics*, I–III, v. ii, p. 5):

> Discussion of the nature of light belongs to the natural sciences, and the discussion of the manner of radiation of light depends upon the mathematical sciences on account of the lines on which the lights extend. Again, discussion of the nature of ray belongs to the natural sciences, and the discussion of its shape and structure to the mathematical sciences. And similarly with regard to the transparent bodies through which lights pass: discussion of the nature of their transparency belongs to the natural sciences, and discussion of how (*kayfiyya*) light extends through them belongs to the mathematical sciences. *Therefore, the discussion of the light and of the ray and of transparency must be composed (murakkab) of the natural and the mathematical sciences.*

d. Ibn al-Haytham, *Qaws Quzaḥ wa-l-Hāla* ("On the Rainbow and The Halo") (English translation: A. I. Sabra in "The Physical and the Mathematical in Ibn al-Haytham's Theory of Light and Vision," *ibid.*, p. 4, quoted in Sabra, The *Optics*, I–III, v. ii, p. 4):

> Everything whose nature is made subject of inquiry must be investigated in a manner conformable to its kind: if the thing is simple (*basīṭ*), then (it must be investigated) by a simple reasoning (*naẓar*), and if composite, then by a composite (*murakkab*) reasoning. Now among the things which men have aspired to know about, and which have given to much perplexity of thought, are the two effects known as the halo and the rainbow . . . since their subject is air, their investigation (*naẓar*) must be physical, and since their shape is round, they must also be investigated mathematically.

e. Al-Khāzinī, *Mīzān al-ḥikma* ("Balance of Wisdom") (Hyderabad edn., 1359 [1940–41]; N. Khanikoff, "Analysis and Extracts of *Kitāb Mīzān al-ḥikma*," *Journal of the American Oriental Society*, 6 (1859), pp. 10–11):

> Every craft is combined (*murakkab*) of geometrical and natural crafts through the two complementary (*jāmiʿ*) entities of quantity (*kamm*) and quality (*kayf*) . . . This Just balance (*al-mīzan al-ʿadl*) is founded upon geometrical demonstrations (*al-barāhīn al-handasiyya*) and deduced (*mustanbiṭ*) from physical cases (*al-ʿilal al-ṭabīʿiyya*), in two points:
>
> [1] As it implies centers of gravity (*marākiz al-athqāl*), which constitutes the most elevated and noble department of the exact [mathematical] sciences (*al-ʿulūm al-riyāḍiyya*), namely the knowledge that the weights of heavy bodies vary according to difference of distance from a point in common-the foundation of a steelyard.
> [2] As it implies a knowledge that weights of heavy bodies vary according to difference in rarity or density of the liquids in which the body weighed is immersed—the foundation of the balance of wisdom.

Appendix III. Early Classifications: Organization and Transmission

a. Early Classifications:

Qusṭā ibn Lūqā (d. c. 300/912–913), *Aṣnāf al-ṣināʿāt* ('Classes of crafts'), in Arabic:

> Collective (*jāmiʿ*) crafts/sciences: Philosophical crafts/sciences, mathematical and mixed mathematical crafts/sciences, only by extension.

al-Fārābī (d. 339/950), *Iḥṣāʾ al-ʿulūm* ("Enumeration of the Sciences") in Arabic:

> Mathematical sciences (*taʿālīm*) include, as part of the four sciences of arithmetic, geometry, astronomy and music, optics (between geometry and astronomy), and after them, the sciences of devices (*ḥiyal*) and weights (*athqāl*) as parts of mechanics.

al-Khwārizmī (ca. 367/977), *Mafātiḥ al-ʿulūm* ("Keys to the Sciences"), in Arabic:

> Mathematical sciences (*taʿālim*) include, right after the four sciences of arithmetic, geometry, astronomy and music, only mechanics (*ḥiyal*), itself in two chapters: sciences of lifting weights (*jarr al-athqāl*) and wonderous instruments (*ālāt ʿajība*).

b. Later Classifications:

Ibn Sīnā (d. 428/1037), *Dānish-nama-yi ʿAlāʾī* ("Book of Knowledge dedicated to ʿAlāʾ-al-Dawla") in Persian (ed. with introduction and commentary by Muḥammad Muʾīn, Tehran, 1331 H.sh./1952), pp. 1–10:

> Mathematical sciences (*ʿilm-i riyāḍī*) include, in addition to the four intermediate (*miyāngīn*) sciences of arithmetic, geometry, astronomy and music, optics and mechanics, and mechanics in both subdivisions, and in both cases as a subdivision (*furūʿ*) themselves.

Nāṣir al-Dīn al-Ṭūsī (d. 620/1274), *Akhlāq-i Nāṣirī* ("Nāṣirean Ethics") in Persian, Translated by G. M. Wickens, London: Allen and Unwin, 1964:

> Mathematical sciences (*ʿilm-i riyāḍī*) include, in addition to the four sciences of arithmetic, geometry, astronomy and music, both optics and mechanics—mechanics in only one of its subdivisions (*ʿilm al-athqāl*), and in both cases as subdivisions (*furūʿ*).

Quṭb al-Dīn al-Shīrāzī (d. 711/1311), *Durrat al-tāj* ("Pearl of the Crown") in Persian, edited by M. Mishkat (Tehran, 1317 H.sh./1939), vol. I, p. 74:

Mathematical sciences (*ʿilm-i riyāḍī*) include, in addition to the four intermediate (*awsaṭ*) sciences of arithmetic, geometry, astronomy and music, both optics and mechanics—mechanics in only one of its subdivisions (*ʿilm al-athqāl*), and in both cases as subdivisions (*furūʿ*).

c. Abū Naṣr Al-Fārābī's (d. 339/950 A.D.), *Iḥṣāʾ al-ʿulīm* ("Enumeration of the Sciences"), ed. ʿUthmān Amīn [= Osman Amine], (Cairo: Librairie Anglo-Égyptienne, 1968), 79–84; English translation: A. I. Sabra's *The Optics of Ibn al-Haytham*, vol. II, pp. lvi–lvii).

> *The science of optics* (ʿilm al-manāẓir) *investigates the same things as does the science of geometry (handasa) such as figures, magnitudes, order, position, equality and inequality*. But there was a need for a separate science of optics . . . because many of the things which are proved to be of a certain shape or position or order or the like, acquire opposite properties when they become objects of vision . . . *By means of this science discrimination is made between what is seen as different from what it truly is and what is seen as it truly is; and the reason why all this should be so are established by certain demonstrations* (barāhīn al-yaqīniyya) . . .

d. Abū Naṣr Al-Fārābī's (d. 339/950 A.D.), *Iḥṣāʾ al-ʿulūm* ("Enumeration of the Sciences"), ed. ʿUthmān Amīn [= Osman Amine] (Cairo: Librairie Anglo-Égyptienne, 1968), 88–89; English translation: George Saliba, "The Function of Mechanical Devices in Medieval Islamic Society," in *Science and Technology in Medieval Society*, ed. Pamela O. Lang (*Annals of the New York Academy*, 441 [1985], 141–151) pp. 145–46:

> *The science of mechanics* (ʿilm al-ḥiyal) *is the knowledge of the procedure by which one applies all that* which *is proven to exist in the mathematical sciences that were mentioned above in statements and proofs* (barāhīn) *unto the natural* (ṭabīʿī) *bodies, and [the act of] locating [all that] and establishing it in actuality* (fiʿl). The reason for that is that these mathematical sciences look into lines, surfaces, volumes, numbers, and all their subject matter is intelligible on its own and in isolation from natural (*ṭabīʿī*) bodies . . . The material and perceptible bodies have special conditions that prohibit them from accepting [the ideas] that were demonstrated by proofs (*bārāhīn*) from being located in them as one pleases to do. On the contrary, these natural (*ṭabīʿī*) bodies have to be prepared to accept what one seeks to establish in them, and one has to contrive to remove the obstruction . . . *The sciences of mechanics* (ʿulūm al-ḥiyal) *are therefore those that supply the knowledge of the methods* (ṭuruq) *and procedures* (tadābīr) *by which one can contrive to find this applicability and to demonstrate it in actuality* (fiʿl) *in the natural* (ṭabīʿī) *bodies that are perceptible to the senses* (maḥsūs).

e. Abū Naṣr al-Fārābī's (d. 339/950 A.D.), *Iḥṣāʾ al-ʿulūm* ("Enumeration of the Sciences"), ed. ʿUthmān Amīn [= Osman Amine] (Cairo:

Librairie Anglo-Égyptienne, 1968, p. 88; English translation of section on "The Science of Weights" in Marshall Clagett, "Some General Aspects of Physics in the Middle Ages," *Isis*, 39 (1948), p. 32):

> The science of weights (*ʿilm al-athqāl*) is concerned with matters of weight in two fashions:
>
> [1] According as it investigates weights from the point of view of their being measured or something being measured with them, i.e., the investigation of the fundamental principles of the discourse on the balance; or
> [2] According as it investigates weights which are moved or something being moved with them, i.e. the investigation of the basic principles of instruments with which heavy things are lifted and upon which they are carried from place to place

f. Abū ʿAbdallāh Muḥammad al-Kātib al-Khwārazmī (d. 387/997), *Mafātīḥ al-ʿulūm* (ed. G. van Vloten, Leiden 1895, repr. 1968), 4–5; English translation (table of contents) by Mahdi Muhaqqiq ('The Classification of the Sciences', *The Different Aspects of Islamic Culture*, v. 4: *Science and Technology in Islam*, part I [UNESCO, 2001]), pp. 116–119:

> Islamic Religious Law (*sharīʿa*) and Associated Arab Sciences (*al-ʿulūm al-ʿArabiyya*);
>
> Non-Arab (*al-ʿajam*) Sciences [from Greek (*al-Yūnāniyyīn*) or other nations (*umam*)]:
>
> Philosophy, Logic, Medicine, Arithmetic, Geometry, Astronomy-Astrology (*nujūm*), Music, Mechanics (*ḥiyal*) in two chapters ["the movement of heavy weights by application of only a slight force . . . [and] the machinery for producing motion and the construction of remarkable vessels"]; see C. E. Bosworth, "A Pioneer Arabic Encyclopedia of the Sciences: al-Khwārizmī's Key of the Sciences," *Isis*, 54 (1963): 341–45.

THE BRETHREN OF PURITY (*IKHWĀN AL-ṢAFĀʾ*) AND THEIR PHILOSOPHICAL TREATISES (*RASĀʾIL*)

Mokdad Arfa
Department of Philosophy, Faculty of Human and Social Sciences, University of Tunis

What is there new to say about the Brethren of Purity? Many studies have been written, much research has been conducted into their way of thinking, many translations of their *Rasāʾil* have been made into European languages, and many commentaries have been produced—while the known sources, which remain few in number, have already been exploited, and no additional sources that could enhance our understanding seem to emerge. Until new evidence turns up that will change this situation, the researcher must be content with carrying on historical and exegetical studies of their philosophy.

The *Rasāʾil*, for which the Brethren are famous, is the most important source for gaining an understanding of their doctrine. We will merely refer here to certain facts, of which some are objective and draw from external sources, the rest being based on an exegesis of the text of the *Rasāʾil*, in an effort to define certain aspects of their doctrine and shed light on their intentions and the path they advocated through them. We will explain how they conceived the *Rasāʾil*, the role of the treatises in the achievement of their aims, and the extent to which they are a compendium of knowledge, and an encyclopædic work.

Definitive Elements

The work of Abū Ḥayyān al-Tawḥīdī (d. 400/1023), *Kitāb al-Imtāʿ wal-muʾānasa*, is the most important independent source for gaining an insight into the identity and position of the Brethren of Purity, the originators of the *Rasāʾil*, given that the author was their contemporary as well as a friend of Zayd ibn Rifāʿa, one of their leading exponents.[1] To this one should add the contribution made by the Qāḍī ʿAbd al-Jabbār al-Hamadhānī (d. 415/1025), a prominent and distinguished figure of the Muʿtazilite school, in his work, *Tathbīt dalāʾil al-nubuwwa*.

These sources show that the "Brethren of Purity and Friends in the True Faith" basically lived in Basra during the 4th Islamic century (10th century C.E.), which is considered one of the most fertile periods in Islamic history. It witnessed the break-up of the Abbasid empire into tutelages, including that of the Būyid dynasty in Iraq, under whom the Shiite doctrine prevailed. Within an Ismāʿīlī environment, to be more precise, the Brethren established a philosophical and religious society, which embraced a doctrine that those committed to secrecy and concealment were called upon to adopt. They refer in their *Rasāʾil* to their own assembly, "where they discuss their sciences and deliberate upon their secrets."[2] They make mention of their order, which is divided into various degrees.[3] On this al-Tawḥīdī says, "This group was harmonious in companionship, sincere in friendship and united in holiness, purity and sincere counsel. They set up for themselves a doctrine by which they claimed to have come close to attaining God's grace and the path to His Paradise."[4]

Such secrecy has been the reason why their numbers cannot be definitively determined, let alone our being able to identify all or only a part of them.[5] Fortunately, al-Tawḥīdī in *al-Imtāʿ wa-l-muʾānasa*[6] and al-Qāḍī ʿAbd al-Jabbār have preserved for us the names of their most important members, including Abū Sulaymān Muḥammad Ibn Maʿshar al-Bustī (or al-Bistī), also known as al-Muqaddasī, al-Qāḍī Abū l-Ḥasan ʿAli ibn Hārūn al-Zanjānī, Abū Aḥmad al-Nahrajūrī al-ʿArūḍī, also known as al-Mihrajānī, al-ʿAwfi and Zayd ibn Rifāʿa,

[1] Al-Qifṭī refers us to al-Tawḥīdī's *al-Imtaʿ wal-muʾānasa*, see *Taʾrīkh al-ḥukamaʾ*, ed. Julius Lippert (Leipzig, 1903), p. 82ff.

[2] *Rasāʾil Ikhwān al-Ṣafāʾ* (Beirut: Dār Bayrūt / Dār Ṣādir, 1376 H/1957), vol. 4, p. 41.

[3] *Ibid.*, vol. 4, p. 57.

[4] Abū Ḥayyān al-Tawḥīdī, *al-Imtaʿ wal-muʾānasa*, ed. Aḥmad Amīn & Aḥmad al-Zayn (Cairo, 1939–44), 2, p. 5.

[5] According to al-Qifṭī (*Taʾrīkh al-ḥukamaʾ*, p. 82), "Since their compilers kept them [the *Rasaʾil*] secret, people disagreed over who had written them and everyone had their say on the basis of guesswork and conjecture . . . I continued to research diligently in order to identify their author until I came across the remarks of Abū Ḥayyān al-Tawḥīdī."

[6] *Al-Imtaʿ wal-muʾānasa*, 2, pp. 3–5.

the *kātib*.[7] It seems these five were the core around which a group of scholars assembled, and they compiled the famous *Rasāʾil* during the second half of the 4th Islamic century (10th century C.E.), a total of fifty-one treatises, to which is added the so-called Comprehensive Treatise (*al-Risāla al-jāmiʿa*). Who compiled the *Rasāʾil* and, more precisely, how many were the authors, are still matters for debate; al-Bayhaqī (d. 565/1169), for instance, goes as far as to say that the text of the *Rasāʾil* belongs to a single author, namely al-Maqdisī.[8]

Doctrinal Elements

To set out the various aspects of the doctrine of the Brethren of Purity as it appears in the *Rasāʾil* is to go beyond the scope of this article and our present purpose, since there are enough studies already to spare us this task. We will limit ourselves to referring briefly to some of the theoretical principles that will give us an insight into the spirit that motivated the Brethren of Purity to compile the *Rasāʾil* and that gave these treatises a particular orientation, including their theories of existence, and the nature and destiny of mankind.

The Brethren derive the order of existence principally from a combination of Neo-Platonism and Neo-Pythagoreanism, mixed with Hermeticism as well as a number of other influences. The former taught a cosmic order that regulates existence in an emanative, uniform and discriminate way essentially on the basis of defining a specific relationship between beings and their creator, from whom all of them issue forth by emanation. Pythagoreanism states that the world is created, that beings arise from the First in the same way as the numbers that arise from the One and that beings are commensurable in terms of the nature of number.[9] Thus is achieved a

[7] Al-Qāḍī ʿAbd al-Jabbār ibn Aḥmad al-Hamadhānī says of al-Zanjānī, *qāḍī* of the Shīʿites, "He is a chief among their chiefs and has followers, secretaries and leaders . . . and he is eminent among them". Of them he then mentions Abū Muḥammad ibn Abī l-Baghl, the writer and astrologer, adding, "These are living in Basra, and others are elsewhere" (*Tathbīt dalāʾil al-nubuwwa*, ed. ʿAbd al-Karīm ʿUthmān, Beirut, 1386 H/1966, pp. 610–611).

[8] *Taʾrīkh ḥukamāʾ al-Islām*, ed. Muḥammad Kurd ʿAlī (Damascus, 1964), pp. 35–36.

[9] See, for example, *Faṣl fī maʿnā qawl al-Fīthāghūriyīn anna l-mawjūdāt bi-ḥasab ṭabīʿat al-ʿadad* (vol. 3, pp. 200ff.).

graduated order of beings, from the First, to the Intellect, to the Universal Soul and then Nature so as to cover all of creation, from humans to the most inferior of beings. This entire order of existence is governed by a divine providence and a wise, divine policy that arranges it in its smallest detail. The Universal Soul is deemed to be the soul of this world and Nature is just one of the forces of this soul, in which it flows through many individual souls, to the extent that everything that happens in Nature is merely the acts of individual souls.[10]

Man occupies a central position in this order of existence and his soul is merely one of these individual souls, that is, one of the forces of the Universal Soul. The Brethren always stressed mankind's position, which lies midway along the scale of existence, emphasising its dual nature in terms of being an amalgamation of two distinct essences, a material body and spiritual soul, and these are two fundamental elements in the concept of his destiny. Just as the body has its own peculiar traits, so too does the soul, given that it comes from the divine things that constitute forms devoid of primordial matter. These are enduring and eternal essences that are incorruptible and unassailable. The soul therefore is a spiritual, divine, self-existent essence with a thorough knowledge of the force, possessing intellect, knowledge and laudable qualities.[11]

Connected with this spiritual anthropology is the dual concept of destiny. The destiny of the soul when it is separated from the body depends on the behaviour exhibited by the person in this life and the morality he has displayed.[12] Either the soul sinks down in pursuit of this world with the body and descends into the Sea of Primordial Matter, which prevents it from receiving the emanation from the Universal Soul, in which case its destiny is hardship, or it aspires to the after-life by seeking knowledge,[13] in which case it is delivered from the Sea of Primordial Matter and the bonds of nature, ascending to the heavenly host and thereby achieving everlasting happiness. We often see in the *Rasāʾil* descriptions of the soul's stages of development until it becomes an angel and attains happiness,[14] as

[10] *Rasāʾil*, 2, p. 130.
[11] *Rasāʾil*, 1, p. 260.
[12] *Rasāʾil*, 2, p. 50.
[13] *Rasāʾil*, 1, p. 261.
[14] *Rasāʾil*, 1, p. 448.

well as accounts of the entry of the pure, spiritual soul into Paradise, the World of Souls.[15]

We can now understand the extreme importance of knowledge of the soul and the Brethren's entreaty, reiterated throughout the *Rasā'il*, to attain knowledge of the soul, its essence and its beginning and end.[16] They ascribe to such knowledge certain diverse and crucial functions, including those of epistemology, whereby knowledge of the soul became the root of the sciences, the constituent element of wisdom and the basis for all the scientific and practical arts.[17] Knowledge of the soul then is the first stage in studying the divine sciences . . . and it is a path to knowing God.[18] Ignorance of the soul gives rise to all those errors and fallacies about the knowledge of existence that occur within the various doctrines.[19] Without this, we would find it hard to understand the Brethren's constant criticism of the theologians (*mutakallimūn*), whom they refer to as "disputing over religion".[20] Most of them went on to refute the doctrine of the essential nature of the soul although, if this doctrine is refuted, then all the other doctrines dependent upon it are also refuted.[21]

The Philosophical Path

The path advocated by the Brethren is linked to their theories on existence and its order, on mankind and his position within existence and on the soul and its destiny.[22] This points to a doctrine of concurrence between behaviour in this world, which focuses on asceticism, and the acquisition of learning and knowledge, which all comes together to form a theory on knowledge, learning and education.[23] It also brings us to two fundamental issues, namely, an epistemological theory linking science to existence and a particular conceptualisation of the history of human knowledge.

[15] *Rasā'il*, 1, p. 451.
[16] *Rasā'il*, 2, p. 59.
[17] *Rasā'il*, 1, p. 101.
[18] *Rasā'il*, 1, p. 71.
[19] *Rasā'il*, 2, p. 13.
[20] *Rasā'il*, 3, p. 535.
[21] *Rasā'il*, 2, p. 238.
[22] *Rasā'il*, 1, p. 399.
[23] *Rasā'il*, 1, p. 399.

With regard to the first of these issues, we often see science in the *Rasā'il* being defined as the acquisition of the form of the known in the knower.[24] It is generally said that it comes from the doctrine of the Brethren of Purity and is in fact their definition of the way in which the order of existence occurs in the human soul, which, according to the Brethren, happens "by studying all the sciences of creation that exist in the world, from the substances, accidents, elements, abstracts and compounds, and by examining their origins, the number of their genera and species and their specific characteristics, their arrangement and order as they are now and how they occur and develop from a single cause, a single principle and a single creator."[25]

In terms of the second issue, i.e. the history of human knowledge, the Brethren identify two stages or states, attributing the first state to those of the earlier period, who endeavoured to acquire the sciences until they had done so. On this matter, the Brethren say that all arts were developed by the wisdom of the sages and that the people then learned from them and from each other so that a legacy was passed on by the sages to the ordinary people, from scholars to students and from teachers to pupils.[26] The second state, however, is one of retrogression, in which these sciences were lost and the acquisition of knowledge foundered. We are thus able to see in the ideas of the Brethren of Purity and their programme of teaching an adherence to the old practice of acquiring and imparting wisdom and its use in a new cause. This return to and emulation of those who went before, the knowledge they acquired, their categorisation and classification of it, their view on the function of the sciences in salvation and their educational curricula, by which they graduated their pupils, are significant.[27]

Since the *Rasā'il* advocate a return to and revival of this former wisdom, they are thereby calling for the adoption of the classification of sciences as they had been according to this wisdom. The *Rasā'il* contain many instances where the sciences are divided up and classified and, in this respect, we will refer first of all to what appears to us to be a general framework, that is, the division of all the human

[24] *Rasā'il*, 1, p. 262; 2, p. 9.
[25] *Rasā'il*, 1, pp. 48 and 158.
[26] *Rasā'il*, 1, p. 186.
[27] *Rasā'il*, 1, pp. 75–77.

arts into spiritual, scientific arts, which are the types of science, and physical, scientific arts, which are the types of art.[28] Then comes the division of the sciences, which mankind breaks down into three types:[29]

(1) The propædeutic and mathematical sciences, which are the humanities and most of which have been established for the purpose of pursuing one's livelihood and improving one's lot in this world, and are sub-divided into nine categories: reading and writing; lexicography and grammar; arithmetic and commerce; poetry and prosody; augury, divination and the like; magic, talismans, alchemy, mechanical artifices and the like; trades and handicrafts; buying and selling, trading, human civilisation; biography and history.

(2) The religious and "conventional" sciences, established for the healing of the soul and the quest for the after-life, divided into six categories: revelation; exegesis; narrative and reporting; jurisprudence, traditional practices and precepts; commemoration, exhortation, asceticism and mysticism; the interpretation of dreams.

(3) The philosophical and "true" sciences, in four categories: mathematics, which is of four disciplines: the science of number, geometry, astronomy and music; the logical disciplines, divided into five arts: the arts of poetry, rhetoric, dialectic, demonstration, and sophistry; the natural sciences, in seven disciplines: the sciences of physical principles, the heaven and the world, generation and corruption, meteorology, mineralogy, botany and zoology; theology, in five disciplines: knowledge of the Creator, of the spiritual entities, psychology, politics, and eschatology.[30]

All these sciences fall within the scope of the philosophy, for which the Brethren reiterate the well-known, conventional definition, namely, that it is the emulation of God according to man's capacity,[31] specifying its various stages, of which the beginning is the love of the sciences, the middle one is knowledge of the true nature of creation according to man's capacity, and the final stage is speaking and acting in keeping with science.[32] The ultimate purpose behind acquiring

[28] *Rasā'il,* 1, p. 183.
[29] *Rasā'il,* 1, p. 266.
[30] See also *Rasā'il,* 1, pp. 48–49 and see the reference to these sciences and their principles, vol. 1, pp. 78–79, vol. 2, pp. 19–21.
[31] *Rasā'il,* 2, p. 10.
[32] *Rasā'il,* 1, p. 48.

these philosophical sciences is to "improve the essence of the soul and to refine, complete and perfect its moral nature in order to survive in the after-life."[33] To this end, mathematics is entrusted with a specific and fundamental role, given that the Brethren insisted on following the Pythagorean scholars, not only in the mathematical view of the world, as stated earlier, but also in terms of giving precedence to mathematics within the scale of the philosophical sciences and the order that has to be followed when teaching them. If every science assists the soul in its development, the ultimate purpose of studying the mathematical sciences, in particular, is to train the souls of the students so that they may grasp the forms of things perceived by the senses, until they may inform the essence of the soul.[34] The study of the geometry of sensible objects, for instance, leads to proficiency in all the practical arts, and studying intellectual geometry leads to proficiency in the theoretical arts.[35] Many benefits are also derived from a knowledge of the stars,[36] prompting the soul to seek to rise up to the heavens and rid itself of the body.[37] Such development of the soul is also the reason for studying geography.[38]

Theology, however, remains the ultimate purpose and goal, beyond which there is no other goal in terms of the soul's development and its progression up the scale of the sciences. According to the Brethren, "The divine sciences are the ultimate purpose of the sages and the end to which they are raised up with true knowledge."[39]

The Brethren attempted to arrange the *Rasāʾil* according to the above classification of the sciences, devoting to each science a treatise "as a kind of gateway and introduction" to it,[40] thereby following an educational programme, in which the *Rasāʾil* are arranged according to man's progress in acquiring knowledge. It starts therefore with the educational, mathematical *Rasāʾil*, followed by the natural, physical *Rasāʾil*, the intellectual, psychological *Rasāʾil* and then, lastly, the divine, moral *Rasāʾil*.[41]

---

[33] *Rasāʾil*, 1, p. 258.
[34] *Rasāʾil*, 1, p. 103.
[35] *Rasāʾil*, 1, pp. 101, 113, and also the need for geometry of bodily, three-dimensional objects (vol. 1, pp. 98–99).
[36] *Rasāʾil*, 1, p. 156.
[37] *Rasāʾil*, 1, p. 137.
[38] *Rasāʾil*, 1, p. 159.
[39] *Rasāʾil*, 1, pp. 75–76, and also vol. 2, p. 21.
[40] *Rasāʾil*, 1, p. 268.
[41] *Rasāʾil*, 4, pp. 283–284, and see the *al-Rasāʾil* table of contents, vol. 1, p. 21.

The doctrine of the Brethren of Purity does not depend on philosophical knowledge alone. In fact, they stress throughout the *Rasāʾil* the need to combine wisdom and prophecy, given that the teachings of the prophets are merely to heal the soul while religious precepts are there simply to save the soul. Wisdom and the Sharīʿa (religious law) come together as part of the ultimate, desired goal, which is to refine the soul and seek its salvation. Furthermore, the Sharīʿa has both a literal and a hidden meaning and both of these dimensions should be regarded as the truth.[42] The literal meaning of the Sharīʿa consists merely of representations, which refer to a hidden meaning that is understood through philosophical interpretation. Hell, for instance, is understood as being the world of generation and corruption and Paradise as the world of souls. Resurrection of the soul is seen as awakening from the sleep of indifference, rousing from the slumber of ignorance, and salvation.[43] The Brethren portray their fundamental task as being one of interpreting the divine books.[44]

Comments

In their compilation of the *Rasāʾil*, the Brethren were to some extent imbued with a spirit of pessimism and held a negative view of a specific historical situation, i.e. that of their political, social and intellectual community, and of the status of man, undoubtedly stemming from a spiritual concept that sees its material and worldly side as a temporary state, which has to be managed carefully in order to escape from it. Life in this world is important only because it is necessary for perfecting the qualities of the soul through philosophy and law.[45] The Brethren certainly do have an optimism that believes "the state of good will follow the state of evil",[46] and that man can achieve salvation if he does what is required in that respect and seeks to save himself. They produced the *Rasāʾil* as an exposition and explanation of their order, their ethics, their views and their deeds for

[42] *Rasāʾil*, 1, p. 365.
[43] *Rasāʾil*, 3, p. 301.
[44] *Rasāʾil*, 3, p. 78.
[45] *Rasāʾil*, 2, p. 452.
[46] *Rasāʾil*, 1, p. 181.

the purpose of achieving this goal.[47] To what extent then do they possess the specifications for an encyclopædia arranged through an undertaking on the part of the artisans and those with the expertise and skills to provide the knowledge, which is collected, sifted and arranged with a critical eye according to a particular historical perspective, and that employs the elements of accumulation and comprehensiveness and is regarded as a source worthy of recognition?

Dealing with the issue of salvation was, in the view of the Brethren of Purity, urgent and imperative and was done by retrieving the knowledge of the ancient philosophers and gradually making progress in it according to a specific arrangement of the sciences and a specific didacticism and pedagogy.[48] Knowledge of the soul is the crux of the matter in this endeavour, which can only be achieved within a limited, unanimous and harmonious human group that is determined to attain salvation of the soul and bring about a spiritual kingdom. The Brethren often call for people to join with them in order to form such a group.[49] The *Rasāʾil* are the appropriate means of achieving this goal. In them, the Brethren set out the categories and subcategories of the sciences and their authoritative and dedicated texts, merely referring to scientific principles and providing brief descriptions of them so that it might be a "guide for students to attain their goals and achieve their aspirations because the soul's desire for the various sciences and the literary arts are like the body's appetites for various foods, for taste, colour and smell."[50] They followed in the presentation of knowledge an arrangement that was predominant and mathematics was given priority because of its ability to assist with the understanding of creation and the gradual training of the soul. This idea is what lends weight to the consideration of the *Rasāʾil* as a compendium of knowledge, the compilers of which believed they were inheritors of wisdom and were acting as its custodians in order to preserve it so that it might be passed from master to pupil according to certain pedagogic methods, seeking to impart wisdom and make knowledge accessible as well as simplifying, classifying and setting it out according to the sciences and devoting a treatise to each one. The *Rasāʾil* are therefore seen as a gateway to the sciences.[51]

---

[47] *Rasāʾil*, 3, p. 75.
[48] *Rasāʾil*, 1, p. 44.
[49] See, for example, vol. 2, p. 476.
[50] *Rasāʾil*, 1, p. 266.
[51] *Rasāʾil*, 3, p. 538. The Brethren say, "We have devised fifty-one treatises on

However, there are some aspects that preclude the *Rasāʾil* from being an encyclopædia in the strict sense. Among these is the fact that we cannot see in a programme of salvation any encyclopædic exposition of human knowledge. In the *Rasāʾil*, the Brethren are endeavouring to be "students, who are influenced by wisdom, who want salvation and who choose redemption."[52] Any encyclopædia does indeed try to impart to us the knowledge that is available and create an authoritative and reliable source of reference as it seeks to achieve an ideal in terms of knowledge and optimising man's development. Even if there are such aspects in the *Rasāʾil* of the Brethren of Purity, they revolve principally around the quest for salvation and casting off the affairs of this world, being guided in that by Pythagoreanism with its combination of science and mysticism.

In this connection, the preferential arrangement of the *Rasāʾil* is "commensurate with what the grades of the scholars and levels of the benefiting students require."[53] The *Rasāʾil* end with the divine law, "the essences of what we have set out, the treasures of what we have compiled."[54] According to the Brethren, it is, in the final analysis, a preferential arrangement of knowledge based on a gradual development of students and it is hard for conventional encyclopædias to deviate from what is not in keeping with the non-preferential arrangement by which knowledge is normally presented in encyclopædias.

The compilers of encyclopædias generally aim therefore to reach as many people as possible with their publications and so they are usually available to the public and not merely confined to a group that considers itself to be uniquely qualified to acquire this knowledge. In fact, the Brethren often call for their *Rasāʾil* to be disseminated to all "the Brethren", wherever they are in the land,[55] although their environment and the nature of their cause was such that they had to be secretive when compiling, distributing and publishing the *Rasāʾil*, something that the compilers of encyclopædias do not normally have to do. There is a strong exclusivity that renders only a few qualified to receive and benefit from the *Rasāʾil*. The Brethren say

the arts of literature, the wonders of the sciences and the exquisiteness of wisdom, each one a kind of gateway, introduction and model" (vol. 4, p. 186, and see also p. 339).

[52] *Rasāʾil*, 1, p. 43.

[53] *Rasāʾil*, 4, p. 283.

[54] *Rasāʾil*, 4, p. 205.

[55] *Rasāʾil*, 1, pp. 327–328.

in this regard, "We should not offer science to those who are not eligible for it and who do not know its merit. Likewise, it is not permitted, nor is it lawful to withhold it from those who seek guidance and request it."[56] The Brethren say they addressed everyone with what was most appropriate to address them with in their *Rasā'il*.[57] Encyclopædias do not go in for vagueness when setting out their contents but attempt to present knowledge in a way that avoids confusion, whereas the *Rasā'il* stress the secret nature of the teachings and the effort required of those qualified to interpret it, since not everyone is competent to understand and benefit from the contents of the *Rasā'il*. This disparity from the point of view of the literal interpretation and the hidden meaning exists within a single treatise as well as between the *Rasā'il* and the Comprehensive Treatise (*al-Risāla al-jāmiʿa*), since the Brethren say, "We have placed in each treatise a chapter that we devised from the essence and purity of it. He who manages to understand and apply it will attain happiness in this world and the next. We have summarised what we included in our fifty-one treatises in a treatise that is separate from the *Rasā'il*, which we have called 'the Comprehensive One' (*al-Jāmiʿa*) and which falls outside the body of the *Rasā'il*. We included in it an explanation of what we said on the other matters as specifically as we could . . . if [any of our brethren] reads it after reading this, he will be greatly benefited and that which is obscure in the *Rasā'il* will be clear to him. If he finds it and he has missed out on the *Rasā'il* or some of them, he will not forego their benefits."[58] In this way, they are seeking to achieve a hidden truth that is considered more correct and more precise than the literal interpretation. This is what al-Qifṭī was referring to when he talked about the *Rasā'il*, describing it as "a summation of the various types of treatise by means of summary and abridgement, they being fascinating treatises that are not in-depth studies and do not provide any clear evidence or argument, as if they are for pointing to and highlighting the intended meaning the student is to attain for any particular category of wisdom."[59]

---

[56] *Rasā'il*, 4, p. 283.
[57] *Rasā'il*, 4, p. 242.
[58] *Rasā'il*, 4, p. 250. See also what the Ikhwān al-Ṣafa' say about *al-Risāla al-jamī'a* (vol. 1, p. 42).
[59] *Ta'rīkh al-hukamā'*, p. 82.

The *Rasā'il* were therefore supplemented by attending the assemblies at which they were studied in more depth.[60]

There is a further matter, which is that encyclopædias provide knowledge which is organised according to the point human knowledge has reached in any particular historical period, whereas we find in the *Rasā'il* no such awareness of the historical dimension, except for their advocacy of a return to a former stage of human learning, regarded as having exemplary status, in which those of that former period acquired the true knowledge in a definitive way, and which is to be reclaimed in order to create a spiritual kingdom. It has to be acknowledged here that clear evidence of this historical dimension, which presents the sciences and doctrines and their development in the context of their historical setting and their social and political environment, together with an explanation of the theoretical causes for it, is only seen later with Ibn Khaldūn and that represents an objective distance between the compiler and his subject that every encyclopædic work needs.

The Brethren say:

> We include in our books and in our *Rasā'il* such elements of the sciences as will purify the intellect and inform the soul. We have taken from each science as much as could be taken and as time allowed and we endeavoured to do that to the best of our ability. We therefore specified it, recorded it and conveyed it to our brethren.[61]

In fact, in every encyclopædic work a selection of the available knowledge has to be made. Still, the Brethren sought to assemble in their *Rasā'il* all the available knowledge on philosophy, religion, magic and astrology, whatever its nature and source. This led to the juxtaposition and harmonization of conflicting views, and theories that are difficult to reconcile. The *Rasā'il* therefore lack the rational and critical approach that examines the sciences as a critical process, which seeks to select from human knowledge what it regards as the truth. In this respect, the *Rasā'il* of the Brethren of Purity have come in for criticism from a variety of scholarly circles and conventions. Abū Sulaymān al-Manṭiqī al-Sijistānī studied them, and al-Tawḥīdī put his judgement as follows,

---

[60] *Rasā'il*, 4, p. 186.
[61] *Rasā'il*, 4, p. 367.

> They toiled but to no avail, they made great efforts but provided nothing new, they preserved but provided nothing, they sang but did not delight, they wove finely and searched with a fine-tooth comb. They assumed what is not, what is not possible and what cannot be. They believed they could surreptitiously introduce philosophy—consisting of astronomy, astrology, the Almagest, fate and the effects of nature; music, which is a knowledge of melody, rhythms, beats and metres; logic, which is the consideration of premises with attributions, quantities and qualities—into the Sharīʿa and bring religious law and philosophy together.[62]

Indeed, we cannot deprive compilers of encyclopædias of their right to make speculative choices that shape their view of knowledge and to select, arrange and present it. But such a combination of many different teachings derived from the various doctrines makes it difficult to regard the *Rasāʾil* as an encyclopædia in the strict sense.[63] The *Rasāʾil* were essentially a manual that was used by the missionaries to spread the Ismāʿīlī cause and for educational purposes, and to encourage the in-depth study of the sciences, giving students "an introduction to the sciences and their principles so that it might help them to become accomplished in them, and stir them to become thoroughly acquainted with them."[64]

[62] *Al-Imtāʿ wal-muʾānasa*, vol. 2, p. 6.

[63] With regard to the family of the Prophet, the Brethren say they are the depository of the knowledge of God and heirs to the knowledge of the prophecies (vol. 4, p. 186).

[64] *Rasāʾil*, 4, p. 339.

INTEGRATIVE CONCEPTS

AL-QAZWĪNĪ'S *'AJĀ'IB AL-MAKHLŪQĀT*: AN ENCYCLOPÆDIA OF NATURAL HISTORY?

Syrinx von Hees
University of Bonn

This essay focuses on the text *'Ajā'ib al-makhlūqāt wa-gharā'ib al-mawjūdāt* ('The Wonders of Creation and the Peculiarities of Beings'), written in the second half of the 13th century by the Persian jurist Zakariyyā' al-Qazwīnī.[1] Within the present context of studies on *Encyclopædic Activities in the Pre-Eighteenth Century Muslim World*, we want to raise the question: can Qazwīnī's work be classified as an encyclopædia? So far, scholars of Islamic studies who worked on encyclopædias have largely ignored the *'Ajā'ib al-makhlūqāt*.[2] Neither do specialists on

---

[1] For this study the oldest known manuscript of the *Kitāb 'Ajā'ib al-makhlūqāt wa-gharā'ib al-mawjūdāt* has been used as textual basis, because no satisfactory critical edition of this work exists. Today this manuscript is preserved at the Bayerische Staatsbibliothek, Munich, under the signature Cod. arab. 464. For further details about this manuscript, please refer to Syrinx von Hees, *Enzyklopädie als Spiegel des Weltbildes: Qazwīnīs Wunder der Schöpfung—eine Naturkunde des 13. Jahrhunderts* (Wiesbaden, 2002), pp. 91–96. This study, pp. 19–90, contains a detailed account of the life of Zakariyyā' al-Qazwīnī and his cultural background.

[2] Franz Rosenthal, *The Technique and Approach of Muslim Scholarship* (Rome, 1947), pp. 60–63: "Specialization and Encyclopedism"; Charles Pellat, 'Les Encyclopédies dans le Monde Arabe,' in: *Cahiers d'Histoire Mondiale 9* (1966), pp. 631–658; Régis Blachère, 'Quelques Réflexions sur les formes de l'encyclopédisme en Égypte et en Syrie du VIIIe/XIVe siècle a la fin du IXe/XVe siècle,' in: *Bulletin des Études Orientales, 23* (1970), pp. 7–19; Hilary Kilpatrick, 'A Genre in Classical Arabic Literature: The Adab Encyclopedia,' in: Robert Hillenbrand (ed.), *Proceedings of the 10th congress of the UEAI, Edinburgh 1980* (Edinburgh, 1982), pp. 34–42; Christel Hein, *Definition und Einteilung der Philosophie: von der spätantiken Einleitungsliteratur zur arabischen Enzyklopädie* (Frankfurt am Main, 1985); Charles Pellat, 'Mawsū'a, « encyclopædia », 1: in Arabic,' in: *EI²*, vol. 6 (1991), pp. 903–907; Mounira Chapoutot-Remadi, 'L'Encyclopédie arabe au Xe siècle,' in: Annie Becq (ed.): *L'Éncyclopédisme: actes du Colloque de Cæn, 12e–16e janvier 1987* (Paris, 1991), pp. 37–46; Chapoutot-Remadi, Mounira: 'Les encyclopédies arabes de la fin du Moyen Age,' in: Annie Becq (ed.): *L'Éncyclopédisme. Actes du Colloque de Cæn, 12e–16e janvier 1987* (Paris, 1991), pp. 267–279; Gerhard Endress, 'Die wissenschaftliche Literatur, § 8.8.1.6: Enzyklopädie,' in: *GAP*, vol. 3 (Wiesbaden, 1992), pp. 57–61; Hilary Kilpatrick, 'Encyclopedias, medieval,' in: *EAL*, vol. 1 (1998), pp. 208f.; Hans Hinrich Biesterfeldt, 'Medieval Arabic Encyclopedias of Science and Philosophy,' in: Steven Harvey (ed.), *The Medieval Hebrew Encyclopedia of Science and Philosophy* (Dordrecht, 2000), pp. 77–98; id., 'Arabisch-Islamische

Zakariyyā' al-Qazwīnī consider his work as an encyclopædia. Some classify it as belonging to an independent literary genre, called cosmography;[3] while others describe it as belonging to the *'ajā'ib* genre.[4]

Enzyklopädien: Formen und Funktionen,' in: Christel Meier (ed.), *Die Enzyklopädie im Wandel vom Hochmittelalter bis zur Frühen Neuzeit* (München, 2002), pp. 43–83.—Among all these authors, Ch. Pellat in his *EI*[2] article (1991), p. 903f., is the only one who mentions Qazwīnī's work in his discussion of encyclopædias, albeit in passing: ". . . the *Kitāb al-ḥayawān* is far from being a zoological dictionary. . . . It is quite different in the *'Adjā'ib al-makhlūqāt* of al-Qazwīnī (600–82/1202–83), which contains an alphabetical series of notices concerning animals in its section on the description of the universe dealing with terrestrial matters."

There are some exceptions of this general picture, as for example:

Francis E. Peters, *Aristotle and the Arabs: the Aristotelian Tradition in Islam* (New York, 1968), ch. V, pp. 104–120: 'The Diffusion of Aristotelianism, Encyclopedias', p. 118f.: "In the thirteenth century, the high-water mark of Arab encyclopedism, the genre, is represented by the Marvels of Creation of Zakariya ibn Muhammad al-Qazwīnī (d. A.D. 1283), a work which testifies to the degree of differentiation that has taken place in such encyclopedias during the intervening period"; Geert Jan van Gelder, 'Compleat Men, Women and Books: on Medieval Arabic Encyclopædism,' in: Peter Binkley (ed.): *Pre-Modern Encyclopædic Texts: Proceedings of the Second COMERS Congress, Groningen, 1–4 July 1996* (Leiden, 1997), pp. 241–259. He writes, p. 254f.: "Among the more general encyclopædias of the natural sciences is a work of cosmography entitled *The Wondrous Creations* (*'Ajā'ib al-makhlūqāt*) by Zakariyyā al-Qazwīnī (d. 1283). This is not a loose collection of facts and quotations but a systematic encyclopædia on the cosmos, arranged according to the chain of being from the highest heavens to earth, with its mineral, vegetable and animals realms"; Ulrich Marzolph, 'Mirabilia, « Weltwunder » und Gottes Kreatur: zur Weltsicht populärer Enzyklopädien des arabisch-islamischen Mittelalters,' in: Ingrid Tomkowiak (ed.): *Populäre Enzyklopädien: von der Auswahl, Ordnung und Vermittlung des Wissens* (Zürich, 2002), pp. 85–101, deals also with Qazwīnī's *'Ajā'ib al-makhlūqāt*, but does not discuss its encyclopædic character, instead is concerned with the meaning of wonder in connection with the author's world-view. Thus this article belongs more to the group of texts discussing *'ajā'ib* (see note 4), than to those just mentioned, discussing 'encyclopædia'.

[3] Maria Kowalska, 'Bericht über die Funktion der arabischen kosmographischen Literatur des Mittelalters,' in: *Folia Orientalia 11* (1969), pp. 175–180; Alma Giese in the introduction, especially pp. 9–11, to her translation: *Al-Qazwīnī. Die Wunder des Himmels und der Erde* (Stuttgart, 1986); Bernd Radtke, 'Die älteste islamische Kosmographie: Muḥammad-i Ṭūsīs 'Ajā'ib ul-makhlūqāt,' in: *Der Islam 64,2* (1987), pp. 278–288; Bernd Radtke, 'Persian Cosmography, Early Tafsir and Nestorian Exegesis,' in: Živa Vesel (ed.), *La science dans le Monde Iranien* (Teheran, 1998), pp. 323–335; Remke Kruk, Review of Hees (2002), in: *Bibliotheca Orientalis* 59, 5–6 (2002), is "not altogether happy" with my classification of Qazwīnī's work as an encyclopædia and states, p. 649: "In the case of Qazwīnī the matter seems to me fairly simple: he sets out to give a popular description of all the phenomena of the natural world, and the form he chooses is that of the cosmography."

[4] For an evaluation of the concept of *'ajā'ib*-literature, see Syrinx von Hees, 'The Astonishing: a critique and re-reading of *'Ajā'ib*-Literature,' in: *MEL* 8,2 (2005), pp. 101–120. Carra de Vaux, Bernard: 'Introduction,' dated Novembre 1897, in: André Miquel (ed.), *L'Abrégé des Merveilles*, traduit de l'arabe et annoté par Carra de Vaux, préface d'André Miquel (Paris, 1984), p. 19f.; César E. Dubler, "Adjā'ib," in: *EI*[2], vol. I (1960), p. 203; Tawfiq Fahd, 'Le Merveilleux dans la faune, la flore et les

In the following I want to prove that Qazwīnī's text is a full-fledged encyclopædia. This is of importance because it will allow us to appreciate and evaluate the work *'Ajā'ib al-makhlūqāt* far more precisely than has so far been the case. At the same time, it will contribute to our understanding of encyclopædic writing.

I will follow the criteria for a definition of the literary genre 'encyclopædia' developed by recent medievalist research, as for example the studies of Christel Meier and Bernard Ribémont.[5] It is now well known that the word 'encyclopædia' is a relatively modern European coinage of the late 15th century, which became commonly used in the 18th century in France.[6] In medieval times, in Latin, English, French, German, Italian, Arabic and Persian literature, the term was not known. Nevertheless medieval Western literature has been examined in the light of the early modern concept of 'encyclopædia' and its criteria. A number of enlightening publications appeared as an outcome of this inquiry.[7] I will investigate whether these criteria apply to the text *'Ajā'ib al-makhlūqāt*.

minéraux,' in: Mohamed Arkoun (ed.), *L'Étrange et le merveilleux dans l'Islam médiéval* (Paris, 1978), p. 119; André Miquel in the introduction of his edition: *L'Abrégé des Merveilles* (*v. supra*), p. 13; Guy Ducatez, 'La *Tuḥfa al-albāb* d'Abū Ḥāmid al-Andalusī al-Ġarnāṭī. traduction annotée,' in: *REI*, 53 (1985), p. 141; C. E. Bosworth, "Ajā'eb al-Makhlūqāt,' in: *Encyclopaedia Iranica*, vol. I (1985), p. 696f.; Lutz Richter-Bernburg, "Ajā'ib literature', in: *EAL*, vol. 1, (1998), p. 65f.; Marzolph (2002), p. 94.

[5] Christel Meier, 'Grundzüge der mittelalterlichen Enzyklopädik: zu Inhalten, Formen und Funktionen einer problematischen Gattung,' in: Ludger Grenzmann, Karl Stackmann (eds.), *Literatur und Laienbildung im Spätmittelalter und in der Reformationszeit. Symposion Wolfenbüttel 1981* (Stuttgart, 1984), pp. 467–503; Bernard Ribémont, 'On the Definition of an Encyclopædic Genre in the Middle Ages,' in: Peter Binkley (ed.), *Pre-Modern Encyclopædic Texts: Proceedings of the Second COMERS Congress, Groningen, 1–4 July 1996* (Leiden, 1997), pp. 47–61.

[6] Robert L. Fowler, 'Encyclopædias: Definitions and Theoretical Problems,' in: Peter Binkley (ed.): *Pre-Modern Encyclopædic Texts* [as quoted *supra*, n. 5], pp. 3–29.

[7] Annie Becq (ed.), *L'Encyclopédisme. Actes du Colloque de Cæn, 12–16 janvier 1987.* (Paris, 1991); Michelangelo Picone, (ed.), *L'Enciclopedismo Medievale* (Ravenna, 1994); Franz M. Eybl, et al (ed.), *Enzyklopädien der Frühen Neuzeit: Beiträge zu ihrer Erforschung* (Tübingen, 1995); Peter Binkley (ed.), *Pre-Modern Encyclopædic Texts. Proceedings of the Second COMERS Congress, Groningen, 1–4 July 1996* (Leiden, 1997); Steven Harvey, (ed.), *The Medieval Hebrew Encyclopedia of Science and Philosophy* (Dordrecht, 2000); Bernard Ribémont, *Les Origines des encyclopédies médievales: d'Isidore de Séville aux Carolingiens* (Paris, 2001); *id. La "Renaissance" du XIIe siècle et l'encyclopédisme* (Paris, 2002); Christel Meier (ed.), *Die Enzyklopädie im Wandel vom Hochmittelalter bis zur Frühen Neuzeit* (München, 2002); Ingrid Tomkowiak (ed.), *Populäre Enzyklopädien: von der Auswahl, Ordnung und Vermittlung des Wissens* (Zürich, 2002).

First Criterion

An encyclopædia is an organised compendium of knowledge. The aim of its author is to present knowledge in accordance with its own systematics.[8] Qazwīnī's work matches this first criterion. *ʿAjāʾib al-makhlūqāt* presents nature as God's creation in a hierarchical arrangement that corresponds to his contemporary understanding of the system of the natural beings. He divides the creatures of the world, *ʿālam* in the upper ones, *ʿulwiyyāt* and the lower ones, *sufliyyāt*; that is to say, he separates the supra-lunar from the sub-lunar phenomena. Those things that God has created below the lunar sphere are subdivided according to the four elements, fire, *nār*, air, *hawāʾ*, water, *māʾ*, and earth, *arḍ*. The largest part of the work is dedicated to the Three Natural Kingdoms, called *al-kāʾināt* by Qazwīnī, divided into minerals, *maʿādin*, plants, *nabāt* and animals, *ḥayawān*; human beings are included in the last kingdom. This structure of Qazwīnī's work is hierarchical, clear and intelligible and corresponds to the established system of natural history, the knowledge of which Qazwīnī wants to transmit to his readers. This hierarchical order of the material allows the user of the book to relate each and every piece of information to its proper position in the system.

[8] Meier (1984), pp. 481–483, concluding on p. 483: "Der vorherrschende Eindruck bei der Betrachtung des jeweiligen Gesamtwerkes ist in der Regel . . . der einer geschlossenen, vollen Ordnung. Hier vollzieht sich also eine Art qualitativer Sprung, indem die quantitative Vielfalt des Materials aller Art als qualitative Fülle und Vollkommenheit erscheint . . ."; Ribémont (1997), p. 48: "the idea of an organised compendium of knowledge"; Fowler (1997), p. 13: "schematic organisation by subject of most earlier encyclopædias" as opposed to the alphabetical order of the entries; Christel Meier, 'Organisation of Knowledge and Encyclopædic Ordo: Functions and Purposes of a Universal Literary Genre,' in: Peter Binkley (ed.), *Pre-Modern Encyclopædic Texts* [as quoted *supra*, n. 5], p. 104: "In the Middle Ages encyclopædists made use of two general systems of classification to arrange information and to illustrate the interdependence of the different arts and sciences (later on they proceeded to alphabetical order). These systems were based either on traditional conceptions of the order of the world or on rational and scientific approaches to knowledge, i.e. on disciplines or on a system of sciences": "ordo rerum" and "ordo artium".

Second Criterion

The author of an encyclopædia wants to present serious,[9] but concise knowledge in manageable brevity.[10] It is the seriousness of the content of Qazwīnī's book that some researchers have doubted. They maintain that Qazwīnī's book deals with fabulous stories and anecdotes that cannot be taken seriously. They claim that his book is the epitome of the decadence of the Arabic-Islamic sciences.[11] I will try to refute this statement at a later point in this essay. For now a reference to Qazwīnī's own claim of seriousness might suffice. In his preface he emphasizes: "I swear by God, that I have not made up anything (I wrote), but written down everything as I have perused it".[12] He adds that he is concerned with "discernment or deep insight" of creation.[13]

---

[9] Meier (1987), p. 111: "By definition an encyclopædia is a book of universal knowledge".

[10] Meier (1984), p. 475: "Die . . . mittelalterliche Enzyklopädie hat auch eine praktische Seite . . ." Sie ist "eine Bibliothek", ein Buch, das "in sich den Inhalt vieler Bücher" vereint.; and p. 489: ". . . Forderung nach einem knappen Kompendium der Dinge aller Wissensbereiche (besonders der Natur) . . ."; p. 491: "der Kompilationscharakter mit der entsprechenden Kürze bei gleichzeitiger Darbietung des maßgeblichen, . . . Wissens . . ."; Ribémont (1997), p. 59: "we can define the medieval encyclopædia as a « brief compendium »", plus the following quotations.

[11] Dubler (1960), p. 203f.: "The Arabic literature of the 4th/10th centuries, called 'classical', is characterized by an equilibrium between erudition and æsthetic creation. When this equilibrium was disturbed by the decadence of Arabic literature, the writers increasingly disregarded science; the 'adja'ib thus came into greater favour and reached their full development in the cosmographies of the 8th/14th century (sic.). The greatest author of this period was al-Ḳazwini . . ."; and p. 204: "At this epoch the cosmographical works increasingly neglect geography . . ."; and "As the scientific interest decreased, however, and the popular interest in amusing literature grew, the data lost their precision and their exact geographical localization"; Kowalska (1969), p. 178: "Die hier erwähnten kosmographischen Werke sind von vielen Standpunkten (aus gesehen) typisch für die Endperiode der Geschichte der mittelalterlichen Literatur der Araber, weil sie fast ausschließlich Kompilationen aus den Werken der früheren Verfasser sind, und nur im geringen Maße originelle Informationen bringen, die noch weniger ein Resultat der eigenen Beobachtungen des Verfassers bilden."

[12] Munich, Cod. arab. 464, fol. 2v, 9.

[13] Munich, Cod. arab. 464, fol. 3r, 2: *yanẓur bi-ʿayn al-baṣīra.* This expression seemed important to a later reader who gives at the margin the Ottoman translation as: *gönül gözü.*

The criterion of brevity no doubt applies to Qazwīnī's work: he managed to compress the knowledge on God's creatures into one volume. The earliest preserved manuscript of *ʿAjāʾib al-makhlūqāt*, written in Wāsiṭ in 1280, is 424 pages long.[14] Qazwīnī is conscious of having to limit the knowledge he presents. For example, he stresses: "The wonders of the heavens are so numerous that I don't aspire to name a tenth of a tenth of them";[15] or "A human being should look at himself, for there are wonders in him, a lifetime is not long enough to comprehend a tenth of a tenth thereof".[16]

Brevity also characterises the method of his citation. Qazwīnī shortens most of his quotations, citing the main idea while leaving parts of long sentences out. This manner of citation enables him to include many reports and to present them in a more concise manner than the way they were presented in his sources, which is indicative of the encyclopædic genre.[17]

Third Criterion

The aim of an encyclopædia is essentially didactic. The author wants to educate.[18] Qazwīnī does not use any word that conveys the notion of education in his preface, but one of the stated aims of his book is to lead the reader to the feeling of astonishment in front of God's

[14] Munich, Cod. arab. 464.

[15] Munich, Cod. arab. 464, fol. 3r, 17f.

[16] Munich, Cod. arab. 464, fol. 4r, 2f.

[17] Hees (2002), p. 243: "Die meisten Zitate hat Qazwīnī verkürzt, indem er aus einem längeren Abschnitt bei Ǧāḥiẓ immer wieder einzelne Satzteile wegläßt und nur die Hauptlinie des Gedankens oder der Geschichte aufgreift. Manchmal nimmt Qazwīnī dabei leichte Änderungen vor, hauptsächlich in der Wortstellung. Insgesamt kann er durch diese Art des Zitierens viele Nachrichten aufgreifen und sie dem Leser in einer im Vergleich zu Ǧāḥiẓ bündigen, einfachen und eben nicht ausschweifenden Form präsentieren."

[18] Meier (1984), p. 488: "die Enzyklopädie ist Hilfe zum Bücherlesen"; p. 489: die "Gattung . . . trägt also von ihrer Seite auch zur Kenntnis der Welt, d.h. der Werke des Schöpfers bei . . ."; p. 491: "vielmehr soll dem Schüler und Confrater Hilfe geleistet werden."; "Aus dem Charakter der Gattung läßt sich so im deduktiven Verfahren ihre Eignung auch als Bildungsmittel für das im Spätmittelalter rasch starkende lesende Laienpublikum schließen"; ". . . das universale, für alle Menschen gleich wichtige Bildungsziel"; Ribémont (1987), p. 50: "In fact, the encyclopædist aimed at transmitting learned knowledge to a reader who was assumed to expect it. Thus there is *action* in the sphere of learning and knowledge"; p. 55: "We find (in the prologues of encyclopædias) a lexical field with terms like *mores*, *edificatio*, *evigilatio*, *vivere in Domino*, etc."

creation. According to Qazwīnī this feeling is originally innate in the human being, but it is gradually lost due to different preoccupations. Qazwīnī hopes that the reading of his book will revive this feeling of astonishment and will stimulate the reader to contemplate the greatness of God's creation.[19] This can be considered a very clear pedagogical message.

Fourth Criterion

The author of an encyclopædia wants to make specialized knowledge verified by authorities and contemporaries accessible to his public. Such specialized knowledge is usually difficult to access and to comprehend by a general public. The users of an encyclopædia expect such a simplified presentation. Ribémont calls this the didactic transposition.[20] In order to fulfil this aim properly, the author of an encyclopædia should firstly be able to sift and collect the most significant contents from many different specialized books and secondly to systematize and order these collected bits of information in an accessible manner.[21] Qazwīnī is aware of this working process. He states: "It is now incumbent upon the one who studies my book to imagine the efforts I have undertaken in order to collect what was scattered, *fī jam'i mā kāna mubaddadan* and to put together what was cut into pieces, *fī talfīqi mā kāna mushattatan*."[22] In this phrase the two central concepts of the encyclopædic working appear: to collect and order.

I want to investigate to what extent Qazwīnī in his treatment of the material fulfills his stated claims concerning collecting and ordering. As an example, I choose his presentation of the Third Natural Kingdom, the animals, *al-ḥayawān*.[23]

[19] Munich, Cod. arab. 464, fol. 2v, 16–fol. 3r, 2.
[20] Ribémont (1987), pp. 50–53.
[21] Meier (1984), pp. 476–477.
[22] Munich, Cod. arab. 464, fol. 2r, 27–fol. 2v, 1.
[23] In this study I do not consider Qazwīnīs discussion of the human being, the djinn and the animals of wondrous appearances and forms, but concentrate on the remaining animals, Munich, Cod. arab. 464, fol. 168v–fol. 207r; plus the water animals that are treated at the end of the discussion about the third element, namely 'water', fol. 72r–fol. 78v. For a detailed analysis of Qazwīnī's treatment of the animals, please refer to Hees (2002), pp. 115–253.

In this case, we can observe that Qazwīnī indeed collected material from a large number of sources with very different scopes and nature. In his treatment of the animal kingdom he classifies the animals according to different categories, such as the beasts of burden, cattle, birds and so on. He gives a description of each specific animal, followed by a presentation of the medical properties of its body parts. For the physical descriptions, he uses Jāḥiẓ's *Kitāb al-ḥayawān* frequently,[24] Bīrūnī's *Āthār al-bāqiya*, Ibn Faḍlān's *Riḥla*,[25] an anonymous work *Tuḥfat al-gharāʾib* less frequently[26] and most probably a Persian work on natural history by Shāhmardān.[27] For his presentations on the medical properties, he relies on Ibn Sīnā's *al-Qānūn fī l-ṭibb*, most probably the lost work *Kitāb al-khawāṣṣ* by Bālīnās as well as the work of Shāhmardān.[28] For each animal category, he writes a general introduction using information from a philosophical encyclopædia, namely *Rasāʾil Ikhwān al-Ṣafāʾ*.[29] It is evident that he uses specialized sources for his presentation of the animal kingdom. He derives relevant information from them and then reassembles it in his own order. At least material from three separate fields of knowledge, namely philosophy, natural history and medicine are combined and presented.

His act of compilation is also evident in the large number of individual animals that he was able to collect. The most impressive is his collection of birds. He presents 57 different species.[30]

His description of the eagle stands as an example for his "putting together what was cut into pieces". Al-Jāḥiẓ in his voluminous work *Kitāb al-ḥayawān* has a number of reports on the eagle. These reports are scattered throughout his work. Qazwīnī knew the entire work of Jāḥiẓ and painstakingly collected and selected information on the eagle from the different volumes and presented it in a coherent text under the rubric *ʿuqāb*.[31] This is a concrete example of how Qazwīnī

[24] Hees (2002), pp. 242–244.
[25] Hees (2002), p. 246.
[26] Hees (2002), p. 245f.
[27] Hees (2002), pp. 240–242; one must be of course very careful about such claims of dependence as Remke Kruk points out in her review (2002), p. 651f.
[28] Hees (2002), pp. 247–249.
[29] Hees (2002), p. 239.
[30] Munich, Cod. arab. 464, fol. 185v–fol. 197r. For a table, comparing Qazwīnī's impressive list with other sources dealing with birds, please see Hees (2002), p. 136f., where it becomes visible that Qazwīnī made an exceptional effort to be as comprehensive as possible in this regard.
[31] Munich, Cod. arab. 464, fol. 192v, 9–fol. 193r, 4. Concerning the eagle,

managed to make the scattered material on the eagle more accessible to his reader.[32]

In the same manner Qazwīnī uses Ibn Sīnā's *al-Qānūn fī l-ṭibb*. This is most evident in his entry on the frog.[33] He derives information from Ibn Sīnā's section on the frog in making simple remedies as well as from his treatise on 'Potions from animal poison'.[34] Therefore, Qazwīnī must have studied this entire medical work thoroughly. He collected information from different parts of this work and then assembled it under the appropriate rubric.[35]

We can observe how Qazwīnī was able to shape an integral whole out of the collected quotations. His description of the eagle for example is well structured. First, Qazwīnī assembles traditions about its hunting behaviour, then on the age of the eagle, and finally on some special behaviour by young eagles. He gave special care to the lucidity of his text.[36]

No doubt, Qazwīnī was successful in collecting and rearranging the results of his research.

Fifth Criterion

The author of an encyclopædia seeks to make his book as user friendly as possible. To facilitate the use of his book, the author can include one or more of the following: a detailed table of contents, a clearly marked hierarchical structure, numerical or alphabetical lists, introductions, summaries, glossaries or cross-references.[37] Qazwīnī uses some of these devices in his text.

Qazwīnī quotes from Jāḥiẓ the following information: catching of the black wolf (V 550), pursuit of the armies (VI 322 and VII 21), telling by the huntsmen (VI 407), Iraq-Yemen (VII 37), feather pipes (VII 25), saying by the Beduins (VII 24). The numbers in brackets indicate volume and page of the edition by 'Abd as-Salām Muḥammad Hārūn, Cairo, 1385/1965–1389/1969, of the *Kitāb al-ḥayawān*. For a full discussion of Qazwīnī's presentation of the eagle, please refer to Hees (2002), pp. 151–176.

[32] Cf. Hees (2002), pp. 243; 251.

[33] Munich, Cod. arab. 464, fol. 76r, 23–fol. 76v, 23. For a full discussion of Qazwīnī's presentation of the frog, please refer to Hees (2002), pp. 189–204.

[34] Ibn Sīnā, *al-Qānūn fī l-ṭibb* (Būlāq, 1294 H., repr. Beirut: Dār Ṣādir, n.d.), vol. III, p. 232f., and vol. I, p. 466.

[35] Cf. Hees (2002), p. 248.

[36] Cf. Hees (2002), p. 170.

[37] Ribémont (1987), p. 58: "For this reason we can measure the evolution of the encyclopædic tradition by the writer's use of more and more indices, alphabetical

He presents a detailed table of contents, *fihrist*, filling two and a half pages.[38] This table of contents illustrates the hierarchical structure of the book, divided into two main parts, *al-maqāla al-ūla* and *al-maqāla al-thāniya*; subdivided into numbered subjects, *al-naẓar al-awwal, al-naẓar al-thāni*. These are further divided into sections, *anwāʿ*, and sub-sections, *fuṣūl*, that are alphabetically enumerated, *alif, bāʾ* and so on. The investigation about the human being has additional structuring features, namely divisions, *aqsām*, subdivided into kinds, *aṣnāf*.

These pages show another aspect of the user-friendliness of this text, namely, the optical design that marks the hierarchical structure through framed, particularly large and bold headings. Beneath these come subheadings in a slightly smaller script, written in red ink. Within the body of the text, new sections and quotations are indicated by a word written in an elongated script, in most cases in red ink. This way of highlighting the headings is used throughout the Wāsiṭ manuscript, which was inscribed during the lifetime of Qazwīnī in the city he lived in.[39]

For the subdivision of the single subjects, Qazwīnī chooses to arrange them in hierarchical order: in the case of the animals he begins with the "most noble", the beasts of burden, ending with the "less noble", the insects. Most of these subdivisions are arranged in alphabetical order. Such a system allows the user of the book to find the information desired as quickly as possible.

In addition to these practical features, Qazwīnī writes introductions for each and every new section of investigation.[40] He gives an overview of the following content including a definition of the living species to be discussed.

tables, etc." A nice example of an analysis of a work along these lines is: Maaike van Berkel, 'The Attitude towards Knowledge in Mamlūk Egypt: Organisation and Structure of the *Ṣubḥ al-aʿshā* by al-Qalqashandī (1355–1418),' in: Peter Binkley (ed.): *Pre-Modern Encyclopædic Texts. Proceedings of the Second COMERS Congress, Groningen, 1–4 July 1996* (Leiden, 1997), pp. 159–168. She argues that the *Ṣubḥ al-aʿshā* was meant as a manual, a work of reference, intended for consultation, because al-Qalqashandī uses the above-mentioned features in order to facilitate the use of his book.

[38] Munich, Cod. arab. 464, fol. 7v–fol. 8v.

[39] Cf. Hees (2002), pp. 83–85.

[40] This is the case for the animals in general, *fī l-ḥayawān*, Munich, Cod. arab. 464, fol. 144r, 9–fol. 144v, 10; but also for each animal category, such as the beasts of burden, *ad-dawābb*, fol. 168v, 21–fol. 169r, 8; cattle, *an-naʿam*, fol. 171r, 4–23; wild animals, *as-sibāʿ*, fol. 175v, 15–25; birds, *aṭ-ṭayr*, fol. 185v, 17–fol. 186r, 14;

Sixth Criterion

In order to help the reader in visualizing the condensed basic knowledge, the author of an encyclopædia uses examples, narrations and illustrations.[41] This criterion for the literary genre 'encyclopædia' is clearly present in Qazwīnī's text. For example, in order to illustrate the cleverness of young eagles more vividly, he contrasts them with more familiar domesticated birds.[42]

Qazwīnī's narration of stories achieves a lively style of presentation. Under the rubric frog, for example, he narrates an orally transmitted anecdote on an emir from Mosul complaining about the croaking of the frogs in his pond, a story that ends with a surprising solution to this problem.[43]

Of course, the illustrations are the most obvious visual feature of the work. In the Wāsiṭ manuscript, 44 drawings and 467 coloured illustrations enrich the text.[44] The illustrations make the text more colourful, and more importantly, they give supplementary information and are indeed at times more lucid than the text itself. The animal illustrations for example substitute the description of the animal in the text, which is missing in most cases. This is how the illustrations facilitate the precise identification of the creature in question, thus bestowing upon the work more scientific value.[45]

insects, *al-hawāmm wa-l-ḥasharāt*, fol. 197r, 21–fol. 197v, 13, and the water animals, *ḥayawanāt al-mā'*, fol. 72r, 4–15. For a discussion of the general introduction about the animals, please see Hees (2002), pp. 144–150.

[41] Meier (1984), p. 471; 480f., concluding, p. 481: "Der Bestandteil Illustration entspricht, insgesamt gesehen, dem Werktyp Enzyklopädie"; Ribémont (1987), p. 52: "His desire is not to incorporate his knowledge into a narrative structure, or even a discourse that is both didactic and logical, whose aim is to demonstrate (in an almost mathematical or philosophical way). The didacticism of the author manifests itself only through example, illustration and images."

[42] Munich, Cod. arab. 464, fol. 192v, 24. In this case, Qazwīnī took the notion of the young eagles who do not move in their nest high up in the mountains and therefore never fall out, from Jāḥiẓ, but his further comment: "If one would put an ordinary bird's young one like a chicken or a partridge in a prey bird's nest, it would immediately crash down", is not to be found in the text of Jāḥiẓ.

[43] Munich, Cod. arab. 464, fol. 76v, 14–17. Qazwīnī reported that it was recommended to the emir that he should cover the pond with a huge cooking pot. Note, that Qazwīnī lived and studied in Mosul for about ten years during the 1220s. Cf. Hees (2002), pp. 49–66. For another example of such orally transmitted anecdotes, see fol. 184v, 2–10.

[44] For a study on the style of these illustrations see for example Hans-Caspar Graf von Bothmer, *Die Illustrationen des "Münchener Qazwīnī" von 1280. (Cod. Monac, arab. 464). Ein Beitrag zur Kenntnis ihres Stils* (München, 1971).

[45] Cf. Hees (2002), p. 346f.; Syrinx von Hees and Edward Schwartz, 'The bird

Seventh Criterion

In order to convince the readership of the credibility of the offered basic knowledge, it is important for the author of an encyclopædia to stress his faithfulness in dealing with his sources and his commitment to tradition.[46] He has to quote authorities and formulate his sentences as definite statements that need not be proved anymore.[47] In this matter also, Qazwīnī's text corresponds to the expectations of a user of an encyclopædia. Throughout his text he employs citations of well-known authorities that are introduced by "he said", *qāla*. In the Wāsiṭ manuscript, a technique in the calligraphy is used to indicate the beginning of a quotation: the letter *qāf* in the word *qāla* is consistently written longer than usual. In the case of the animal description, the authorities mostly quoted are Ibn Sīnā (named 48 times), Bālīnās, the author of *Kitāb al-Khawāṣṣ* (31 times), and al-Jāḥiẓ (26 times).[48] Qazwīnī also mentions authorities he did not consult directly, but had quoted already in his sources. ʿAbdallah Ibn ʿUmar as a ḥadīth-authority,[49] or more general authorities like the hunters, the Bedouins or the Indians, as well as the names of poets with their poems are derived from Jāḥiẓ and cited in Qazwīnī as direct sources.[50]

The style of Qazwīnī's text corresponds to clear encyclopædic statement sentences. He strives with great effort to be unambiguous about his subjects, thus consciously avoiding disputed contents. For instance his sources describe in different ways how the eagle is able

illustrations of a thirteenth-century Arab natural history', in: *Interdisciplinary Science Reviews* 29,3 (2004), pp. 231–247.

[46] Meier (1984), p. 477: "Seine Verbindlichkeit gewinnt das dargestellte Wissen erst durch seine Authentizität, d.h. durch die authentische Wiedergabe der Lehre der Fachautoritäten, womöglich der *inventores* jedes Wissensgebietes. Traditionsgebundenheit und Quellentreue der Enzyklopädie sind also Tugenden, nicht Mängel."

[47] Ribémont (1987), p. 52: ". . . the encyclopædic discourse is characterised by the presence of certain elements. These include, first of all, continual references and quotations which make the text seem like an *accessus ad auctores*, as shown by the recurrence of expressions such as *ut dixit*, "sicomme dit", or the appearance, often abrupt, of the name of an *auctor* followed by a quotation. Furthermore, the encyclopædist's mode of expression is that of statement and definition."

[48] For a precise list of these occurrences in Qazwīnī's text, please refer to Hees (2002), p. 247, fn. 494; p. 248, fn. 499; and p. 242, fn. 474.

[49] Fol. 76r, 25. For a commentary, see Hees (2002), p. 195. Another example would be the naming of the anonymous *Ṣāḥib al-filāḥa*, fol. 192v, 11, a quotation most probably taken over from Ibn Qutayba, cf. Hees (2002), p. 167.

[50] See Hees (2002), p. 243 with fn. 476.

to catch a hare or a fox. Qazwīnī avoids details and restricts his statement to the surely established fact, that "it hunts small wild animals like hares and foxes".[51] Qazwīnī tries not to digress from the main subject. He avoids citing information which might be equally valid in entries on other animals, as in the case of the eagle.[52]

It became evident that authorities are abundant in Qazwīnī's work and that he tries to formulate his sentences as clear and undisputed statements, avoiding any possible confusion or ambiguity, assuring his reader of the credibility of the offered knowledge.

Eighth Criterion

The encyclopædia is meant to aid the general cultural memory.[53] This idea is expressed by Qazwīnī in his preface, where he says: "I wanted to write down (the astonishing peculiarities) to make them lasting. I detested to forget them lest they would be lost".[54]

Ninth Criterion

Both Christel Meier and Bernard Ribémont underline the central position of natural history in the Western medieval works they studied.[55] These encyclopædias with a special focus on nature were abundant during the 13th century.[56] They present the *res naturales* as God's creation. The purpose of writing theses encyclopædias was to guide

[51] Munich, Cod. arab., fol. 192v, 9. For a detailed reference to the other sources that were compared with this quotation (Aristotle; Jāḥiẓ; Ibn Qutayba; Ibn Sīnā; Shahmardān), please see Hees (2002), p. 166, fn. 129.

[52] See Hees (2202), p. 167f. In another case, Qazwīnī notes the well-known tradition of the hare changing his sex yearly, but ignores the disputed opinion, that this might be the way the hares reproduce themselves. See Hees (2002), pp. 177–179.

[53] Ribémont (1987), p. 53: "The encyclopædic text is a *locus memoriæ* . . ."; p. 58.

[54] Munich, Cod. arab., fol. 2r, 26f.

[55] Meier (1984), p. 479: ". . . die elementare Form der Enzyklopädie, die nur den Kosmos, die natürliche Welt darstellt"; p. 487: ". . . die Kosmographie (die unabdingbar in eine Enzyklopädie gehört)"; Ribémont (1987), p. 53: "Any medieval encyclopædia presents knowledge . . . with a particular orientation: to present the properties of *res naturales*, that is to say, practically all the elements of Creation, elements that are always considered as coming from the will of God."

[56] Cf. Jacques Le Goff, 'Pourquoi le XIIIe siècle a-t-il été plus particulièrement un siècle d'encyclopédisme?', in: *Picone* (1994), pp. 23–40.

the reader through the study of nature to the knowledge of God.[57] This corresponds to Qazwīnī's main concern. Qazwīnī concentrates in his work on the presentation of natural history devoting most of his attention to the description of the Three Natural Kingdoms. He reports how he "passionately fell in love with the wonderful works of God the Sublime in his creations and with the extraordinary creative ability in his creatures".[58] He is convinced that his book on nature as God's creation is able to lead the reader to the knowledge of God. This is reflected in his words: "Whenever one ponders over (the physical perceptible creations of God), one gains through God right guidance, certainty, enlightenment and wisdom";[59] or: "Therein lies enlightenment and remembrance for each repentant servant of God";[60] completing his discussion of the harmonious functions of the human organs he says: "Neither the creator nor his devices are to be seen. Glory be to Him, how great he is and how evident is his proof."[61] Thus nature becomes a convincing proof of God's greatness. This use of the study of nature is expressed throughout the whole book.[62]

With this investigation of the distinguishing features of the encyclopædic genre, I hope to have made evident that the book *ʿAjāʾib al-makhlūqāt* by Zakariyyāʾ al-Qazwīnī is a full-fledged encyclopædia in medieval terms. His work fulfils to a large extent the criteria developed by medievalists for the literary genre 'encyclopædia'. Arguably this book is more of an encyclopædia than *Kitāb Shifāʾ an-nafs* by Ibn Sīnā.[63] While the latter text has received its due attention from schol-

[57] Meier (1984), p. 474: "... das Naturstudium als Weg zur Gotteserkenntnis"; p. 488: "die Enzyklopädie ist Hilfe zum Bücherlesen und sie führt zur Gotteserkenntnis".

[58] Munich, Cod. arab. 464, fol. 1v, 16f.

[59] Munich, Cod. arab. 464, fol. 2r, 4f.

[60] Munich, Cod. arab. 464, fol. 3r, 18.

[61] Munich, Cod. arab. 464, fol. 5r, 8.

[62] Another example would be Munich, Cod. Arab. 464, fol. 3v, 22: "From the earth germinates no leaf without that therein lies one or more profit, that man's intellect knows without understanding". His detailed description of the medical, cosmetic and hygienic properties of the animal parts and of the plants, make it very clear and especially graphic to the reader, how great the profit of God's created things is to him. Qazwīnī offers this possibility of interpretation through his outstanding combination of natural history with medicine. Cf. Hees (2002), p. 240.

[63] Compare the argument put forward by Charles E. Butterworth, 'In what sense is Averroes an encyclopedist?', in: Stefen Harvey (ed.): *The Medieval Hebrew Encyclopedia of Science and Philosophy* (Leiden, 2000), pp. 99–119.

ars discussing Arabic encyclopædias, the former has been largely ignored by scholars.

With regard to the content, the text is no doubt an encyclopædia of natural history. It seems to be the first encyclopædia of natural history in Arabic. However, Qazwīnī had the possibility to follow Persian models with special emphasis on natural history. Živa Vesel treated four Persian encyclopædias on natural history in her study on Persian encyclopædic writing.[64] Three of these works were composed in the 12th century prior to Qazwīnī's *ʿAjāʾib al-makhlūqāt*. In comparison to these Persian encyclopædias Qazwīnī's presentation of God's creation stands out for its extraordinarily clear hierarchical structure. The system he used follows closely the Aristotelian system of nature as developed in the parts on natural history, *al-ʿilm aṭ-ṭabīʿī* of the philosophical encyclopædias.[65]

Qazwīnī's choice of title for his encyclopædia, *ʿAjāʾib al-makhlūqāt*, The Wonders of Creation, refers to nature as a convincing wonder of God. It is a commonly expressed view by some authors that the term *ʿajāʾib* carries the meaning of fantastic and unrealistic, and consequently is conceived of as belonging to an unscientific context. Contrary to this view, I firmly believe that the combined notion of *ʿajāʾib al-makhlūqāt* indicates nothing unrealistic, but refers to living beings, that is to say to nature, as a sign of God.[66] This should not be seen to disqualify the serious research that went into the work, nor the accessibility of the work to readers of the time.

Classifying the work *ʿAjāʾib al-makhlūqāt* as an 'encyclopædia' greatly helps in understanding the purpose of this book better and to describe its position and function in Arabic literary history. There is no need anymore for dismissive phrases such as "there is nothing original in this work", "it is just a compilation", "it disregards science", "it deals only with learning, not with science", "it is a typical example of the decadence of Arabic literature". When we understand Qazwīnī's work as an encyclopædia, it becomes clear that his purpose was to transmit basic knowledge drawn from authoritative specialized works and this is what he actually did. Thus, his purpose was not to be

[64] Živa Vesel, *Les encyclopédies persanes. Essai de typologie et de classification des sciences* (Paris, 1986), pp. 27–34; 46f.

[65] See Vesel (1986), p. 46f.; Hees (2002), pp. 103–109.

[66] For a full development of this argument, see Syrinx von Hees, 'The Astonishing: a critique and re-reading of *ʿAjāʾib* Literature', in: *MEL* 8,2 (2005), pp. 101–120.

original, but to provide a good compilation of verified information, offered in a clear and intelligible structure. The purpose was to offer a learning tool for his readers. It is this didactical transposition that Qazwīnī mastered in an exemplary manner. In this way he did not disregard science, but made scientific knowledge available for a broader public.

For whom did Qazwīnī write his book? Who actually used such organized compendia of basic knowledge? Is it possible to read such a systematic encyclopædia from beginning to end with pleasure? Could it be used to study the material in a systematic way? Or, was it specifically meant to be used as a reference work? Until now information on the history of the reception of *ʿAjāʾib al-makhlūqāt* and similar works is missing. Such an investigation would enhance our understanding of pre-modern encyclopædias. I don't want to jump to conclusions concerning the reception of *ʿAjāʾib al-makhlūqāt*, but it is remarkable and worth mentioning that a large number of illustrated and un-illustrated manuscripts are preserved to the present day. The work *ʿAjāʾib al-makhlūqāt* was translated into Persian and Ottoman Turkish. This testifies to the high popularity of Qazwīnī's encyclopædia on natural history. The readership must have been relatively huge. The intention of the author of such a general work on 'scientific subjects' was not to replace the specialized literature on which the author based his work. It was directed to a broad, non-specialized readership. Students could use such a book to get a first overview of the material, scholars of all specialties could profit from such a general reading and most probably literates who were not engaged in research professionally, could consult such a book. The existence of an encyclopædic text such as this one is itself testimony to a broad readership. In any case, a book addressing a large number of learned people should not be taken as a sign of the decadence of the Arabic-Islamic sciences.

L'ENCYCLOPÉDISME DANS L'HISTORIOGRAPHIE: RÉFLEXIONS SUR LE CAS D'IBN KHALDŪN

Abdesselam Cheddadi
Institut Universitaire de la Recherche Scientifique,
Université Mohammed V, Rabat, Morocco

On sait que le mouvement encyclopédique qui a fleuri dans la culture islamique a connu deux périodes privilégiées : la première se situe à l'époque de l'islam classique, entre le IXe et le XIe siècle et est localisée principalement autour de Bagdad; la seconde se situe au Moyen Âge tardif, entre le XIIIe et le XVe siècle, et est localisée en Égypte et en Syrie. Au cours de ces deux périodes, les sociétés musulmanes ont pu voir s'épanouir ce que Franz Rosenthal a appelé « knowledge triumphant », inaugurant la première tentative historique de mise en œuvre, à une relative grande échelle, de l'idéal d'un « être de savoir » dont nous pouvons reconnaître un des derniers avatars dans le slogan « pour une société du savoir » que la Banque mondiale et le PNUD, tout récemment, ont tenté de promouvoir à travers le monde, de la Corée du Sud et de la Chine jusqu'au Maroc.

Mon propos ici est de présenter quelques réflexions sur l'encyclopédisme d'Ibn Khaldūn, qui se situe au milieu de la seconde période. Mais il ne serait peut-être pas inutile d'esquisser, avant cela, fût-ce très sommairement, un rappel de ce qu'était cette version tardive de l'encyclopédisme musulman, du fait qu'il constitue l'immédiat arrière-plan d'Ibn Khaldūn. Je me contenterai de fournir des indications sur le contexte intellectuel, social et politique où des œuvres à caractère encyclopédique ont pu voir le jour, et sur les principales fonctions qu'elles étaient censées remplir.

L'arrière-plan d'Ibn Khaldūn

Comparé à l'encyclopédisme de l'époque de l'islam classique, l'encyclopédisme des XIIIe, XIVe et XVe siècles en Égypte et en Syrie accuse un recul à la fois au niveau du champ du savoir couvert et du public auquel il s'adresse, ce qui s'explique aisément par la situation historique du monde islamique d'alors, profondément divisé et souffrant encore des effets dévastateurs des diverses vagues du déferlement mongol. L'ouverture au savoir et la créativité scientifique s'étant, par ailleurs, rétrécie—sans véritablement disparaître, comme on l'a parfois avancé—, la dimension épistémologique de systématisation et d'organisation des connaissances ne se justifie plus, et les préoccupations philosophiques et religieuses de l'esprit encyclopédique s'atténuent considérablement. Seul résiste, et même se renforce un encyclopédisme utilitaire, qui s'adresse de façon privilégiée aux secrétaires et aux hauts fonctionnaires. Mais là encore, il se développe géographiquement de façon restrictive, dans le seul royaume mamelouk, qui était, il est vrai, la région du monde musulman qui connaissait alors la plus grande stabilité politique et la plus grande prospérité économique.

Si les grandes sommes philosophiques et religieuses des siècles précédents ne sont pas renouvelées, en revanche d'importantes compilations sont réalisées dans les domaines littéraire, géographique et historique. Parmi les œuvres encyclopédiques les plus significatives on peut citer le grand dictionnaire de Yāqūt sur la toponymie du monde connu et celui d'al-Samʿānī sur l'onomastique ethnique, les dictionnaires biographiques d'Ibn Khallikān, d'al-Ṣafadī, d'al-Dhahabī et d'Ibn Ḥajar, les monographies biographiques centrées sur les capitales du Proche-Orient comme Bagdad, Damas et Alep, et, enfin, les histoires universelles telles que celles d'Ibn al-Athīr ou d'Ibn Kathīr. Pour les savants, les érudits, les écrivains, les fonctionnaires, ces ouvrages représentaient d'indispensables instruments de travail. Ils constituaient aussi une mine de matériaux à partir desquels des synthèses s'avéraient possibles. C'est dans ce climat que se situe la démarche encyclopédique d'al-Nuwayrī, d'al-ʿUmarī et d'al-Qalqashandī. Une présentation rapide de leurs œuvres permettra de préciser quelques traits du contexte dans lequel s'inscrit la vision encyclopédique d'Ibn Khaldūn, même si celui-ci ne s'y réfère jamais explicitement.

Al-Nuwayrī, né en 1279, est mort en 1332, l'année de naissance d'Ibn Khaldūn. Haut fonctionnaire sous le règne du sultan mamelouk Muḥammad Qalāwūn, son ouvrage encyclopédique, le *Nihāyat al-arab fī ʿuyūn al-adab*, qui connaît une large diffusion de son vivant, est destiné à procurer à ses pairs un instrument de référence, de vérification et d'information dans l'exercice de leur charge. En fait, il dépasse le public des *kuttāb* pour s'adresser à tout homme ayant le souci de se cultiver. En plus des aspects touchant directement l'administration, il réserve une très grande place aux sciences religieuses et à la culture littéraire au sens large.

Érudit sans cesse en éveil, savant avide de confrontations, al-ʿUmarī est plus original et moins soucieux des autorités que ne le fut al-Nuwayrī, son prédécesseur immédiat. Il adopte, dans son *Masālik al-abṣār fī mamālik al-amṣār*, une approche plus critique que livresque. Son ouvrage est divisé en deux grandes parties, dont l'une est consacrée à la description de la terre, et l'autre à l'homme en tant qu'être vivant en société et se livrant, de ce fait, à la culture de l'esprit. Dans sa cosmographie et sa géographie, il renoue avec la grande tradition des auteurs irakiens des IXe et Xe siècles. Se voulant plus qu'un simple compilateur, il complète son information sur les pays et les royaumes par d'amples enquêtes menées avec rigueur, tout en consacrant à l'histoire et aux annales des chapitres très développés et fort documentés. Une grande partie de son ouvrage est dominée par l'esprit d'*adab* : plusieurs volumes sont consacrés à des biographies de savants, de juristes, d'écrivains et de poètes. Il y présente aussi une vaste anthologie littéraire s'étendant à toutes les grandes régions du monde islamique.

Avec al-Qalqashandī, plus jeune qu'Ibn Khaldūn d'une vingtaine d'années, nous avons affaire à un auteur qui s'adresse plus franchement au milieu des fonctionnaires de la haute administration, comme l'indique d'ailleurs le titre de son ouvrage : *Subh al-aʿshā fī ṣināʿat al-inshāʾ*, sur l'art de la chancellerie. Mais on y voit bien combien était large et exigeante la culture des secrétaires. Si rien n'est négligé de ce qui touche à la chancellerie—art de la prose, technique et règles de l'art du secrétaire, normes imposées par l'usage et le protocole dans l'exercice de ses fonctions, itinéraires et état politique des royaumes dans le passé jusqu'à l'époque mamelouke—quatre des sept volumes qui constituent le *Ṣubḥ al-aʿshā* sont réservés à une vaste anthologie embrassant l'ensemble de la culture islamique.

Ainsi, il semble bien que, dans ce second grand moment que connaît l'encyclopédisme en islam, c'est un idéal de culture moyenne pratique qui l'emporte, moins tourné vers la philosophie et la religion, le savoir pour le savoir, et s'adressant en priorité aux différentes couches sociales qui participent de près ou de loin à la gestion et à l'administration des affaires publiques. En revanche, les deux anciennes dimensions de l'ouverture sur le monde et de la maîtrise de la langue et de la littérature sont conservées, et l'esprit universaliste demeure vigoureusement affirmé.

L'encyclopédisme chez Ibn Khaldūn

Ibn Khaldūn ne s'oppose nullement à cet idéal culturel. Pensant son époque comme celle où la culture islamique a achevé son développement et où le pouvoir et la civilisation urbaine se trouvent au terme de leur cycle d'évolution, il y voit, au contraire, la réalisation de ce que pouvait être, en son temps, une culture citadine prospère. Issu d'une famille de hauts fonctionnaires, serviteur zélé de l'État—aussi bien pendant la première période de sa vie, passée jusqu'à l'âge de cinquante ans dans l'Occident musulman, que durant son séjour de vingt-cinq ans en Égypte—, il adhère parfaitement à cette culture des *kuttāb* qui se donnait pour *la* culture. Cependant, si cet idéal culturel peut trouver une justification théorique dans sa pensée, sa conception propre de l'encyclopédisme se situe ailleurs et revêt une forme inédite sous les deux aspects théorique et historique où elle s'est exprimée.

Comme on le sait, Ibn Khaldūn, dans la lignée d'historiens comme al-Masʿūdī et Ibn al-Athīr, est l'auteur d'une histoire universelle monumentale, 'Le Livre des Exemples' (*Kitāb al-ʿIbar*), qui peut être considéré comme une des dernières grandes sommes historiques de la culture islamique. À ce titre, son entreprise en tant que tentative de totalisation et de présentation systématique des connaissances historiques s'inscrit incontestablement dans le sillage des œuvres encyclopédiques similaires qui ont marqué l'historiographie des XIIIe et XIVe siècles, comme celles d'Ibn Kathīr, d'al-Dhahabī ou d'Ibn Abī l-Dam, ainsi que celles de bien d'autres auteurs de cette époque. Mais, avec la *Muqaddima*, premier volume du *Livre des Exemples*, qui en constitue l'introduction théorique, Ibn Khaldūn propose une totalisation et une présentation du savoir humain effectuées à partir d'un point de vue nouveau. C'est cet aspect que je vais d'abord aborder brièvement.

Précisons, en premier lieu, que le savoir encyclopédique qu'on peut découvrir dans la *Muqaddima* déborde le cadre de celui qu'on rencontre dans les formes connues de l'encyclopédisme musulman. En effet, en plus de l'exposé systématique sur les sciences religieuses, les sciences philosophiques, les sciences occultes, et les sciences en rapport avec la langue et la littérature, contenu dans le sixième chapitre consacré aux sciences et à l'enseignement, on y trouve trois autres sommes à caractère systématiques : premièrement, une description géographique complète de la terre habitée; deuxièmement, un tableau des institutions religieuses et politiques musulmanes mais aussi, juives et chrétiennes auquel s'ajoute une présentation détaillée des emblèmes du pouvoir; et, troisièmement, un tableau, unique en son genre dans la culture islamique, des arts et des métiers pratiqués dans les sociétés humaines.

N'ayant pas une visée purement cognitive et explicative, la *Muqaddima* a une vision plus compréhensive que toutes les approches encyclopédistes qui l'ont précédée, y compris l'approche philosophique. Elle peut de la sorte échapper à la relation circulaire, héritée de la tradition aristotélicienne, entre ontologie, système des connaissances humaines, et exposition didactique de celles-ci. La théorie de la société et de la civilisation qu'elle développe, qui comprend à la fois le système des connaissances et le système des pratiques humaines, est instrumentale : elle se veut l'outil de l'écriture et de l'explication de l'histoire.

Le changement de perspective par rapport à la tradition philosophique gréco-arabe est radical : le point de vue auquel Ibn Khaldūn se place n'est pas celui de l'être, mais de l'homme en tant qu'animal social. Chez lui, l'anthropologie et la sociologie passent avant l'ontologie, et c'est à travers les deux premières et non la troisième, comme chez les philosophes, qu'il examine le système des connaissances ainsi que l'ensemble des activités humaines. La pensée, qui est dit-il, la caractéristique propre à l'homme, n'est pas chez lui dépendante d'une émanation de l'intellect actif, comme chez al-Fārābī, Ibn Sīnā et Ibn Rushd, mais elle résulte simplement des activités des organes corporels de l'homme, les sens et le cerveau. Sans nier l'existence d'un monde surnaturel des essences spirituelles, il affirme qu'il n'est pas accessible à l'homme, si ce n'est d'une façon restrictive à travers la révélation prophétique, et seulement en vue de la loi religieuse.

À partir de là, Ibn Khaldūn propose une cosmologie, une théorie de la connaissance et une classification des sciences qui opèrent une rupture fondamentale avec les conceptions philosophiques qui l'ont précédé, même s'il utilise souvent les mêmes matériaux que celles-ci. Sa cosmologie met l'accent sur la place spécifique qu'occupe l'homme dans la chaîne hiérarchisée des êtres. Grâce à elle, il peut d'une part marquer les limites de l'homme et, de l'autre, expliquer le phénomène crucial que constitue la révélation. Située entre le monde des sens qui lui est immédiatement inférieur et le monde des esprits ou des essences spirituelles qui lui est immédiatement supérieur, l'âme humaine, qui a une nature double, animale et angélique, peut avoir accès sous certaines conditions et pour des types particuliers d'hommes aux réalités surnaturelles. C'est ainsi que s'explique la révélation prophétique.

Dans la théorie de la connaissance qu'Ibn Khaldūn échafaude sur la base de cette cosmologie, il établit une distinction entre les deux types de connaissances qui sont permises à l'homme : le premier type, celui de la connaissance qui provient de la pensée, est ouvert à tous les hommes en général. Il est fondé uniquement sur les facultés corporelles de l'homme. Ibn Khaldūn souligne la fonctionnalité au point de vue anthropologique de ce type de connaissance. La pensée, dit-il, comporte trois degrés d'intelligence—l'intelligence discernante (*al-ʿaql al-tamyīzī*), l'intelligence empirique (*al-ʿaql al-tajribī*), et l'intelligence théorique ou spéculative (*al-ʿaql al-naẓarī*)—, liés respectivement aux trois sphères d'activité de l'homme : celle de l'action sur le monde et de la fabrication des objets; celle des relations interpersonnelles et sociales; et, enfin, celle des activités théoriques ou scientifiques.

Le second type de connaissance, celle qui provient de la vision des essences spirituelles, est réservé à certaines catégories d'hommes qui ont une disposition naturelle à se hisser de la condition humaine à la condition angélique en un bref instant et dans des circonstances particulières. Ce second type de connaissance comporte également plusieurs niveaux. Le niveau le plus élevé est celui des prophètes, qui réalisent une vision complète et authentique des essences spirituelles grâce à une disposition naturelle que Dieu a mise en eux. Ensuite, il y a le niveau des saints et des mystiques qui, grâce aux exercices spirituels qu'ils pratiquent et à leur piété, peuvent écarter le voile des sens et avoir également une vision authentique des essences spirituelles. Puis, on a une troisième catégorie, qui comporte les divers types de devins, de magiciens et de sorciers : eux aussi ont une disposition naturelle à accéder à l'invisible, mais c'est une disposition imparfaite, ce qui fait que leur vision des essences spirituelles est obscurcie et affaiblie, et que les connaissances qu'ils obtiennent sont incertaines et mêlent souvent le vrai et le faux. Enfin, il y a un dernier niveau de vision des essences spirituelles, qui est en principe accessible à tous les hommes dans certaines situations particulières comme le rêve, la proximité du sommeil ou de la mort, ou chez les fous. Ce niveau s'explique par le fait que, dans tous ces états, l'âme se détache d'une certaine façon et jusqu'à un certain point du corps, et peut, par conséquent, accéder au monde des esprits. Mais la vision des essences y est aléatoire et échappe au vouloir de l'homme.

Pour ce qui est de la classification des sciences que propose Ibn Khaldūn, elle repose à la fois sur sa cosmologie et sur sa théorie de la connaissance. Voici comment il commence son exposé sur les sciences, dans le fameux sixième chapitre de la *Muqaddima* :

> Les sciences que cultivent les hommes et qui sont apprises et enseignées dans les villes sont de deux sortes. Les unes sont naturelles à l'homme : il en trouve le chemin grâce à sa pensée. Les autres sont traditionnelles : il les reçoit de ceux qui les ont fondées. La première catégorie est celle des sciences de la sagesse et des sciences philosophiques. Ce sont celles que l'homme peut appréhender en vertu de la nature de sa pensée. [. . .] La seconde catégorie est celle des sciences traditionnelles positives. Elles s'appuient toutes sur une information issue de l'institution religieuse.[1]

Ce texte montre que la classification que propose Ibn Khaldūn marque une double différence avec la tradition philosophique : d'un côté elle se présente comme une simple description du système des connaissances, basée sur l'observation des réalités anthropologiques et historiques. De l'autre côté, comme on le voit à travers sa division des sciences en « sciences rationnelles », qui « sont naturelles à l'homme » et qu'il appréhende « en vertu de la nature de sa pensée », et en « sciences traditionnelles . . . qui s'appuient sur une information issue de l'institution religieuse », répudiant les conceptions ontologiques de la philosophie traditionnelle, elle se réfère clairement à la cosmologie et à la théorie de la connaissance propres à Ibn Khaldūn.

Dans la suite de l'exposé sur les sciences, ce qui est mis en évidence, ce sont les aspects humains d'organisation, de développement et d'enseignement de celles-ci. Ibn Khaldūn n'expose pas seulement les *uṣūl* et les *furū*ᶜ, ainsi que les *masāʾil* (fondements, développements dérivés, questions ou thèmes) de chacune des sciences considérées, mais en fait un historique souvent détaillé, en mentionnant

[1] Cf. *Le Livre des Exemples*, I, édition Gallimard, La Bibliothèque de la Pléiade, Paris, 2002, p. 851.

les principales autorités et les œuvres maîtresses, et en précisant les conditions de transmission et d'enseignement dans les différentes parties du monde musulman.

Cette première forme d'expression de l'encyclopédisme d'Ibn Khaldūn se situe donc dans une nouvelle perspective épistémologique : prenant ses distances aussi bien par rapport à la visée ontologique des philosophies d'al-Fārābī, d'Ibn Sīnā et d'Ibn Rushd, au souci du salut religieux présent par exemple chez les Ikhwān al-Ṣafā' ou chez al-Ghazāli, que par rapport à la préoccupation utilitaire et pédagogique prépondérante dans la dernière forme d'encyclopédisme en Égypte et en Syrie, elle répond à une exigence qui dérive d'une démarche anthropologique. Liée à la science de la société et de la civilisation dont Ibn Khaldūn se proclame à juste titre l'inventeur, et se voulant purement humaine, elle se rapproche peut-être le plus de l'esprit encyclopédiste moderne qui s'est développé à partir du siècle des lumières.

La seconde expression de l'encyclopédisme chez Ibn Khaldūn concerne plus précisément le domaine de l'histoire. Tout d'abord, il est clair que l'auteur du "Livre des Exemples" partage la perspective de totalisation et d'universalisme des plus grands historiens des XIIIe et XIVe siècles, comme Ibn al-Athīr et Ibn Kathīr, qu'il connaît et qu'il a consultés. Il est également évident qu'il s'inscrit dans le courant historiographique critique tel qu'il est illustré par exemple par des auteurs comme al-Ījī ou al-Kāfiyajī et que, tout en défendant la discipline de l'histoire en raison des fonctions vitales qu'elle assume dans la culture islamique, il vise la restauration d'une historiographie plus rigoureuse et plus scientifique. Mais là s'arrêtent les similitudes que l'on peut établir entre ses préoccupations et celles de l'historiographie de son temps. Sur la conception de l'objet de l'histoire et de ses méthodes, sur la forme donnée à l'histoire universelle, il se situe, là aussi, dans un espace radicalement neuf. Je me contenterai, pour illustrer cette nouveauté, de citer deux aspects : la définition de l'objet de l'histoire, et la forme de structuration du récit et de l'œuvre historique.

Prenons d'abord la définition de l'objet de l'histoire. Dans leurs réflexions épistémologiques sur la nature de l'histoire, les auteurs des XIVe et XVe siècles présentent l'objet de l'histoire comme une multiplicité de choses indépendantes les unes des autres, qu'ils ont du mal à classer. Al-Kāfiyajī, par exemple, propose trois rubriques : (1) événements relatifs au Prophète, (2) événements célestes, (3) événements terrestres.[2] On trouve une classification différente chez al-Sakhāwī : (1) agents du savoir et de la loi, (2) grands événements, (3) événements relatifs au passé reculé et à la fin du monde, (4) événements de moindre importance.[3] Chez d'autres auteurs encore, on trouve des distinctions plus générales, comme celles entre événements marquants, biographies, dates de décès (*aḥdāth, tarājim, wafayāt*).

Le plus souvent, l'objet de l'histoire, comme on le voit, n'est pas pensé dans la catégorie de l'unité. Et sa diversité elle-même est présentée selon des critères hétérogènes et extérieurs, tout juste pour mettre un peu d'ordre sur une liste de choses qui se sont ajoutées les unes aux autres au cours du temps. Le *mawḍūʿ*, l'objet, se donne plutôt comme un agglomérat d'objets. S'il arrive que l'on cherche à subsumer l'ensemble des objets de l'histoire sous une rubrique générale, on choisit celles d'homme et de temps. L'histoire, dit al-Sakhāwī, « a pour objet l'homme et le temps ».[4] De son côté, al-Kāfiyajī déclare que l'objet propre de l'histoire est « d'appréhender l'homme de façon appropriée. » Il classe ensuite les hommes en trois catégories : une catégorie supérieure, qui comprend les prophètes; une catégorie moyenne, qui comprend les saints; et une catégorie inférieure, qui comprend le reste des hommes. L'histoire, conclut-il, est l'ensemble des récits relatifs à ces trois catégories.[5]

Ainsi, si l'histoire a pour objet l'homme, l'homme n'est pas appréhendé comme un concept, mais comme une classe d'objets. Il est remarquable qu'Ibn Khaldun part aussi, dans sa définition de l'histoire, de l'homme. Mais s'il le fait, c'est pour établir une relation nécessaire entre la nature humaine, la société et la civilisation humaine. Il n'appréhende pas l'homme au sens d'une classe d'objets, mais à celui d'un concept. Du même coup, l'histoire n'a plus affaire à un agglomérat d'objets disparates qu'on ordonne selon des catégories, mais à un objet unifié, la civilisation humaine (*al-ʿumrān al-basharī*).

---

[2] Voir al-Kāfiyajī, *al-Mukhtasar fī ʿilm al-tārīkh*, in Franz Rosenthal, *ʿIlm al-tārīkh ʿind al-muslimīn*, trad. arabe par Ṣāliḥ Aḥmad al-ʿAlī (Beyrouth: Mu'assasat al-Risāla, 1403/1983), pp. 237–238.

[3] Voir al-Sakhāwī, *al-Iʿlān bi-l-tawbīkh li-man dhamma ahl al-tārīkh*, in Franz Rosenthal, *ʿIlm al-tārīkh ʿind al-muslimīn*, trad. arabe par Ṣāliḥ Aḥmad al-ʿAlī (Beyrouth: Mu'assasat al-Risāla, 1403/1983), p. 385.

[4] Cf. al-Sakhāwī, *op. cit.*

[5] Cf. al-Kāfiyajī, *op. cit.*, p. 251.

Comme il le dit dans la préface au "Livre des Exemples", l'histoire qu'Ibn Khaldūn projette d'écrire a maintenant un objet bien défini et complètement inédit : c'est une histoire de la civilisation humaine depuis les origines jusqu'à son époque. Cette nouvelle conception de l'objet de l'histoire a une profonde répercussion sur la structuration du récit et de l'œuvre historiques. Chez les plus grands historiens antérieurs, comme al-Masʿūdī, al-Ṭabarī, et Ibn al-Athīr, par exemple, l'œuvre historique se présente essentiellement sous la forme d'une juxtaposition d'objets constitués au cours du temps selon l'ordre chronologique ou l'affinité thématique. Les coupures sur l'axe temporel, la succession des thèmes, n'emportent aucune conséquence sur l'organisation du récit ou de l'œuvre. L'adoption de la forme d'exposition annalistique accentue encore cette organisation de simple juxtaposition. Même lorsque l'œuvre est clairement marquée par des choix idéologiques ou politiques, ceux-ci ne se manifestent que dans le détail ou l'épisode et ne jouent aucun rôle notable dans la structuration du récit d'ensemble.

L'œuvre historique d'Ibn Khaldūn est organisée tout autrement. Comme on l'a vu, l'histoire qu'il veut écrire est une histoire de la civilisation humaine :

> Dans sa vérité, dit-il, l'histoire nous informe sur la société humaine, c'est-à-dire la civilisation du monde et toutes les conditions qui l'affectent de par sa nature : la vie en groupes isolés et la vie en communauté, les formes de solidarité, les types de domination des hommes les uns sur les autres, le pouvoir et les États engendrés par cette domination, les catégories de ces États, les modes d'acquisition et les moyens d'existence, les sciences et les arts auxquels les hommes consacrent leurs travaux et leurs efforts.[6]

Notons ici l'emploi du mot *aḥwāl* (conditions, états) qu'Ibn Khaldūn donne comme synonyme de *aʿrāḍ* ou *ʿawāriḍ*, accidents. Comme il l'énonce à plusieurs reprises dans l'introduction à la *Muqaddima*, l'étude de la civilisation se ramène à l'explication de ses « conditions essentielles » (*al-aḥwāl al-dhātiyya*), ou de « ses accidents essentiels » (*al-ʿawāriḍ al-dhātiyya*). Alors que dans la *Muqaddima*, il présente ces « conditions » ou ces « accidents » à un niveau théorique et de façon systématique, dans l'histoire à proprement parler, il fait le récit de leurs manifestations concrètes dans le cadre de ce qu'il appelle les

[6] *Idem*, p. 251.

« nations » (*al-umam*). Cela le conduit à observer vis-à-vis des récits ou des informations historiques traditionnelles, les *akhbār*, une attitude nouvelle.

Pour écrire l'histoire, il ne s'intéresse pas aux informations historiques en elles-mêmes, mais aux « conditions » qu'elles représentent ou qu'elles illustrent, ce qu'il appelle les « *aḥwāl* ». Et pour atteindre ces « conditions », il va au-delà de la juxtaposition thématique et chronologique des récits, il fait éclater les objets traditionnels spontanément constitués, et il forme un nouveau et unique objet : les nations (*al-umam*).

Bien entendu, ni le mot ni la chose n'étaient ignorés des historiens antérieurs à Ibn Khaldūn. Son apport, c'est d'avoir élevé la notion au niveau du concept. Pour Ibn Khaldūn, une nation (*umma*) est une entité ethnique qui est identifiée par une généalogie (*nasab*) et un nom propre (qui est souvent celui du fondateur ou ancêtre éponyme), spécifiée par un territoire (*mawāṭin*), des « marques distinctives » (*shaʿāʾir*), des coutumes et des croyances, et rendue digne de mémoire (*dhikr*) par des hauts faits dont la forme la plus achevée est la détention du pouvoir souverain (*mulk*). S'il puise ses matériaux dans les récits traditionnels, il le fait en brisant les anciens objets constitués pour en incorporer les éléments dans l'unique objet qu'il choisit pour son histoire. C'est de cette façon qu'il procède pour les informations d'ordre géographique, généalogique, biographique et politique. Aussi pourrait-on dire, en un sens, qu'il a inventé les Arabes et les Berbères en tant qu'objets d'histoire.

Et c'est à travers le récit relatif à ce nouvel objet, les nations, que se structurent le récit et l'œuvre historiques. En effet, le "Livre des Exemples" se présente comme une histoire des nations : l'histoire des Arabes et des Berbères, et celle des nations qui leur étaient contemporaines. Les modes d'intégration du récit sont ceux-là mêmes qui servent à reconnaître, à définir et à suivre le développement d'une nation : la généalogie (*nasab*), le territoire et le mode de vie (*mawāṭin, aḥwāl al-maʿāsh*), mais surtout, le pouvoir (*al-mulk*). Comme on le sait, le pouvoir est présenté, dans la *Muqaddima*, comme l'élément fondamental de l'évolution sociale et de la civilisation. Étant de nature éphémère, il passe d'une nation à l'autre, d'un groupe de nations à un autre groupe de nations. D'où la notion de *dawla*, où l'on reconnaît l'idée première de rotation et de changement. Le rôle de distribution économique et de structuration sociale du pouvoir fait de lui le facteur principal du passage de la civilisation rurale à la civilisation urbaine. La marche même du récit est rythmée par les phases qui marquent la progression des formations politiques ou *duwal*, constituées en nations, de leur état initial de « ruralité » (*al-badāwa*) à l'apogée du pouvoir qu'elles atteignent dans la « civilisation urbaine » (*al-ḥaḍāra*), et à leur chute.

A EUROPEANIST'S PERSPECTIVE

A EUROPEANIST'S PERSPECTIVE

Ann Blair
Dept of History, Harvard University

The Term "Encyclopedia"

"Encyclopedia" is a term coined in Latin and shortly thereafter in various European vernaculars by humanist writers ca. 1470–1530, on the model of what they thought was a Greek term, *enkuklopaideia*, for "circle of learning".[1] The term and its supposed etymology have been rich in history, inspiring authors over many centuries to expatiate on the metaphor of the "circle of learning" in any number of organizational schemes.[2] Even as recently as its latest print edition (the 15th), the *Encyclopædia Britannica* for example described its purview as the circle of learning, which was presented in the *Propaedia* in a circular table with 10 subdivisions.[3] Philological work of the last half century has established, however, that the etymology from *enkuklopaideia* is false, based on a corruption of the Greek expression *enkuklios paideia*, which designated common education or general culture.[4] My point is not to invalidate analyses of the metaphors based on the "circle of learning" which are clearly of great historical significance,

[1] For a list of early appearances of the term, in addition to a general discussion of the term, see Robert L. Fowler, "Encyclopædias: definitions and theoretical problems", in *Pre-modern encyclopædic texts. proceedings of the second COMERS congress*, Groningen, 1–4 July 1996, ed. Peter Binkley (Leiden: Brill, 1997). The introduction of the word in French is attributed to Rabelais in 1532 (see for example Jean Céard, "Le commentaire ou l'encyclopédisme non méthodique de la Renaissance", in *L'Entreprise encyclopédique*, Littérales 21 [1997], pp. 79–95, p. 79); the *Oxford English Dictionary* dates the first English use to 1531 (Sir Thomas Elyot, The Governour, I, xiii).

[2] For a valuable explication of the circle metaphor see Jean Céard, "Encyclopédie et encyclopédisme à la Renaissance" in *Encyclopédisme: actes du colloque de Caen* (1991), ed. Annie Becq (Paris: Aux Amateurs de Livres, 1991), pp. 57–67.

[3] *Encyclopædia Britannica*, 15th edition (Chicago, 1994; first published 1974), *Propaedia*, pp. 5–8 (section by Mortimer J. Adler).

[4] See L. M. de Rijk, "Egkuklios paideia. A Study of Its Original Meaning," *Vivarium* 3 (1965): 24–93; H. Fuchs, "Enkyklios Paideia," *Reallexikon für Antike und Christentum*, 5 (1962), pp. 366–98.

but to remind us that even in the European context the term "encyclopedia" is a relatively recent linguistic construct.[5]

Even once the term was coined, "encyclopedia" occurred only rarely in book titles before the 18th century.[6] Johann Heinrich Alsted's *Encyclopædia* of 1630 was one of the first to associate the title with a work which we would consider encyclopedic: a four-volume folio work which offered pedagogical presentations (akin to a textbook) of all the traditional disciplines as well as a long list of new disciplines which Alsted often coined for the first time in an attempt to cover exhaustively all areas of human endeavor. His encyclopedia combined in this way a focus on essential and ordered knowledge with completeness in scope. Though it was reprinted once in 1649, Alsted's *Encyclopædia* did not generate any imitators. The fad for works entitled encyclopedia took off in the 18th century, with Ephraim Chambers' *Cyclopædia* and the work that Diderot first began as a translation of Chambers into French, but which grew into the 17-volume *Encyclopédie* (1751–65).[7] Although the *Encyclopédie* did not have the afterlife of the *Encyclopædia Britannica* (1768–71), the latter started as a much more modest three-volume work compiled by one man, William Smellie, who "used to say jocularly, that he had made a Dictionary of Arts and Sciences with a pair of scissors, clipping out from various book a quantum sufficit of matter for the printer."[8] Instead, the *Encyclopédie*

[5] For a useful history of the term see Ulrich Dierse, *Enzyklopädie: zur Geschichte eines philosophischen und wissenschaftstheoretischen Begriffs* (Bonn: Bouvier Verlag Herbert Grundmann, 1977).

[6] Early examples include Joachim Ringelberg, *Lucubrationes vel potius absolutissima kyklopaideia* (Basel: Westhemerus, 1538) and Paul Scalich de Lika, *Encyclopædiae, seu Orbis disciplinarum, tam sacrarum quam prophanarum, Epistemon* (Basel: Ioannes Oporinus, 1559); the colophon to Gregor Reisch, *Margarita philosophica* refers to the book as a "cyclopædia" as early as 1508, though the term only appears as a subtitle in 1583. Alfredo Serrai, *Storia della Bibliografia I: Bibliografia e Cabala: le enciclopedie rinascimentali*, ed. Maria Cochetti (Roma: Bulzoni, 1988), p. 146.

[7] For a fine study of Chambers and his context, see Richard Yeo, *Encyclopedic Visions: Scientific Dictionaries and Enlightenment Culture* (Cambridge: Cambridge University Press, 2001). The literature on the *Encyclopédie* is so vast as to defie summary; for a recent survey, see Frank Kafker, "Some observations on five interpretations of the Encyclopédie", *Diderot Studies*, XXIII, ed. Otis Fellow and Diana Guiragossian Carr (Geneva: Droz, 1988), pp. 85–100.

[8] Robert Kerr, *Memoirs of the Life, Writings and Correspondence of William Smellie*, 2 vols (Edinburgh: John Anderson, 1811), I, pp. 362–63 (emphases in the original). On the fortunae of the two works, see Frank Kafker, "The Tortoise and the Hare: A Comparison of the longevity of the *Encyclopædia Britannica* with the *Encyclopédie*", in *Scotland and France in the Enlightenment*, ed. Deidre Dawson and Pierre Morère (Lewisburg, PA: Bucknell University Press, 2004), 161–74.

established the format for the modern encyclopedia which is still current today, as a multi-author, multi-volume, illustrated and alphabetized reference work.

There was no genre of the "encyclopedia" before the 18th century, but historians have long since used this category to describe works which presented neither the title nor the form of the modern encyclopedia, but which presented encyclopedic features—typically a classification of knowledge and a synthesis of an ambitious or exhaustive scope of knowledge. Since the beginning of the 19th century in particular historians have described as "encyclopedias" a series of medieval works from Isidore of Seville to Thomas of Cantimpré, including Vincent of Beauvais' *Speculum maius*.[9] The designation, though anachronistic, has proved effective because it has been consistently applied to a canon of works that strove to synthesize and summarize much knowledge, despite differences in purpose and context.[10]

For Cassiodorus (ca. 490–585) and Isidore of Seville (ca. 600–636), principal authors in the first wave of "medieval encyclopedias", the point was to preserve what was useful from ancient learning for the training of monks and preachers respectively and to bring together and transmit an essential core of knowledge. These authors self-consciously spared the basics of ancient learning, from arithmetic to the meanings of terms through their etymology, from the destruction and loss of access that was befalling the more complex and voluminous ancient originals. The second wave of medieval encyclopedias, in the 13th to 15th centuries, was a response to a different set of circumstances. These authors were inspired not by the fear of loss, but by the awareness of an overabundant accumulation of knowledge. Historians can attribute this overload to a few different factors, including the sudden influx of Aristotelian and other texts

[9] For an interesting survey of the association of the term "encyclopedia" with Vincent of Beauvais, see Jürgen Henningsen, "« Enzyklopädie »: zur Sprach- und Bedeutungsgeschichte eines pädagogischen Begriffs", in *Archiv für Begriffsgeschichte*, 10 (1966): 271–362, esp. pp. 321–24. He points out that when the 1624 printed edition of the *Speculum maius* uses the term "encyclopedia" it is not to designate the whole four-volume work, but only the volume devoted to the arts and sciences.

[10] See, most recently, Bernard Ribémont, "On the definition of an encyclopedic genre in the Middle Ages," in *Pre-Modern Encyclopedic Texts*, ed. Binkley, pp. 47–61 and *De natura rerum: études sur les encyclopédies médiévales* (Orléans: Paradigme, 1995). A number of classic studies of individual encyclopedias appeared in "Encyclopédies et Civilisations", *Cahiers d'histoire mondiale* 3 (1966): 431–851 and Maurice de Gandillac et al., *La pensée encyclopédique au Moyen Age* (Neuchâtel: Éditions de la Baconnière, 1966).

transmitted from the Islamic world, the increasing bulk of materials generated by university teaching, and the growth of historical writing, among other genres cultivated outside the universities. Thus Vincent of Beauvais articulated his motivations elegantly in the preface to his four-volume *Speculum maius* (1255):

> Since the multitude of books, the shortness of time and the slipperiness of memory do not allow all things which are written to be equally retained in the mind, I decided to reduce in one volume in a compendium and in summary order some flowers selected according to my talents from all the authors I was able to read.[11]

His four-volume encyclopedia offered short chapters on a myriad topics, gathered from Vincent's wide reading.[12] His purpose was to paraphrase and abridge, to bring together in one place and in orderly fashion material which would otherwise be difficult of access because too abundant, dispersed and time-consuming to master.

The term "encyclopedia" has proved a useful category to European medievalists because there has been an impressive consensus around a canon of "medieval encyclopedias" since that expression was first coined. The period for which the use of the term has proved more problematic is the early modern period, ca. 1450–1700, because there has been no functional agreement among early modernists on a canon of encyclopedias before the *Encyclopédie*. The problem lies partly in the great number and diversity of works that could be considered encyclopedic, both increased by the impact of printing. In addition, the enthusiasm of early modern authors for the term and ideal of the "encyclopedia" further complicates its use by historians—in the early modern period the term is not just a historical category, but also an actors' category or rather the category of many actors who emphasize different aspects of its multivalence.

The lack of generic markers for the encyclopedia in early modern Europe is not only a function of historians' imprecision; it is rooted in the multiple conceptions of the encyclopedia that one finds among the early modern authors themselves. For example, an undisputedly

---

[11] Vincent of Beauvais, *Bibliotheca mundi* (Douai: Baltazar Beller, 1624), I: Speculum naturale, Prologue, 1.

[12] For an entry into the literature on Vincent of Beauvais see *Vincent de Beauvais: intentions et réceptions d'une oeuvre encyclopédique au Moyen Age*, Actes du XIVe colloque de l'Institut d'Etudes médiévales (1988), ed. Monique Paulmier-Foucart, Serge Lusignan et Alain Nadeau (Saint-Laurent: Maison Bellarmin, 1990).

central figure in any study of early modern encyclopedism, Johann Heinrich Alsted devotes a long section of the preface to his Encyclopedia of 1630 to the works that he considers to have preceded him in his task. Alsted lists some 15 works, dating mostly from the preceding half-century, whose "heroic labor" in "presenting all of philosophy in one syntagma" inspired him, he explains. These works range from 150-page octavo volumes to thousand-page folios, from purely diagrammatic systems of knowledge (such as Freigius' Ramist tables) to texts which offer only a table of contents to guide the reader through their continuous prose, from lullist and cabbalistic schemes of knowledge (like Cornelius Gemma on the Cyclognomic art) to compilations of famous quotations on all possible topics (like Theodor Zwinger's *Theatrum vitae humanae*).[13] So Alsted himself traces his encyclopedia to a dual inspiration, from systematic but skeletal presentations of knowledge on the one hand and bulky but jumbled compilations of actual material on the other.

Similarly, historians have studied as "encyclopedias" elaborate classifications of knowledge sometimes without even any content as well as large informative books arranged arbitrarily according to the alphabet or even miscellaneously.[14] Among the many interpretations

[13] "Quod precatus sum a Deo immortali cum professio philosophiae mihi demandaretur, ut pro ineffabili sua gratia mihi concederet ea docere, quae ad liberalium ingeniorum culturam et ad philosophiae decus pertinerent: id toto illo duodecim annorum decursu . . ., id, inquam, toto professionis meae tempore ante oculos habui. Sic enim semper institui rationes meas, ut aliorum commodis inservire, ac unius Dei gloriam amplificare possem. Hinc mihi natae sunt variae lucubrationes: e quibus multae diversis temporibus lucem aspexerunt. Tandem subiit animum meum haec cogitatio, magnum fore operae pretium si latifundium regni philosophici uno syntagmate delinearem: quod ante me fecisse videbam viros omni exceptione majores Fortium videl. Ringelbergium in Encyclopædia, Hieronymum Cardanum in libris de Subtilitate, itemque de varietate rerum, Theodorum Zwingerum in Theatro vitae humanae, Petrum Ramum in Professione regia, authorem margaritae philosophicae et catenae scientiarum, Thomam Freigium in Paedagogo, Antonium Possevinum in Bibliotheca selecta, Gregorium Tholozanum in Syntaxi artis mirabilis, Cornelium Gemmam in Cyclognomicis, Jacobum Lorhardum in Heptade philosophica, Wowerium in Polymathia, Matthiam Martinium in Encyclopædia, Bartholomaeum Keckermannum et Clementem Timplerum in variis Systematis, Robertum Flud in Macrocosmo et Microcosmo, Johannem Colle de Idea et theatro imitatricium et imitabilium ad omnes intellectus, facultates, scientias et artes. Horum authorum heroico labore, ac utilitate rei longe maxima adductus, sumsi animum, cumque animo calamum et duce Scriptura sacra, comite ratione recta et experientia certa, teste denique conscientia, elucubravi hoc, quod vides, opus." Alsted, *Encyclopedia septem tomis distincta* (Herborn, 1630), vol. I, sigs. iiiv–iiijr.

[14] On the contrast between encyclopedic ordering and the miscellany see Neil

of the term between these two poles, none seems to me particularly more legitimate than another. But the European case suggests that it is helpful to understand how these categories were formed and first applied to works in pre-modern Islam. When and by whom was the term "enyclopedia" first applied to the Islamic context?[15] Is there, as for the Latin Middle Ages, a "canon" of works which specialists have long agreed to call "encyclopedias"? If not, then attempting to create a hard-and-fast definition will no doubt prove difficult. But to proceed at first with a broad interpretation of "encyclopedia" might be the best tactic, pending a consensus on how to settle on a narrower definition.

Reference Works in Early Modern Europe

In pursuing my own research in early modern "encyclopedias" I have decided to avoid the term and the definitional difficulties it poses and to focus instead on a genre defined by its intended use. Of the different kinds of "encyclopedias" the elegant classifications of knowledge have received comparatively more study than the unwieldy tomes so often based on compilation.[16] I am at work on a typology of the latter genres, which I call "reference books". That term is equally anachronistic (first used in the early-19th century) and not even canonical, but I would argue that it does correspond to a contemporary conception and practice of reading, based on consultation rather than continuous reading. Of course actual use need not correspond to intended use: it is possible to read the dictionary straight through and to consult even a short work on just a particular point. Nonetheless one can identify the intended use of a

Kenny, *The Palace of Secrets: Béroalde de Verville and Renaissance Conceptions of Knowledge* (Oxford: Clarendon Press, 1991).

[15] Dierse attributes this step to J. von Hammer-Purgstall, *Über die Enzyklopädie der Araber, Perser und Türken* (Vienna, 1857) and his article entitled "Enzyklopädie" in J. S. Ersch and J. G. Gruber, *Allgemeine Enzyklopädie der Wissenschaften und Künste*, section I, part 34 (Leipzig, 1840), pp. 206–8; see Dierse, p. 4. n. 14.

[16] See for example Jean-Louis Taffarelli, *Les systèmes de classification des ouvrages encyclopédiques* (Villeurbanne: École normale supérieure des bibliothèques, 1980); and *The Structure of Knowledge: Classifications of Science and Learning since the Renaissance*, ed. Tore Frängsmyr (Berkeley: Office for the History of Science and Technology, University of California, 2001); also Robert McRae, *The Problem of the Unity of the Sciences: Bacon to Kant* (Toronto: University of Toronto Press, 1961).

work from its presentation and finding devices, and at times from authorial statements. Thus the Swiss naturalist and bibliographer Conrad Gesner explained in justifying the alphabetical arrangement of his four-folio-volume *Historia animalium* (1551) that the "utility of lexica" like his "comes not from reading it from beginning to end, which would be more tedious than useful, but from consulting it from time to time (*ut consulat ea per intervalla*)."[17] Although there is no widespread term to designate these kinds of books nor a special place for them in libraries in the early modern period, contemporaries nonetheless were well aware of the increased availability and use of such works, for better and for worse.

From the "better" perspective, Gabriel Naudé, in his *Advice for erecting a library* (1627; here as translated into English in 1661 by John Evelyn) called for the purchase of such works as necessary in any good library:

> Neither must you forget all sorts of commonplaces, dictionaries, mixtures, several lections, collections of sentences and other like repertories. In earnest, for my part, I esteem these collections extreamly profitable and necessary, considering [that] the brevity of our life and the multitude of things which we are now obliged to know, e're one can be reckoned amongst the number of learned men, do not permit us to do all of ourselves.[18]

But others saw in these aids to learning the very cause of the imminent decline of civilization. Thus Meric Casaubon, writing in 1668, traced a steady decline in learning since its highpoint ca. 1600 and blamed it on the time wasted on "methods" that promised "a shorter way".[19] The French philologist Pierre-Daniel Huet (1630–1721), as reported in the posthumous *Huetiana* (1722), elaborated on this tragic story of unintended consequences:

> One cannot praise too much those who wanted to impart to their contemporaries and descendants the good things which had cost them so many sleepless nights and who sought to abbreviate and smooth the path of learning. But their success was too great and a good cause

[17] Conrad Gesner, *Historia Animalium, lib. I de Quadrupedibus viviparis* (Zurich: Froschauer, 1551), sig. beta 1v.

[18] Gabriel Naudé, *Instructions Concerning Erecting of a Library*, tr. John Evelyn (1661; repr. Cambridge, MA: Houghton, Mifflin and Co., 1903), 60–61.

[19] Meric Casaubon, *Generall Learning*, ed. Richard Serjeantson (Cambridge, UK: Renaissance Texts from Manuscript, 1999), p. 21.

> has produced a very bad result—we are satisfied with the false erudition which is at the foot of the mountain and spare ourselves the effort of climbing to the top where true erudition is. So many summaries, so many new methods, so many indexes, so many dictionaries have slowed the live ardor which made men learned . . . All the sciences today are reduced to dictionaries and no one seeks other keys to enter them.[20]

Whether they were perceived as useful aids or as the agents of the decline of civilization, the genres that I propose to call reference books were clearly a noticeable presence in early modern intellectual culture.

These assessments, both friendly and hostile, provide good specifics on the kinds of works in use as reference books ca. 1500–1700. Early modern dictionaries, like Calepino's *Dictionarium* that went through 150 editions in the 200 years after its publication in 1502, typically contained many encyclopedic elements in addition to linguistic definitions and increasingly polyglot translations.[21] They followed medieval antecedents (such as Giovanni Balbi's *Catholicon,* composed ca. 1286) in including such information as the gestation period of an elephant or the curative virtues of cabbage under these respective terms. This encyclopedic content is also remarkably impervious to change: the entry in the Calepino for "terra," for example, explains that the earth is the heaviest element, stationary in the middle of the world, even as late as 1746, after the international acceptance of Newton's *Principia* (first published in 1687). At first I attributed the long persistence of this position to the notoriously conservative nature of the dictionary genre, which always starts by recycling the contents of earlier editions. But I now see it also as inherent in the purpose of the Calepino, which was designed, as one preface explains, as an aid to reading the classical canon; since the classical texts all assumed that the earth was the heaviest element and stationary, this was the relevant information to include in this particular dictionary, rather than the latest scientific consensus.[22]

---

[20] *Huetiana ou pensées diverses de M. Huet* (Paris: Jacques Estienne, 1722), #74, p. 171.

[21] Ambrogio Calepino's Latin *Dictionarium* began in 1503 as a Latin-Latin encyclopedic dictionary, then added synonyms in Greek and numerous vernaculars for a total of 6 then 8 and finally 11 languages. See Albert Labarre, *Bibliographie du Dictionarium d'Ambrogio Calepino* (1520–1779) (Baden-Baden: Koerner, 1975).

[22] "Ut instar communis commentarii in plerosque scriptores, hic liber sit". Calepino, *Dictionarium* (Basel: Henricpetri, 1616), "De triplici utlitate hujus Operis".

Dictionaries of proper names, which experienced such a rich fortuna in the Islamic world, first appeared relatively later than other reference genres in the Latin West, despite ancient models such as Diogenes Laertius.[23] The genre developed only slowly in the 16th century, both in the form of the biographical dictionary focused on the great figures of a nation or a profession, and, to accompany the dictionary of common names, as an aid in reading classical texts by explaining the names of places, persons and gods encountered there.[24]

A category of reference work that bulks particularly large from the 13th century on consists, in Naudé's words, of "commonplaces and collections of sentences and other like repertories". The florilegium collected the "flowers" or best quotations from important authorities sorted under topical headings (typically the vices and virtues and various religious topics). First developed as an aid to preachers who needed quotations to flesh out their sermons, the florilegium initially focused on the Bible and Church fathers; from the Renaissance on the genre was adapted to serve the needs of schoolboys and included a range of classical authors as models of classical Latinity as well as moral probity.[25] Other collections of material sorted under headings offered edifying anecdotes and exempla from natural and human history, which could serve not only moral instruction but especially the rhetorical needs of those writing letters, orations and treatises. Works in this genre typically used alphabetical order, either as an organizing principle or as a finding device in one or more indexes. Systematic alphabetizing and indexing also began in earnest in the 13th century, notably with the concordance to the Bible completed by the Dominicans at St Jacques by 1239. By the 14th and 15th

[23] Richard and Mary Rouse, "Bibliography before print: the medieval De viris illustribus", in *The Role of the Book in Mediaeval Culture. Proceedings of the Oxford International Symposium*, ed. Peter Ganz, vol. I (Turnhout, Belgium: Brepols, 1986), 133–53.

[24] See, for examples of the first two types, John Bale, *Illustrium maioris Britanniae scriptorum Summarium* (1548) and Paul Freher, *Theatrum virorum eruditione clarorum* (1688). Dictionaries of the proper names encountered in classical literature began earlier, with Hermannus Torrentinus, *Elucidarius carminum . . . seu vocabularius poeticus*, (first published Deventer, 1498); in the same vein Conrad Gesner's bulkier *Onomasticon* (first published Basel, 1546) was often combined with Calepino's *Dictionarium*.

[25] See Mary Rouse and Richard Rouse, "Statim invenire: Schools, Preachers and New Attitudes to the Printed Page", in *Renaissance and Renewal*, ed. R. L. Benson and G. Constable (Cambridge, Mass: Harvard University Press, 1982), 201–25, and *Authentic witnesses: approaches to medieval texts and manuscripts* (Notre Dame: University of Notre Dame Press, 1991), chs. 6–7; Ann Moss, *Printed Commonplace-Books and the Structuring of Renaissance Thought* (Oxford: Clarendon Press, 1996).

centuries a number of large utilitarian works included indexes, including for example the *Speculum historiale* of Vincent of Beauvais.[26]

Naudé mentions a third general category, which is less well known: his "mixtures or several lections" refers to a genre of work often entitled *variae* or *antiquae lectiones* (various or ancient readings), which typically presented themselves as imitations of Aulus Gellius' *Noctes atticae* and offered a miscellaneously arranged set of commentaries on the languages, literature and culture of classical antiquity. These works originated with the humanist project of looking back to classical antiquity for models of texts to imitate and study, and in pratical terms, were often generated from the notes of teachers of the humanities. Usually massive in size, these works served as storehouses of rhetorical and cultural information made accessible by alphabetical indexing.[27]

A final reference genre, much used by those who built up library collections for themselves or others, is the bibliography. From a few medieval antecedents, the genre developed especially after printing.[28] Gesner's *Bibliotheca universalis* (1545) listed alphabetically by author some 10,000 works, extant and lost, in Latin, Greek and Hebrew; in the accompanying *Pandectae* (1548) Gesner attempted to provide

[26] See Richard and Mary Rouse, "The Verbal Concordance to the Scriptures," *Archivum Fratrum Praedicatorum* 44 (1974), 5–30; on indexing especially see Mary Rouse and Richard Rouse, "Concordances et index", in *Mise en page et mise en texte du livre manuscrit*, ed. Henri-Jean Martin and Jean Vezin (Paris: Editions du Cercle de la Libraire, Promodis, 1990), 219–28. On early modern indexing, see Ann Blair, "Annotating and indexing natural philosophy", in *Books and the Sciences in History*, ed. Marina Frasca-Spada and Nick Jardine (Cambridge: Cambridge University Press, 2000), pp. 69–89.

[27] Examples include Angelo Poliziano's *Miscellanea* (1489), Niccolo Perotti's *Cornucopiae* (1489), Erasmus's *Adages* (first published in 1500, then much enlarged in 1508), Caelius Rhodiginus, *Lectiones antiquae* (1516), Alexander ab Alexandro, *Dies geniales* (1522). On this genre see Jean-Marc Mandosio, "La miscellanée: histoire d'un genre", in *Ouvrages miscellanées et théories de la connaissance à la Renaissance*, ed. Dominique de Courcelles (Paris: Ecole des Chartres, 2003); Raphaële Mouren, "La varietas des philologues au XVIe siècle" in *La varietas à la Renaissance*, ed. Dominique de Courcelles (Paris: Ecole des Chartes, 2001), pp. 5–31; Jean-Marc Chatelain, "Encyclopédisme et forme rhapsodique au XVIe siècle", in *L'entreprise encyclopédique*, ed. Jean Bouffartigue and Françoise Mélonio, Littérales 21 (Paris: Centre des Sciences de la Littérature, Université Paris X-Nanterre, 1997), pp. 97–111; and Ann Blair, "The Collective Commentary as Reference Genre", in: *Der Kommentar in der Frühen Neuzeit*. Ed. Ralf Häfner, Markus Völkel. Frühe Neuzeit, 15. Tübingen, 2006.

[28] Richard and Mary Rouse, "Bibliography before print: the medieval De viris illustribus", in *The Role of the Books in Mediaeval Culture*, ed. Peter Ganz, vol. I (Turnhout, Belgium: Brepols, 1986). More generally, Luigi Balsamo, *Bibliography. History of a tradition*, tr. William A. Pettas (Berkeley: Bernard M Rosenthal, Inc, 1990).

a universal topical index to the contents of all these books. He describes his own methods of working, which included cutting and pasting from printed works (where possible, he specifies) and arranging and rearranging notes on slips of paper held on sheets with temporary glue before pasting them in a permanent order for publication. Gesner's bibliographical works were each only printed once but elicited much praise, along with abridgments and imitations in the vernaculars as well as specialized subjects.[29]

In Western Europe the 13th century was a period of renewed development of consultation reading after the decline of classical culture. Many of the reference genres dominant in the early modern period originated then; their legacy can still be identified today, from the dictionary to the dictionary of quotations and the alphabetical index. The precise methods of citation and the elaborate manuscript *ordinatio* characteristic of many scholastic manuscripts further contributed to the ease of retrieval of specific passages in a large volume: running heads, and divisions of the text into books, chapters, quaestiones and distinctiones were generally highlighted by rubrication, numbering, changes in script or marginal signals.[30] It would be fruitful to compare the techniques of text management, from *ordinatio* to finding devices, in the manuscript cultures of the Latin Middle Ages and pre-modern Islam. The work that has been done so far on techniques of scholarship and note-taking indicates many similarities in the ways of working, including the high esteem in which memorization was held, combined with the constant reliance on the written word, from notes taken on slips of paper during oral performances to excerpts copied out while reading.[31] At the same time

---

[29] See Hans Wellisch, *Conrad Gessner. A Bio-Bibliography* (Zug, Switzerland: IDC, 1984); more generally, Archer Taylor, *A History of Bibliographies of Bibliographies* (New Brunswick, NJ: Scarecrow Press, 1955).

[30] Malcolm B. Parkes, "The Influence of the concepts of ordinatio and compilatio on the development of the book", in *Medieval Learning and Literature: essays presented to Richard William Hunt*, ed. J. J. G. Aexander and M. T. Gibson (Oxford: Clarendon Press, 1976).

[31] Franz Rosenthal, *The Technique and Approach of Muslim Scholarship* (Rome: Pontificium Institutum Biblicum, 1947), pp. 6–7ff. On note-taking from sermons and lectures (reportationes), see Nicole Bériou, "La réportation des sermons parisiens à la fin du XIIIe siècle", *Medioevo e rinascimento*, 3 (1989), 87–123; Beryl Smalley, *The Study of the Bible in the Middle Ages* (Oxford: Basil Blackwell, 1952), 201ff. For some explicit comparison with Islamic note-taking see George Makdisi, *The Rise of Colleges: Institutions of Learning in Islam and the West* (Edinburgh: Edinburgh University Press, 1981), pp. 244ff.

the much longer continuities in the reception of pre-modern Islamic encyclopedias (which in some cases are still in print and use today) and the long survival of a "pure" manuscript culture in Islam offer rich areas for examining the divergence between these two cultures. Whereas Islamic culture seems to have continued on a steady course, Western Europe experienced printing (mid-15th century) and a "quarrel of the ancients and the moderns" which was resolved in favor of the latter (late-17th century).

The invention and rapid spread of printing in the mid-15th century introduced new problems and possibilities. Considerable historiographical controversy has been generated by attempts to assess the impact of printing (on Protestantism, scientific revolution, a public political sphere etc).[32] One consequence of printing, however, seems undeniable: printing generated a large and cumulative increase in the availability of books. Personal and institutional libraries grew much faster than ever before. By the mid-16th century and in ever louder tones thereafter Europeans were complaining about the abundance of books, which seemed a deleterious overabundance, including (as noted above) an overabundance of those books which were designed to offer shortcuts to the ever-increasing mass of reading material. In addition to reference books, which were printed and reprinted at remarkable rates despite their expense to the buyer, new kinds of advice books were also designed to help, from Naudé's manual on how to select books for one's library to advice on how to read books or take notes most efficiently.[33]

The cheapening of books also made possible some new methods of work, including, to spare the labor of copying, cutting out passages from printed books, for inclusion in personal notebooks as well as in the composition of new works. But such destructive methods of working no doubt remained the exception, though one article in

[32] See Elizabeth Eisenstein, *The Printing Press as an Agent of Change: Communications and Cultural Transformations in Early Modern Europe* (Cambridge: Cambridge University Press, 1980). For two different kinds of critiques see Anthony Grafton, "The Importance of Being Printed", *Journal of Interdisciplinary History*, 11 (1980): 265–86, and Adrian Johns, *The Nature of the Book: Print and Knowledge in the Making* (Chicago: University of Chicago Press, 1998). See the forum featuring these authors in *American Historical Review*, 107 (2002): 84–128.

[33] For more on this topic see Ann Blair, "Reading Strategies for Coping with Information Overload, ca. 1550–1700", *Journal of the History of Ideas*, 64 (2003): 11–28.

the *Encyclopédie* portrays the ideal reader as pruning his books down to those few pages that were genuinely useful, consigning the rest of the book to the flames.[34] A more widespread method for coping with overload was to delegate and share the tasks of reading, note-taking and writing. Recent work has shed light on the collaborative nature of much intellectual work in the early modern period in Europe, quite possibly continuing medieval practices that are not yet well studied.[35] Scholars and students, as well as members of the ruling elite, hired scribes to make fresh copies but also amanuenses or readers who would read and take notes in one's stead.[36] Groups formed by students, literary societies or a governing elite could devise collective reading and/or writing projects which pooled intellectual tasks and resources.[37] Such collaborative ventures often involved hierarchies of tasks and persons.[38] A particularly elaborate example is the team of people engaged in a massive compilation of ecclesiastical history launched in mid-16th century by the Protestant Flaccius

[34] "S'il achètte par exemple, un ouvrage en douze volumes, où il n'y ait que six pages qui méritent d'être lûes, il sépare ces six pages du reste et jette l'ouvrage au feu". Article "Bibliomanie", in Diderot ed., *Encyclopédie,* tome II (Paris: Briasson et al., 1751), p. 228 as discussed in Daniel Désormeaux, *La figure du bibliomane: histoire du livre et strategie littéraire au XIXe siècle* (St Genouph: Nizet, 2001), ch. 3.

[35] See for example Kathryn Kerby-Fulton and Maidie Hilmo, *The Medieval Professional Reader at Work: evidence from manuscripts of Chaucer, Langland, Kempe and Gower* (Victoria, Canada: English Literature Studies, 2001). A seminal article inspiring this recent research is Steven Shapin, "The Invisible Technician", *American Scientist,* 77 (1989): 554–563.

[36] For an example of a professional reader active in early 17th-century England, see Lisa Jardine and Anthony Grafton, "Studied for Action: How Gabriel Harvey Read his Livy", *Past and Present,* 129 (1990): 30–78. Another form of evidence includes advice on hiring helpers of different kinds, as in Vernon F. Snow, "Francis Bacon's Advice to Fulke Greville on Research Techniques", *Huntington Library Quarterly,* 23 (1960): 369–79, 370; or Daniel Georg Morhof, *Polyhistor,* 3rd ed. (Lübeck: Petrus Boeckmannus, 1732), I, 1, 21 #12, p. 239. Finally, criticisms of such hiring also constitutes evidence that it was a well-known practice, as in Jeremias Drexel SJ, *Aurifodina artium et scientiarum omnium. Excerpendi sollertia, omnibus litterarum amantibus monstrata* (Antwerp: Vidua Iaonnis Cnobbari, 1638), p. 58.

[37] The Hamburg professor Vincent Placcius boasted for example of the utility of a closet he advocated for storing notes on slips of paper sorted under headings because it facilitated the collective accumulation and use of reading notes. Vincent Placcius, *De arte excerpendi, vom Gelährten Buchhalten liber singularis quo genera et praecepta excerpendi* (Stockholm and Hamburg: Gottfried Liebezeit, 1689), pp. 129, 145–6.

[38] Erasmus for example distinguished between young men whom he hired as scribes and his more mature helpers or amanuenses who exercised judgment in reading and note-taking; see Franz Bierlaire, *La familia d'Erasme: contribution à l'histoire de l'humanisme* (Paris: Vrin, 1968), e.g. pp. 28–29.

Illyricus. Flaccius explains how he spent the funding obtained from princely patrons on seven students who made excerpts from the authors assigned to them, two masters of arts "of outstanding maturity" who assessed and arranged these materials into a coherent historical narrative, five inspectors responsible for selecting and assigning the works to be studied and generally managing the project; and one copyist to make fair copies.[39] Printed reference books also offered ready-made the kinds of notes that one might have wanted to take for oneself or to hire another to compile.[40]

Given the vast bulk of many of the encyclopedic works composed in pre-modern Islam, one can surmise that collaborative work was involved there too. While printing accelerated the process manyfold, a manuscript culture also generates in fairly short order more works than any single person can master. Did Islamic scholars articulate concerns about overabundance? How did they cope with the ever-increasing accumulation of works to cite and master? Were there periodic moments of contraction during which some works from the past were set aside and forgotten? By the end of the 17th century Western Europe had in most contexts shifted away from the massive accumulations of classical quotations, exempla and information and toward a new set of topics and authorities. The Latin reference books I have described so far were generally no longer or barely reprinted after 1710.[41] Instead, starting in the last decades of the 17th century, vernacular dictionaries canonized a new set of authors who became "classics" and offered encyclopedic information about contemporary culture and recent scientific developments.[42] Commentaries on Aristotle's physics were still being dictated to students at a university near Barcelona as late as the end of the 18th century, and the Calepino was reprinted 5 more times in the 18th century

---

[39] Anthony Grafton, "Where was Salomon's House? Ecclesiastical History and the Intellectual Origins of Bacon's New Atlantis", in *Die europäische Gelehrtenrepublik im Zeitalter des Konfessionalismus*, ed. Herbert Jaumann (Wiesbaden: Harrassowitz Verlag, 2001), 21–38, pp. 29–30.

[40] For more discussion on this general theme, see Ann Blair, "Note-taking as an art of transmission", *Critical Inquiry* 31 (2004), 85–107.

[41] One widely reprinted florilegium, Domenico Nanni Mirabelli's *Polyanthea*, was in print from 1503 to 1686; Caelius Rhodiginus' *Lectiones antiquae* were printed down to 1666; the sequel to Zwinger's *Theatrum Humanae Vitae*, the *Magnum theatrum* was last reprinted in 1707.

[42] Notable examples include the *Dictionaire* [sic] of Antoine Furetière (1690) or the *Lexicon Technicum* of John Harris (1710).

for the Seminary of Padua, but the new reference books now focused on the mechanical philosophy and a new set of authorities from Descartes to Newton and their followers.[43]

The shift from ancient to modern authorities in European culture generated more rapidly than ever an overabundance of works in the new vein and of shortcuts to them. In addition to old genres filled with new material, new genres also appeared, notably the learned journal and the book reviews that often filled their pages.[44] Islam by contrast experienced a much greater continuity of traditional culture throughout this period, perpetuating much longer, indeed down to the present day in some cases, the active life of encyclopedic works composed in the pre-modern period. This much more continuous *longue durée* of genres and of the manuscript working methods which created them offers privileged opportunities for insight into similar practices which were dominant in Europe before the transition to modernity. The "encyclopedia", however loosely we define it, is a particularly fruitful lens through which to examine cultural change and continuity in both European and Islamic contexts. The term and the category of "encyclopedia" have proved remarkably resilient and widespread precisely because they are so adaptable and multivalent.

[43] For a general overview of the transitions in scientific fields which occurred during this period, see the *Cambridge History of Early Modern Science*, ed. Lorraine Daston and Katharine Park, forthcoming Cambridge University Press.

[44] One of the earliest of these was Pierre Bayle's *Nouvelles de la République des Lettres* (1684); for a synthetic introduction to these developments, see Hans Bots and Françoise Waquet, *La République des Lettres* (Paris: Belin, 1997), esp. ch. 5.

BIBLIOGRAPHY

Abiad, Malak. "Origine et développement des dictionnaires biographiques arabes." *Bulletin d'Études Orientales*, 31 (1979 [1980]): 7–15.

Ahlwardt, Wilhelm. *Verzeichniss der arabischen Handschriften*. Die Handschriften-Verzeichnisse der Königlichen Bibliothek zu Berlin, Bd. 17. Berlin 1887–1899.

al-ʿAlawī, Jamāl-al-Dīn. *al-Matn al-rushdī: madkhal li-qirāʾa jadīda*. Casablanca, 1986.

Altmann, Alexander, and Stern, S. M. *Isaac Israeli, a Neoplatonic Philosopher of the Early Tenth Century: His Works, Translated With Comments and an Outline of His Philosophy*. Scripta Judaica, 1. Oxford, 1958.

Aouad, Maroun. "Les fondements de la *Rhétorique* d'Aristote reconsidérés par Fārābī, ou le concept de point de vue immédiat et commun". *Arabic Sciences and Philosophy*, 2 (1992): 133–80.

Arkoun, Mohammed. *Contribution à l'étude de l'humanisme arabe au IVe/Xe siècle: Miskawayh (320/325–421 = 932/936–1030), philosophe et historien*. Études musulmanes, 13. Paris, 1970.

Auchterlonie, Paul. *Arabic Biographical Dictionaries: A Summary Guide and Bibliography*. Durham, 1987.

Balsamo, Luigi. *Bibliography: History of a Tradition*. Trans. William A. Pettas. Berkeley, 1990.

Bausani, Alessandro. *L'enciclopedia dei Fratelli della Purità: riassunto, con introduzione e breve commento, dei 52 trattati o epistole degli Ikhwān aṣ-Ṣafāʾ*. Istituto Universitario Orientale, Seminario di Studi Asiatici, series minor, 4. Napoli, 1978.

Becq, Annie (ed.). *L'encyclopédisme. actes du colloque de Caen, 12–16 janvier 1987*. Paris, 1991.

Bergé, Marc. "Épître sur les sciences (*Risāla fī l-ʿulūm*) d'Abū Ḥayyān at-Tawḥīdī". *Bulletin d'études orientales*, 18 (1963–4): 241–300; 21 (1968): 313–46.

Berggren, J. L. "The Mathematical Sciences." In: *History of Civilizations in Central Asia*, vol. 4: *The Age of Achievement: A.D. 750 to the End of the Fifteenth Century*, part 2, ed. by. C. E. Bosworth, M. S. Asimov. Paris, 1992, 182–193.

——, and Robert S. D. Thomas. "Mathematical Astronomy in the Fourth Century B.C. as Found in Euclid's *Phaenomena*." In: *Studi E Ricerche*. Firenze, 1992, 29, 1: 7–33.

Bériou, Nicole. "La réportation des sermons parisiens à la fin du XIIIe siècle. *Medioevo e rinascimento*, 3 (1989): 87–123.

Berkel, Maaike van. "The Attitude Towards Knowledge in Mamluk Egypt: Organisation and Structure of the *Subḥ al-aʿshā* by al-Qalqashandī (1355–1418)." In: Binkley, Peter (ed.): *Pre-Modern Encyclopædic Texts. Proceedings of the Second COMERS Congress, Groningen, 1–4 July 1996*. Leiden, 1997, 159–168.

Bernand, Marie. "Al-Ghazālī, artisan de la fusion des systèmes de pensée." *Journal asiatique*, 278 (1990): 223–51.

Bierlaire, Franz. *La familia d'Erasme: contribution à l'histoire de l'humanisme*. Paris, 1968.

Biesterfeldt, Hans Hinrich. "Arabisch-islamische Enzyklopädien: Formen und Funktionen". In: Christel Meier (ed.), *Die Enzyklopädie im Mittelalter vom Hochmittelalter bis zur frühen Neuzeit*. München, 2002.

—— "Medieval Arabic encyclopædias of science and philosophy". In: *The Medieval Hebrew Encyclopedias of Science and Philosophy*, ed. by Steven Harvey. Dordrecht [etc.], 2000, 77–98.

Binkley, Peter (ed.). *Pre-Modern Encyclopædic Texts: Proceedings of the Second COMERS*

[Centre for Classical, Oriental, Medieval and Renaissance Studies] *Congress, Groningen, 1–4 July 1996.* Brill's Studies in Intellectual History, 79. Leiden [etc.], 1997.

Blachère, Régis. "Quelques Réflexions sur les formes de l'encyclopédisme en Égypte et en Syrie du VIIIe/XIVe siècle a la fin du IXe/XVe siècle." *Bulletin des Études Orientales*, 23 (1970): 7–19.

Blair, Ann. "Annotating and Indexing Natural Philosophy". In: *Books and the Sciences in History*, ed. Marina Frasca-Spada and Nick Jardine. Cambridge, 2000.

——. "Note-Taking as an Art of Transmission", *Critical Inquiry*, 31 (2004): 85–107.

——. "Reading Strategies for Coping with Information Overload, ca. 1550–1700". *Journal of the History of Ideas*, 64 (2003) 11–28.

——. "The Collective Commentary as Reference Genre". In: *Der Kommentar in der Frühen Neuzeit.* Ed. Ralf Häfner, Markus Völkel. Frühe Neuzeit, 15. Tübingen, 2006.

Bosworth, C. E. "ʿAjā'eb al-Makhlūqāt." In: *Encylopaedia Iranica*, ed. by Ehsan Yarshater, vol. 1 (1985): 696f.

——. "The Persian Impact on Arabic Literature". In: A. F. L. Beeston et al. eds., *Arabic Literature to the End of the Umayyad Period.* Cambridge, 1983, 483–496.

——. "A Pioneer Arabic Encylopaedia of the Sciences: al-Khwārizmī's Keys of the Sciences". *Isis*, 54 (1963): 97–111.

Bothmer, Hans-Caspar Graf von. *Die Illustrationen des „Münchener Qazwīnī" von 1280. (cod. Monac, arab. 464): ein Beitrag zur Kenntnis ihres Stils.* München, 1971.

Bots, Hans; Waquet, Françoise. *La République des Lettres.* Paris, 1997.

Brockelmann, Carl. *Geschichte der arabischen Litteratur.* Zweite, den Supplementbänden angepaßte Auflage, vol. 1–2 {with] Supplement, vol. 1–3. *(GAL).* Leiden, 1943–49; supplement, 1937–42 [= *GAL*^{2}, *GAL S*].

Butterworth, Charles E. "In what sense is Averroes an encyclopedist?". In: Stefen Harvey (ed.): *The Medieval Hebrew Encyclopedia of Science and Philosophy.* Leiden, 2000, 99–119.

Carra de Vaux, Bernard. "Introduction". In: André Miquel (ed.), *L'Abrégé des Merveilles.* Paris, 1984, 19f.

Céard, Jean. "Encyclopédie et encyclopédisme à la Renaissance". In: Annie Becq (ed.), *L'Encyclopédisme: actes du colloque de Caen, 12e–16e janvier 1987.* Paris, 1991, 57–67.

——. "Le commentaire ou l'encyclopédisme non méthodique de la Renaissance." In: *L'Entreprise encyclopédique, Littérales*, 21 (1997): 79–95.

Chapoutot-Remadi, Mounira. "L'Encyclopédie arabe au Xe siècle". In: Annie Becq (ed.), *L'Encyclopédisme: actes du Colloque de Cæn, 12e–16e janvier 1987.* Paris, 1991, 37–46.

——. "Les encyclopédies arabes de la fin du Moyen Age". In: Annie Becq (ed.): *L'Encyclopédisme. Actes du Colloque de Cæn, 12e–16e janvier 1987.* Paris, 1991, 267–279.

Chatelain, Jean-Marc. "Encyclopédisme et forme rhapsodique au XVIe siècle." *L'entreprise encyclopédique*, ed. Jean Bouffartigue and Françoise Mélonio, *Littérales*, 21 (Paris, 1997), 97–111.

Cooperson, Michael. *Classical Arabic Biography.* Cambridge, 2000.

Cortabarria Beitia, A., O.P., "La Classification des sciences chez al-Kindi". *Institut Dominicain d'Etudes Orientales, Mélanges*, 11 (Cairo, 1972): 49–76.

Crombie, Robert A. *Grosseteste and the Origins of Experimental Science 1100–1700.* Oxford, 1962.

Crone, P. "Did al-Ghazālī Write a Mirror for Princes? On the Authorship of *Naṣīḥat al-mulūk.*" *Jerusalem Studies in Arabic and Islam*, 10 (1987): 167ff.

Dabashi, Hamīd. "Dānesh-nāma." In: *Encyclopaedia Iranica*, 6 (1993): 651–652.

Daiber, Hans. *Aëtius Arabus. Die Vorsokratiker in arabischer Überlieferung.* Akademie der Wissenschaften und der Literatur, Veröffentlichungen der Orientalischen Kommission, 33. Wiesbaden 1980.

——. "Qosṭā ibn Lūqā (9. Jh.) über die Einteilung der Wissenschaften." *Zeitschrift für Geschichte der Arabisch-Islamischen Wissenschaften*, 50 (1990): 93–129.
Désormeaux, Daniel. *La figure du bibliomane: histoire du livre et strategie littéraire au XIXe siècle.* St Genouph, 2001.
Dictionary of Scientific Biograph, ed. Charles Coulston Gillispie. Vol. 1–16. New York, 1970–1980; repr. 1981 [*DSB*].
Dierse, Ulrich. *Enzyklopädie: zur Geschichte eines philosophischen und wissenschaftstheoretischen Begriffs.* Bonn, 1977.
Dieterici, Friedrich. *Die Abhandlungen der Ichwan es-safa in Auswahl: zum ersten Mal aus arabischen Handschriften herausgegeben.* 3 vols. Leipzig, 1883–6.
Dihle, Albrecht. *Philosophie als Lebenskunst.* Rheinisch-Westfälische Akademie der Wissenschaften, Vorträge, G 304. Opladen, 1990.
——. "Philosophie, Fachwissenschaft, Allgemeinbildung". In: *Aspects de la philosophie hellénistique.* Entretiens sur l'Antiquité classique, 32. Vandœuvres-Genève, 1986, 188–232.
Drachmann, A. G. *The Mechanical Technology of Greek and Roman Antiquity.* Copenhagen, 1963.
Druart, Thérèse-Anne. "Le traité d'al-Farabi sur les buts de la Métaphysique d'Aristote". In: *Bulletin de philosophie médiévale*, 24 (1982): 38–43.
Dubler, César E. "Adjā'ib". In: *EI²*, 1 (Leiden, 1960): 203.
Ducatez, Guy. 'La *Tuḥfa al-albāb* d'Abū Ḥāmid al-Andalusī al-Ġarnāṭī: traduction annotée,' *Revue d'études islamiques*, 53 (1985): 141–241.
EI v. Encyclopædia of Islam.
Eickelman, F. "Tardjama". In: *Encyclopaedia of Islam*, new ed., 10 (1998): 224–225.
Eisenstein, Elizabeth. *The Printing Press as an Agent of Change: Communications and Cultural Transformations in Early Modern Europe.* Cambridge, 1980.
Encyclopædia Britannica, 15th edition. Chicago, 1994 (first published 1974).
The Encyclopaedia of Islam: A Dictionary of the Geography, Ethnography and Biography of the Muhammadan Peoples. Vols. 1–4 and Supplement. Leiden, London, 1913–38. [= *EI*]
The Encyclopaedia of Islam: New Edition. Prepared by a number of leading orientalists, ed. by an editorial committee consisting of H. A. R. Gibb [a. o.]. 12 vols. Leiden, London, 1954–2004. [= *EI²*]
Endress, Gerhard. "L'Aristote arabe: réception, autorité et transformation du Premier Maître". *Medioevo: rivista di storia della filosofia medievale*, 23 (1997): 1–42.
——. "Die dreifache Ancilla: Hermeneutik und Logik im Werk des Sayf-al-Dīn al-Āmidī". In: *Logik und Theologie: das Organon im arabischen und im lateinischen Mittelalter*, ed. Dominik Perler, Ulrich Rudolph. Studien und Texte zur Geistesgeschichte des Mittelalters, 84. Leiden, 2004, 117–45.
——. "The defense of reason: the plea for philosophy in the religious community". *Zeitschrift für Geschichte der arabisch-islamischen Wissenschaften*, 6 (1990): 1–49.
——. "Grammatik und Logik: arabische Philologie und griechische Philosophie im Widerstreit". In: *Sprachphilosophie in Antike und Mittelalter.* Bochumer Studien zur Philosophie, 3. Amsterdam, 1986, 163–299.
——. "Mathematics and philosophy in medieval Islam". In: *The Enterprise of Science in Islam: New Perspectives*, ed. by Jan P. Hogendijk and Abdelhamid I. Sabra, Dibner Institute Studies in the History of Science and Technology. Cambridge, 2003, 121–76.
——. "Die wissenschaftliche Literatur." In: *Grundriss der arabischen Literatur*, ed. Wolfdietrich Fischer, Helnut Gätje, vol. 2 (Wiesbaden, 1987): 400–506; 3 (1992): 3–152.
Ess, Josef van. *Theologie und Gesellschaft im 2. und 3. Jahrhundert Hidschra.* 6 vols. Berlin 1991–1997.
——. *Der Wesir und seine Gelehrten.* Abhandlungen für die Kunde des Morgenlandes XLV, 4. Wiesbaden, 1981.

Eybl, Franz M., et al. (ed.). *Enzyklopädien der frühen Neuzeit: Beiträge zu ihrer Erforschung.* Tübingen, 1995.

Fahd, Tawfiq. "Le Merveilleux dans la faune, la flore et les minéraux". In: Mohamed Arkoun (ed.), *L'Étrange et le merveilleux dans l'Islam médiéval.* Paris, 1978.

Fähndrich, Hartmut. "Compromising the Caliph." *Journal of Arabic Literature*, 8 (1977): 36–47.

——. "The *Wafayāt al-Aʿyān* of Ibn Khallikān: A New Approach". *Journal of the American Oriental Society*, 93 (1973): 432–445.

Fischer, Wolfdietrich; Gätje, Helmut (eds.). *Grundriss der arabischen Philologie.* 2 vols. and Supplement. Wiesbaden, 1987–92 [*GAP*].

Fowler, Robert L. "Encyclopædias: definitions and theoretical problems". In: *Pre-modern Encyclopædic Texts.* Proceedings of the Second COMERS Congress, Groningen, 1–4 July 1996, ed. Peter Binkley. Leiden, 1997, 3–29.

Fuchs, H. "Enkyklios Paideia". In: *Reallexikon für Antike und Christentum*, 5. 1962, 366–98.

GAL v. Brockelmann, *Geschichte der arabischen Litteratur.*

Gandillac, Maurice de, et al. *La pensée encyclopédique au Moyen Age.* Neuchâtel, 1966.

GAP v. Fischer, W.

Gelder, Geert Jan van. "Compleat Men, Women and Books: on Medieval Arabic Encyclopædism." In: Peter Binkley (ed.): *Pre-Modern Encyclopædic Texts: Proceedings of the Second COMERS Congress, Groningen, 1–4 July 1996.* Leiden, 1997, 241–259.

Gibb, Sir Hamilton. "Islamic Biographical Literature". In: *Historians of the Middle East*, ed. B. Lewis and P. M. Holt. London, New York, 1962, 54–58.

——. "Ta'rīkh." In: *Encyclopædia of Islam*, supplement (Leiden, 1938), 233–45.

Giese, Alma. *Al-Qazwīnī: Die Wunder des Himmels und der Erde.* Stuttgart, 1986.

Grafton, Anthony, and Jardine, Lisa. "Studied for Action: How Gabriel Harvey Read his Livy". *Past and Present*, 129 (1990): 30–78.

——. "The Importance of Being Printed". *Journal of Interdisciplinary History*, 11 (1980): 265–86.

——. "Where was Salomon's House? Ecclesiastical History and the Intellectual Origins of Bacon's New Atlantis". In: *Die europäische Gelehrtenrepublik im Zeitalter des Konfessionalismus*, ed. Herbert Jaumann. Wiesbaden, 2001.

Grignaschi, M. "La 'as-Siyāsatu-l-ʿāmmiyah' et l'influence iranienne sur la pensée politique islamique." In: *Monumentum Nyberg III*, Acta Iranica, 6. Leiden, 1975, 33–287.

——. "Les 'Rasā'il Arisṭāṭālīsa ilā l-'Iskandar' de Sālim Abū-l-ʿAlā' et l'activité culturelle à l'époque omayyade". *Bulletin d'Etudes Orientales*, 19 (1965–66): 7–83.

Guidi, M., and Walzer, R. *Studi su al-Kindī, I: Uno scritto introduttivo allo studio di Aristotele.* Rom, 1940.

Gutas, Dimitri. "Ethische Schriften im Islam". In: W. Heinrichs (ed.) *Neues Handbuch der Literaturwissenschaft: Orientalisches Mittelalter.* Wiesbaden, 1990, 346–365.

——. "Ibn Ṭufayl on Ibn Sīnā's Eastern Philosophy". *Oriens*, 34 (1994): 222–41.

——. "Pre-Plotinian Philosophy in Arabic (Other than Platonism and Aristotelianism): A Review of the Sources". In: W. Haase and H. Temporini, eds, *Aufstieg und Niedergang der Römischen Welt.* Part II, Vol. 36.7. Berlin, New York, 1994, 4949–4954.

——. "The 'Alexandria to Baghdad' Complex of Narratives. A Contribution to the Study of Philosophical and Medical Historiography among the Arabs". *Documenti e Studi sulla Tradizione Filosofica Medievale*, 10 (1999): 155–193, 169–174.

——. "The Spurious and the Authentic in the Arabic Lives of Aristotle". In: *Pseudo-Aristotle in the Middle Ages*, Warburg Institute Surveys. London, 1986.

——. *Avicenna and the Aristotelian Tradition.* Leiden, 1988.

——. "Paul the Persian on the Classification of the Parts of Aristotle's Philosophy: A Milestone between Alexandria and Baġdād". *Der Islam*, 60 (1983): 231–267.

Haarmann, Ulrich. "Väter und Söhne im Herrschaftssystem der Mamluken". In: *Berliner Wissenschaftliche Gesellschaft*, Jahrbuch 1995.

Hadot, Ilsetraut. "Les aspects sociaux et institutionels des sciences et de la médecine dans l'Antiquité tardive". *Antiquité tardive*, 6. (Turnhout, 1998): 233–50.
——. *Arts libéraux et philosophie dans la pensée antique*. Paris, 1984.
Hafsi, I. "Recherches sur le genre "*ṭabaqāt*" dans la littératur arabe". In: *Arabica*, 23 (1976): 227–65, and 24 (1977): 1–41, 150–86.
Hall, Robert E. "Al-Khāzinī, Abu'l-Fatḥ ʿAbd al-Raḥmān". In: *Dictionary of Scientific Biography*, VII: 335–351.
Hammer-Purgstall, J. von. "Enzyklopädie". In: J. S. Ersch and J. G. Gruber, *Allgemeine Enzyklopädie der Wissenschaften und Künste*, section I, part 34. Leipzig, 1840.
——. *Über die Enzyklopädie der Araber, Perser und Türken*. Vienna, 1857.
Harris, John. *Lexicon Technicum*. 1710.
Harvey, E. Ruth. "Qusṭā ibn Lūqā," In: *Dictionary of Scientific Biography*, XI, 244–246
Harvey, Steven (ed.). *The Medieval Hebrew Encyclopedias of Science and Philosophy*. Boston, 2000.
Heath, T. L. "The Formal Division of a Euclidean Proposition". In: *The Thirteen Books of Euclid's Elements*. Second Edition, 3 vols. Cambridge, 1926.
Heck, Paul L. *The Construction of Knowledge in lslamic Civilization: Qudāma b. Jaʿfar and his Kitāb al-Kharāj wa-ṣināʿat al-kitāba*. Islamic History and Civilization: Studies and Texts, 42. Leiden, 2002.
Hees, Syrinx von and Schwartz, Edward. "The Bird Illustrations of a Thirteenth-century Arab Natural History". *Interdisciplinary Science Reviews* 29 (2004): 231–47.
——. "The Astonishing: a Critique and Re-reading of *ʿAjāʾib*-Literature". In: *Middle Eastern Literatures* 8 (2005): 101–20.
——. *Enzyklopädie als Spiegel des Weltbildes: Qazwīnīs Wunder der Schöpfung, eine Naturkunde des 13. Jahrhunderts*. Wiesbaden, 2002.
Heffening, Willie. "Ṭabaqāt". In: *Encyclopardia of Islam*. 1927, 214–15.
Hein, Christel. "Definition und Einteilung der Philosophie: von der spätantiken Einteilungsliteratur zur arabischen Enzyklopädie". In: *Europäische Hochschulschriften*, Reihe 20: *Philosophie*. Bd. 177. Frankfurt am Main [etc.], 1985.
Heinrichs, Wolfhart. "Die antike Verknüpfung von *phantasia* und Dichtung bei den Arabern". *ZDMG*, 128 (1978): 252–298.
Henningsen, Jürgen. "Enzyklopädie: zur Sprach- und Bedeutungsgeschichte eines pädagogischen Begriffs". In: *Archiv für Begriffsgeschichte*, 10. 1966, 271–362.
Hermansen, K. and Marcia, D. "Survey Article: Interdisciplinary Approaches to Islamic Biographical Materials". *Religion*, 18 (1988): 163–182.
Hilmo, Maidie and Kerby-Fulton, Kathryn. *The Medieval Professional Reader at Work: evidence from manuscripts of Chaucer, Langland, Kempe and Gower*. Victoria, 2001.
Hoffmann, Birgitt. *Waqf im mongolischen Iran: Rashīduddīns Sorge um Nachruhm und Seelenheil*. Stuttgart, 2000.
Huet, Pierre Daniel. *Huetiana oupensees diverses de M. Huet*. Paris 1722.
Humphreys, R. Stephen. "Taʾrīkh: Historical Writing". In: *Encyclopaedia of Islam* 2, X. 1998, 271–280.
——. *Islamic History: A Framework for Inquiry*. Princeton, 1991.
Janssen, Jules. "An Annotated Bibliography on Ibn Sīnā: First Supplement (1990–1994)". *Textes et études du moyen âge*, 12. Louvain-la-Neuve, 1999, 120–392.
——. "Le Dânesh-nâmeh d'Ibn Sînâ: un texte à revoir?". *Bulletin de philosophie médiévale*, 28 (1986): 163–77.
Jardine, Lisa and Anthony Grafton. "Studied for Action: How Gabriel Harvey Read his Livy". *Past and Present*, 129 (1990), 21–38.
Johns, Adrian. *The Nature of the Book: Print and Knowledge in the Making*. Chicago, 1998.
Jolivet, Jean. "Classification of the Sciences." In: Roshdi Rashed (ed.), *Encyclopedia of the History of Arabic Science*. London: Routledge, 1996, vol. 3: 1008–1025.
Kafker, Frank. "Some Observations on Five Interpretations of the *Encyclopédie*." In: *Diderot Studies*, XXIII, ed. Otis Fellow and Diana Guiragossian Carr. Geneva, 1988, 85–100.

——. "The Tortoise and the Hare: A Comparison of the Longevity of the *Encyclopædia Britannica* with the *Encyclopédie*." In: *Scotland and France in the Enlightenment*, ed. Deidre Dawson and Pièrre Morère. Lewisburg, Penn., 2004, 161–74.

Kenny, Neil. *The Palace of Secrets: Béroalde de Verville and Renaissance Conceptions of Knowledge*. Oxford, 1991.

Kerby-Fulton, Kathryn and Hilmo, Maidie. *The Medieval Professional Reader at Work: Evidence from Manuscripts of Chaucer, Langland, Kempe and Gower*. Victoria, Canada, 2001.

Kerr, Robert. *Memoirs of the Life, Writings and Correspondence of William Smellie*, 2 vols. Edinburgh, 1811.

Khalegi-Motlagh, Dj. "Adab". In: *Encyclopaedia Iranica*, I (London, 1985): 434–435.

Khalidi, Tarif. "Islamic Biographical Dictionaries: A Preliminary Assessment". *Muslim World*, 63 (1973): 53–65.

——. *Arabic Historical Thought*. Cambridge, 1996.

Khalīfa, Ḥājji. *Kashf al-ẓunūn ʿan asāmī l-kutub wa-l-funūn*. Baghdad, 1: 288.

Kheirandish, Elaheh. "Mixed Mathematical Sciences: Optics and Mechanics in the Islamic Middle Ages". In: *The Cambridge History of Science*, 8 vols., vol. 2, eds. David C. Lindberg and Michael Shank, forthcoming.

——. "Qusṭā Ibn Lūqā". In: *Biographical Encyclopedia of Astronomers* (*BEA*, forthcoming).

——. "The Arabic Version of Euclid's Optics: Kitāb Uqlīdis fī Ikhtilāf al-manāẓir", 2 vols. In: *Sources in the History of Mathematics and Physical Sciences*, ed. G. J. Toomer, no. 16. New York, 1999.

——. "The Many Aspects of Appearances: Arabic Optics to 950 AD". In: *The Enterprise of Science in Islam: New Perspectives*, eds. Jan P. Hogendijk and Abdelhamid I. Sabra, *Dibner Institute Studies in the History of Science and Technology*. Cambridge, 2003, 55–83.

Kilpatrick, Hilary. "A Genre in Classical Arabic Literature: The Adab Encyclopedia". In: Robert Hillenbrand (ed.), *Proceedings of the 10th Congress of the UEAI, Edinburgh 1980*. Edinburgh, 1982, 34–42.

——. "Encyclopedias, medieval". In: *EAL*, vol. 1. 1998, 208f.

Kinzinger, Martin. *Wissen wird Macht: Bildung im Mittelalter*. Ostfilder, 2003.

Kowalska, Maria. "Bericht über die Funktion der arabischen kosmographischen Literatur des Mittelalters". *Folia Orientalia*, 11 (1969): 175–180.

Kruk, Remke. Review of Hees (2002). *Bibliotheca Orientalis*, 59 (2002): 5–6.

Kunitzsch, Paul. "al-Nujūm". In: *EI*², VIII. 1992, 97–105.

Labarre, Albert. *Bibliographie du Dictionarium d'Ambrogio Calepino* (1520–1779). Baden-Baden, 1975.

Le Goff, Jacques. "Pourquoi le XIIIᵉ siècle a-t-il été plus particulièrement un siècle d'encyclopédisme?". In: *Picone*. 1994, 23–40.

Leder, Stefan et al. eds. *Ibn an-Nadīm und die mittelalterliche arabische Literatur: Beiträge zum 1. Johann-Fück-Kolloquium (Halle 1987)*. Wiesbaden, 1996.

Levi Della Vida, G. "La traduzione araba delle storie di Orosio". *al-Andalus*, 19 (1954): 257 ff.

——. "Sīra". In: *Encyclopaedia of Islam* (first edition), IV, 439–43.

——. *Fantasmi ritrovati*. Venice 1966.

Lichtenstadter, Ilse. "Arabic and Islamic Historiography". *Muslim World*, 35 (1945): 126–132.

Loth, Otto. "Ursprung und Bedeutung der ṭabaqāt, vornehmlich der des Ibn Saʿd". *Zeitschrift der Deutschen Morgenländischen Gesellschaft*, 23 (1869): 593–614.

MacDonald, Alasdair A., and Arend H. Huussen (eds.). *Scholarly Environments: Centres of Learning and Institutional Contexts 1560–1960*. Groningen studies in cultural change, vol. 7. Leuven [etc.], Peeters, 2004.

MacDonald, Alasdair A., and Michael W. Twomey (eds.). *Schooling and society: the ordering and reording of knowledge in the Western Middle Ages*. Groningen studies in cultural change, v. 6. Leuven [u.a.], 2004.

Mahdi, Muhsin. "Remarks on Alfarabi's *Attainment of Happiness*". In: *Essays on Islamic Philosophy and Science*, ed. by George F. Hourani. Albany, 1975, 47–66.
——. "Science, Philosophy and Religion in Alfarabi's Enumeration of the Sciences". In: *The Cultural Context of Medieval Learning*, ed. J. E. Murdoch, E. D. Sylla. Dordrecht, Boston, 1975, 113–47.
Makdisi, George. *The Rise of Colleges: Institutions of Learning in the Islam and the West*. Edinburgh, 1981.
Malti-Douglas, Fedwa. "Biography, Islamic". In: *Dictonary of the Middle Ages*, II. New York, 1982, 237–239.
——. "Controversy and Its Effects in the Biographical Tradition of al-Khaṭīb al-Baghdādī". *Studia Islamica*, 46 (1977): 115–131.
——. "Dreams, the Blind, and the Semiotics of the Biographical Notice". *Studia Islamica*, 51 (1980): 137–162.
Mandosio, Jean-Marc. "La miscellanée: histoire d'un genre". In: *Ouvrages miscellanées et théories de la connaissance à la Renaissance*, ed. Dominique de Courcelles. Paris, 2003.
Manzalaoui, M. "The Pseudo-Aristotelian *Kitāb Sirr al-asrār*". *Oriens*, 23–24 (1974): 147–257.
Marcia, D. and Hermansen, K. "Survey Article: Interdisciplinary Approaches to Islamic Biographical Materials". *Religion*, 18 (1988): 163–182.
Marmura, Michael E. "Avicenna on the Division of the Sciences in the Isagoge of His *Shifā*'". *Journal of the History of Arabic Science*, 4 (1980): 239–51.
Marzolph, Ulrich. "Mirabilia, «Weltwunder» und Gottes Kreatur: zur Weltsicht populärer Enzyklopädien des arabisch-islamischen Mittelalters". In: Ingrid Tomkowiak (ed.): *Populäre Enzyklopädien: von der Auswahl, Ordnung und Vermittlung des Wissens*. Zürich, 2002, 85–101.
McRae, Robert. *The Problem of the Unity of the Sciences: Bacon to Kant*. Toronto, 1961.
Meier, Christel (ed.). *Die Enzyklopädie im Wandel vom Hochmittelalter bis zur Frühen Neuzeit*. München, 2002.
——. "Grundzüge der mittelalterlichen Enzyklopädik: zu Inhalten, Formen und Funktionen einer problematischen Gattung". In: Ludger Grenzmann, Karl Stackmann (eds.), *Literatur und Laienbildung im Spätmittelalter und in der Reformationszeit. Symposion Wolfenbüttel 1981*. Stuttgart, 1984, 467–503.
Meier-Staubach, Christel. "On the Connection Between Epistemology and Encylopedic 'Ordo' in the Middle Ages and the Early Modern Period." In: *Schooling and scholarshin: the ordering and re-ordering of knowledge in the Western Middle Ages*, vol. 6, ed. by A. A. MacDonald, M. W. Twomey. Leuven 2003, 93–114.
Michot, Jean. "Les sciences physiques et métaphysiques selon la *Risālah fī Aqsām al-ʿulūm* d'Avicenne: essai de traduction critique". *Bulletin de philosophie médiévale*, 22 (1980): 62–73.
Mohaghghegh, Mahdi. "The Classification of the Sciences." In: *The Different Aspects of Islamic Culture*, vol. 4: Science and Technology in Islam, part 1: Science, editor, A. Y. al-Hassan. Paris, 2002, 111–131.
Moraux, Paul. *Der Aristotelismus bei den Griechen*. Band 1: *Von Andronikos bis Alexander von Aphrodisias*. Berlin, 1973.
Moss, Ann. *Printed Commonplace-Books and the Structuring of Renaissance Thought*. Oxford, 1996.
Mouren, Raphaële. "La varietas des philologues au XVIe siècle." In: *La varietas à la Renaissance*, ed. Dominique de Courcelles. Paris, 2001.
Neuwirth, Angelika. *ʿAbd al-Laṭīf al-Baġdādī's Bearbeitung von Buch Lambda der aristotelischen Metaphysik*. Akademie der Wissenschaften und der Literatur, Veröffentlichungen der Orientalischen Kommission, 27. Wiesbaden, 1976.
Parkes, Malcolm B. "The Influence of the concepts of *ordinatio* and *compilatio* on the development of the book." In: *Medieval Learning and Literature: Essays Presented to Richard William Hunt*, ed. J. J. G. Aexander and M. T. Gibson. Oxford, 1976.

Paulmier-Foucart, Monique; Lusignan, Serge; Alain Nadeau. *Vincent de Beauvais, intentions et réceptions d'une œuvre encyclopédique au Moyen Age.* Actes du XIVe colloque de l'Institut d'Etudes médiévales (1988), Saint-Laurent, 1990.
Pellat, Charles. "Les Encyclopédies dans le Monde Arabe". *Cahiers d'Histoire Mondiale,* 9 (1966): 631–658.
——. "Mawsūʿa, «encyclopædia», 1: in Arabic." In: *EI²*, vol. 6 (1991): 903–907.
Peters, Francis E. *Aristoteles Arabus: The Oriental Translations and Commentaries on the Aristotelian Corpus.* Leiden, 1968, 30–34.
——. *Aristotle and the Arabs: The Aristotelian Tradition in Islam.* New York University Studies in Near Eastern Civilization, 10. New York, London, 1968.
Picone, Michelangelo (ed.). *L'Encic lopedismo Medievale.* Ravenna, 1994.
Pingree, David. "ʿIlm al-hayʾa". In: *EI²*, vol. 3 (1970): 1135–1138.
al-Qāḍī, Wadād. "Biographical Dictionaries: Inner Structure and Cultural Significance." In: *The Book in the Islamic World,* ed. George N. Atiyeh. New York, 1995, 93–122.
——. "Dirāsa fī *Kitāb al-Baṣāʾir wa-l-dhakhāʾir*". In: Abū Ḥayyān al-Tawḥīdī, *al-Baṣāʾir wa-l-dhakhāʾir.* 9 vols. Beirut, 1988, 9: 229–305.
——. "Early Islamic State Letters: The Question of Authenticity." In: Averil Cameron and Lawrence I. Conrad (eds.), *The Byzantine and Early Islamic Near East,* 1: *Problems in the Literary Source Material.* Studies in Late Antiquity and Early Islam. Princeton, N.J., 1992, 215–275.
Radtke, Bernd. "Die älteste islamische Kosmographie: Muḥammad-i Ṭūsīs ʿAjāʾib ul-makhlūqāt". *Der Islam,* 64, 2 (1987): 278–288.
——. "Persian Cosmography, Early Tafsir and Nestorian Exegesis". In: Živa Vesel (ed.), *La science dans le Monde Iranien.* Teheran, 1998, 323–335.
——. *Weltgeschichte und Weltbeschreibung im mittelalterlichen Islam.* Beiruter Texte und Studien, 51. Beirut, Stuttgart, 1992.
Ragep, F. Jamil. *Naṣīr al-Dīn al-Ṭūsī's Memoir on Astronomy: al-Tadhkira fī ʿilm al-hayʾa, Edition, Translation and Commentary.*" 2 vols. Sources in the History of Mathematics and Physical Sciences, 12. New York, 1993.
Rashed, Roshdi (ed.). *Encyclopedia of the History of Arabic Science,* 3 vols. London, 1996.
——. "Metaphysics and Mathematics in Classical Islamic Culture: Avicenna and His Successors". In: *God, Life and Cosmos,* ed. by Ted Peters, Muzaffar Iqbal and Syed Nomanul Haq. Aldershot, 2002, 173–193.
Rashed, Roshdi. "Riyāḍiyyāt." In: *EI²*, 8 (1994): 549–562.
Ribémont, Bernard. *De natura rerum: études sur les encyclopédies médiévales.* Orléans, 1995.
——. "Encyclopédies et Civilisations". *Cahiers d'histoire mondiale,* 3 (1966): 431–851.
——. "On the Definition of an Encyclopædic Genre in the Middle Ages". In: Peter Binkley (ed.), *Pre-Modern Encyclopædic Texts: Proceedings of the Second COMERS Congress, Groningen, 1–4 July 1996.* Leiden, 1997, 47–61.
——. *Les Origines des encyclopédies médievales: d'Isidore de Séville aux Carolingiens.* Paris, 2001.
——. *La „Renaissance" du XIIe siècle et l'encyclopédisme.* Paris, 2002.
Richter-Bernburg, Lutz. "ʿAjāʾib Literature". In: *Encyclopedia of Arabic Literature,* ed. by Julie Scott Meisami and Paul Starkey. 2 vols. London, New York, 1998, 1: 65–6.
Rijk, L. M. de. "Egkuklios paideia: A Study of Its Original Meaning." *Vivarium,* 3 (1965): 24–93.
Robinson, Chase. *Islamic Historiography.* Cambridge, 2003.
Roded, Ruth. *Women in Islamic Biographical Collections.* Boulder & London, 1994.
Rosenthal, Franz. "«Blurbs» (taqrīẓ) from fourteenth-century Egypt". *Oriens,* 27–28 (1981): 177–96.
——. *The Classical Heritage in Islam.* London, 1975.
——. *A History of Muslim Historiography.* Leiden, 1968.
——. *Knowledge Triumphant: The Concept of Knowledge in Medieval Islam.* Leiden 1970.

——. "Literature." In: *The Legacy of Islam*, ed. J. Schacht and C. E. Bosworth. Oxford, 1974, 321–349.

——. *The Technique and Approach of Muslim Scholarship*. Rome, 1947.

Rouse, Mary, and Richard Rouse. *Authentic Witnesses: Approaches to Medieval Texts and Manuscripts*. Notre Dame, 1991.

——. "Bibliography before print: the medieval *de viris illustribus*." In: *The Role of the Book in Mediaeval Culture*, ed. Peter Ganz. 2 vols. Bibliologia, 3–4. Turnhout, 1986.

——. "Concordances et index." In: *Mise en page et mise en texte du livre manuscrit*, ed. Henri-Jean Martin and Jean Vezin. Paris, 1990.

——. "Statim invenire: Schools, Preachers and New Attitudes to the Printed Page." In: *Renaissance and Renewal*, ed. R. L. Benson and G. Constable. Cambridge, 1982, 201–25.

——. "The Verbal Concordance to the Scriptures." *Archivum Fratrum Praedicatorum*, 44 (1974): 5–30.

——. Rowson, Everett K. "The Philosopher as Littérateur: al-Tawḥīdī and His Predecessors." *Zeitschrift für Geschichte der Arabisch-Islamischen Wissenschaften*, 6 (1990): 50–92.

——. *An Islamic Philosopher on Death and the Afterlife: Abū l-Ḥasan al-ʿĀmirī's Kitāb al-Amad ʿalā l-abad*. Ametrican Oriental Series, 70. New Haven, 1987.

Ryan, W. F., and C. B. Schmitt (eds.). *Pseudo-Aristotle, The Secret of Secrets. Sources and Influences*. Warburg Institute Surveys and Texts, 11. London, 1982.

Sabra, Abdelhamid I. "Configuring the Universe: Aporetic, Problem Solving, and Kinematic Modeling As Themes of Arabic Astronomy." *Perspectives on Science: Historical, Philosophical, Social*, 6, 3 (1998): 288–330.

——. "Ibn al-Haytham's Revolutionary Project in Optics: The Achievement and the Obstacle". In: *The Enterprise of Science in Islam: New Perspectives*, ed. Jan P. Hogendijk and A. I. Sabra. Dibner Institute Studies in the History of Science and Technology. Cambridge, Mass. (etc.), 2003, 85–118.

——. "Manāẓir, or ʿIlm al-Manāẓir". In: *EI*², 6 (1987): 376–377.

——. "The Physical and the Mathematical in Ibn al-Haytham's Theory of Light and Vision". In: *The Commemoration Volume of Bīrūnī International Congress in Tehran*. Tehran, 1976; repr. in A. I. Sabra, *Optics, Astronomy and Logic*. London, 1994, VII: 1–20.

——. *Optics, Astronomy and Logic: Studies in Arabic Science and Philosophy*. Collected Studies Series, CS 444. London, 1994.

——. *The Optics of Ibn al-Haytham: Books I–III*. Vol. 1: Translation. Vol. 2: Commentary. London, 1989.

Safa, Z. and Shaked, S. "Andarz." In: *Encyclopedia Iranica*, vol. 2. London, New York, 1987: 11–22.

Sarıkaya, Yaşar, "Osmanlı medreselerinde aklî iliumlerin ihmali meselesi üzerine bazı mülahazalar". In *Osmanlı dünyasında bilim ve eğitim: milletlerarası kongresi, Istanbul 1999*. Istanbul, 2001, 145–58.

Schöller, Marco. "Zum Begriff des «islamischen Humanismus»". In: *Zeitschrift der Deutschen Morgenländischen Gesellschaft*, 151 (2001): 275–320.

Schwartz, Edward, and Hees, Syrinx von. "The Bird Illustrations of a Thirteenth-century Arab Natural History". *Interdisciplinary Science Reviews*, 29,3 (2004): 231–47.

Sellheim, Rudolf. *Materialien zur arabischen Literaturgeschichte*. 2 vols. Verzeichnis der Orientalischen Handschriften in Deutschland, Bd. 17, Reihe A. Wiesbaden, 1976–1987.

Serrai, Alfredo. *Storia della Bibliografia I: Bibliografia e Cabala: le enciclopedie rinascimentali*, ed. Maria Cochetti. Roma, 1988.

Shapin, Steven. "The Invisible Technician". *American Scientist*, 77 (1989): 554–63.

Shiloah, Amnon. *The Theory of Music in Arabic Writings (c. 900–1900): Descriptive Catalogue of Manuscripts in Libraries of Europe and the U.S.A.* Répertoire international

des sources musicales/Internationales Quellenlexikon der Musik, Serie B, 10. München 1979.
Smalley, Beryl. *The Study of the Bible in the Middle Ages*. Oxford, 1952.
Snow, Vernon F. "Francis Bacon's Advice to Fulke Greville on Research Techniques". *Huntington Library Quarterly*, 23 (1960): 369–79.
Staden, H. von. "Science As Text, Science As History: Galen on Metaphor". In: Ph. J. van der Eijk et al., eds, *Ancient Medicine in Its Socio-Cultural Context*, Amsterdam, 1995, vol. 2: 499–518.
Steinschneider, Moritz. "Die 'mittleren' Bücher der Araber und ihre Bearbeiter". *Zeitschrift für Mathematik und Physik*, 10 (1865): 456–498.
Stern, Samuel M. "Notes on al-Kindī's Treatise on Definitions". *Journal of the Royal Asiatic Society* (1959), 32–43.
——. *Aristotle and the World State*. Oxford, 1970.
Storey, C. A. *Persian Literature*, vols. I–III; V. London, Leiden, 1927–97.
Taffarelli, Jean-Louis. *Les systèmes de classification des ouvrages encyclopédiques*. Villeurbanne, 1980.
——. *The Structure of Knowledge: Classifications of Science and Learning since the Renaissance*, ed. Tore Frängsmyr. Berkeley, 2001.
Taylor, Archer. *A History of Bibliographies of Bibliographies*. New Brunswick, 1955.
Tomkowiak, Ingrid (ed.). *Populäre Enzyklopädien: von der Auswahl, Ordnung und Vermittlung des Wissens*. Zürich, 2002.
Vesel, Živa. *Les Encyclopédies Persanes. Essai de Typologie et de Classification des Sciences*. Paris, 1986.
——. "Mawsūʿa, 2: In Persian". In: *EI*², 6 (1991): 907–8.
Walzer, Richard, and Guidi, Michelangelo. *Studi su al-Kindī, I: Uno scritto introduttivo allo studio di Aristotele*. Roma, 1940.
——. *Al-Farabi On the Perfect State: Abū Naṣr al-Fārābī's Mabādiʾ ārāʾ ahl al-madīna al-fāḍila*. A revised edition with introduction, translation and commentary. Oxford, 1985.
Waquet, Françoise and Bots, Hans. *La République des Lettres*. Paris, 1997.
Weijers, Olga. *Le maniement du savoir: pratiques intellectuelles à l'époque des premières universités (XIIᵉ–XIVᵉ siècles)*. Studia Artistorum: Subsidia, 3. Turnhout, 1996.
Weisheipl, James A. "The Nature, Scope, and Classification of the Sciences". In: *Science in the Middle Ages*, ed. by David C. Lindberg. The Chicago History of Science and Medicine. Chicago 1991, ²1998, 461–482.
Wellisch, Hans. *Conrad Gessner: A Bio-Bibliography*. Zug, 1984.
Wiedemann, Eilhard. "al-Mīzān". In: *EI*², 7 (1991): 195–204.
Wiet, Gaston. "Les classiques du scribe égyptien au XIᵉ siècle". *Studia Islamica*, 18 (1963): 43–80.
Witkam, Jan Just. *De egyptische arts Ibn al-Akfānī en zijn indeling van de wetenschappen*. Leiden, 1989.
Wright, Owen. "Mūsīqī, later Mūsīqā". In: *EI*², 7 (1992): 681–688.
Yeo, Richard. *Encyclopedic Visions: Scientific Dictionaries and Enlightenment Culture*. Cambridge, 2001.
Young, M. J. L. "Arabic Biographical Writing". In: *Cambridge History of Arabic Literature: Religion, Learning and Science in the ʿAbbasid Period*. Cambridge, 1983, 168–187.
Yūsuf, Zakariyyā. *Muʾallafāt al-Kindī al-mūsīqiyya*. Baghdād, 1962.
Zakeri, M. "ʿAlī ibn ʿUbayda ar-Raiḥānī: A Forgotten Belletrist (*adīb*) and Pahlavi Translator". *Oriens*, 34 (1994): 76–102.

GENERAL INDEX

ISLAMIC PHILOSOPHY, THEOLOGY AND SCIENCE

TEXTS AND STUDIES

ISSN 0169-8729

8. Fakhry, M. *Ethical Theories in Islam.* Second expanded edition. 1994. ISBN 90 04 09300 1
9. Kemal, S. *The Poetics of Alfarabi and Avicenna.* 1991. ISBN 90 04 09371 0
10. Alon, I. *Socrates in Medieval Arabic Literature.* 1991. ISBN 90 04 09349 4
11. Bos, G. *Qusṭā ibn Lūqā's Medical Regime for the Pilgrims to Mecca.* The Risāla fī tadbīr safar al-ḥajj. 1992. ISBN 90 04 09541 1
12. Kohlberg, E. *A Medieval Muslim Scholar at Work.* Ibn Ṭāwūs and his Library. 1992. ISBN 90 04 09549 7
13. Daiber, H. *Naturwissenschaft bei den Arabern im 10. Jahrhundert n. Chr.* Briefe des Abū l-Faḥl Ibn al-ʿAmīd (gest. 360/970) an ʿAḥudaddaula. Herausgegeben mit Einleitung, kommentierter Übersetzung und Glossar. 1993. ISBN 90 04 09755 4
14. Dhanani, A. *The Physical Theory of Kalām.* Atoms, Space, and Void in Basrian Muʿtazilī Cosmology. 1994. ISBN 90 04 09831 3
15. Abū Maʿšar. *The Abbreviation of the Introduction to Astrology.* Together with the Medieval Latin Translation of Adelard of Bath. Edited and Translated by Ch. Burnett, K. Yamamoto and M. Yano. 1994. ISBN 90 04 09997 2
16. Sābūr Ibn Sahl. *Dispensatorium Parvum (al-Aqrābādhīn al-ṣaghīr).* Analysed, Edited and Annotated by O. Kahl. 1994. ISBN 90 04 10004 0
17. Maróth, M. *Die Araber und die antike Wissenschaftstheorie.* Übersetzung aus dem Ungarischen von Johanna Till und Gábor Kerekes. 1994. ISBN 90 04 10008 3
18. Ibn Abī al-Dunyā. *Morality in the Guise of Dreams.* A Critical Edition of *Kitāb al-Manām*, with Introduction, by Leah Kinberg. 1994. ISBN 90 04 09818 6
19. Kügelgen, A. von. *Averroes und die arabische Moderne.* Ansätze zu einer Neubegründung des Rationalismus im Islam. 1994. ISBN 90 04 09955 7
20. Lameer, J. *Al-Fārābī and Aristotelian Syllogistics.* Greek Theory and Islamic Practice. 1994. ISBN 90 04 09884 4
22. Adang, C. *Muslim Writers on Judaism and the Hebrew Bible.* 1996. ISBN 90 04 10034 2
23. Dallal, A.S. *An Islamic Response to Greek Astronomy. Kitāb Taʿdīl Hayʾat al-Aflāk* of Ṣadr al-Shariʿa. Edited with Translation and Commentary. 1995. ISBN 90 04 09968 9
24. Conrad, L.I. (ed.). The World of Ibn Ṭufayl. *Interdisciplinary Perspectives on* Ḥayy ibn Yaqẓān. 1995. ISBN 90 04 10135 7
25. Hermansen, M.K. (tr.). *The Conclusive Argument from God.* Shāh Walī Allāh of Delhi's *Ḥujjat Allāh al-Bāligha.* 1996. ISBN 90 04 10298 1
26. Abrahamov, B. *Anthropomorphism and Interpretation of the Qurʾān in the Theology of al-Qāsim ibn Ibrāhīm.* Kitāb al-Mustarshid. 1996. ISBN 90 04 10408 9

27. Wild, S. (ed.). *The Qur'an as Text*. 1996. ISBN 90 04 10344 9
28. Riddell, P.G. and T. Street (eds.). *Islam: Essays on Scripture, Thought and Society*. A Festschrift in Honour of Anthony H. Johns. 1997. ISBN 90 04 10692 8
29. Jolivet, J. and R. Rashed (eds.). *Œuvres philosophiques et scientifiques d'al-Kindī*. Volume I. *L'Optique et la Catoptrique*. Edited by R. Rashed. 1997. ISBN 90 04 09781 3
30. Rudolph, U. *Al-Māturīdī und die sunnitische Theologie in Samarkand*. 1997. ISBN 90 04 10023 7
31. Endress, G. and J. A. Aertsen (eds.). *Averroes and the Aristotelian Tradition*. Sources, Constitution and Reception of the Philosophy of Ibn Rushd (1126-1198). Proceedings of the Fourth Symposium Averroicum (Cologne, 1996). ISBN 90 04 11308 8
32. Elmore, G.T. *Islamic Sainthood in the Fullness of Time*. Ibn al-ʿArabī's *Book of the Fabulous Gryphon*. 1999. ISBN 90 04 10991 9
33. Abū Maʿšar. *Kitāb al-milal wa-d-duwal*. Arabic text edited by K. Yamamoto with an English translation by K. Yamamoto and Ch. Burnett. 1999. ISBN 90 04 10725 8
34. Albumasar. *De Magnis Coniunctionibus* (On the Great Coniunctions). Latin text edited by Ch. Burnett and Arabic-Latin, Latin Arabic Glossaries by K. Yamamoto and Ch. Burnett. 1999. ISBN 90 04 11074 7
35. Stroumsa, S. *Freethinkers of Medieval Islam*. Ibn al-Rāwandī, Abū Bakr al-Rāzī, and Their Impact on Islamic Thought. 1999. ISBN 90 04 11374 6
36. King, D.A. *World-Maps for Finding the Direction and Distance to Mecca*. Innovation and Tradition in Islamic Science. 1999. ISBN 90 04 11367 3
37. Bar-Asher, M.M. *Scripture and Exegesis in Early Imāmī Shiism*. 1999. ISBN 90 04 11495 5
38. Sayyid Jalāl al-Dīn Āshtiyānī et al. *Consciousness and Reality*. Studies in Memory of Toshihiko Izutsu. 2000. ISBN 90 04 11586 2
39. Schmidtke, S. *Theologie, Philosophie und Mystik im zwölfershiitischen Islam des 9./15. Jahrhunderts*. Die Gedankenwelten des Ibn Abī ṛumhūr al-Aḥsāʾī (um 838/1434-35 — nach 906/1501). 2000. ISBN 90 04 11531 5
40. Griffel, F. *Apostasie und Toleranz im Islam*. Die Entwicklung zu al-Ġazālīs Urteil gegen die Philosophie und die Reaktionen der Philosophen. 2000. ISBN 90 04 11566 8
41. Heemskerk, M.T. *Suffering in the Muʿtazilite Theology*. ʿAbd al-Jabbār's Teaching on Pain and Divine Justice. 2000. ISBN 90 04 11726 1
42. Rashed, R. and H. Bellosta. *Ibrāhīm Ibn Sinān. Logique et Géométrie au Xᵉ Siècle*. 2000. ISBN 90 04 11804 7
43. Tamer, G. *Islamische Philosophie und die Krise der Moderne*. Das Verhältnis von Leo Strauss zu Alfarabi, Avicenna und Averroes. 2001. ISBN 90 04 12029 7
44. Genequand, C. *Alexander of Aphrodisias on the Cosmos*. 2001. ISBN 90 04 11963 9
45. Calverley, E.E. and J.W. Pollock. *Nature, Man and God in Medieval Islam*.
    Volume one. 2002. ISBN 90 04 12381 4
    Volume two. 2002. ISBN 90 04 12382 2

46. Swartz, M. *A Medieval Critique of Anthropomorphism.* Ibn al-Jawzī's Kitāb Akhbār aṣ-Ṣifāt. 2002. ISBN 90 04 12376 8
47. Kusuba, T. and D. Pingree. *Arabic Astronomy in Sanskrit.* Al-Birjandī on Tadhkira II, Chapter 11 and its Sanskrit Translation. 2002. ISBN 90 04 12475 6
48. İskenderoğlu, M. *Fakhr al-dīn al-Rāzī and Thomas Aquinas on the Question of the Eternity of the World.* 2002. ISBN 90 04 12480 2
49. Reisman, D.C. *The making of the Avicennan Tradition.* The Transmission, Contents, and Structure of Ibn Sīnā's al-Mubāḥaṯāt (The Discussions). 2002. ISBN 90 04 12504 3
50. Behloul, S.M. *Ibn Ḥazms Evangelienkritik.* Eine methodische Untersuchung. 2002. ISBN 90 04 12527 2
51. Charette, F. *Mathematical Instrumentation in Fourteenth-Century Egypt and Syria.* The Illustrated Treatise of Najm al-Dīn al-Mīṣrī. 2003. ISBN 90 0413015 2
52. Reisman, D.C. (ed.). *Before and After Avicenna.* Proceedings of the First Conference of the Avicenna Study Group. 2003. ISBN 90 04 12978 2
53. Kahl, O. *Sābūr Ibn Sahl. The Small Dispensatory*. 2003. ISBN 90 04 12996 0
54. Burnett, C., J.P. Hogendijk, K. Plofker and M. Yano. *Studies in the History of the Exact Sciences in Honour of David Pingree*. 2004. ISBN 90 04 13202 3
56. McGinnis, J. (ed.). *Interpreting Avicenna: Science and Philosophy in Medieval Islam*. Proceedings of the Second Conference of the Avicenna Study Group. 2004. ISBN 90 04 13960 5
57. Eschraghi, A. *Frühe Šaiḫī- und Bābī-Theologie*. Die Darlegung der Beweise für Muḥammads besonderes Prophetentum (*Ar-Risāla fī Iṯbat an-Nubūwa al-Ḫāṣṣa*). 2004. ISBN 90 04 14034 4
58. Acar, R. *Talking about God and Talking about Creation*. Avicenna's and Thomas Aquinas' positions. 2005. ISBN 90 04 14477 3
59. Akasoy, A. *Philosophie und Mystik in der späten Almohadenzeit.* Die *Sizilianischen Fragen* des Ibn Sabʿīn. 2006. ISBN 90 04 14522 2
60. Schöck, C. *Koranexegese, Grammatik und Logik.* Zum Verhältnis von arabischer und aristotelischer Urteils-, Konsequenz- und Schlußlehre. 2006. ISBN 90 04 14588 5
61. Endress, G. (ed.). *Organizing Knowledge.* Encyclopædic Activities in the Pre-Eighteenth Century Islamic World. 2006. ISBN-13: 978 90 04 14697 6, ISBN-10: 90 04 14697 0
62. Mourad, S.A. *Early Islam between Myth and History.* Al-Ḥasan al-Baṣrī (d. 110H/728CE) and the Formation of His Legacy in Classical Islamic Scholarship. 2006. ISBN-13: 978 90 04 14829 1, ISBN-10: 90 04 14829 9
63. Bertolacci, A. *The Reception of Aristotle's* Metaphysics *in Avicenna's* Kitāb al-Šifāʾ. A Milestone of Western Metaphysical Thought. 2006. ISBN-13: 978 90 04 14899 4, ISBN-10: 90 04 14899 X,
64. Shihadeh, A. *The Teleological Ethics of Fakhr al-Dīn al-Rāzī*. 2006. ISBN-13: 978 90 04 14991 5, ISBN-10: 90 04 14991 0

65. Pourjavady, R. and S. Schmidtke. *A Jewish Philosopher of Baghdad.* ʿIzz al-Dawla Ibn Kammūna (d. 683/1284-85) and His Writings. 2006.
ISBN-13: 978 90 04 15139 0, ISBN-10: 90 04 15139 7